THE

WORLD

ON

PAPER

....

THE
WORLD
ON
PAPER

....

THE CONCEPTUAL AND
COGNITIVE IMPLICATIONS
OF WRITING AND READING

DAVID R. OLSON

CAMBRIDGE
UNIVERSITY PRESS

Published by the Press Syndicate of the University of Cambridge
The Pitt Building, Trumpington Street, Cambridge CB2 1RP
40 West 20th Street, New York, NY 10011-4211 USA
10 Stamford Road, Oakleigh, Melbourne 3166, Australia

First published 1994
First paperback edition 1996

Printed in Great Britain by Athenæum Press Ltd. Gateshead, Tyne & Wear

A catalogue record for this book is available from the British Library

Library of Congress cataloguing in publication data

Olson, David R.
The world on paper: the conceptual and cognitive implications of
writing and reading / David R. Olson.
     p.   cm.
Includes bibliographical references.
ISBN 0 521 44311 3
1. Written communication. 2. Cognition. I. Title.
P211.O53   1994
302.2'244 – dc20   93–26382 CIP

ISBN 0 521 44311 3 hardback
ISBN 0 521 57558 3 paperback

CE

TO JACK GOODY
who was kept waiting

....

CONTENTS

ILLUSTRATIONS

....

Just outside my office door is a map, more of a schematic really, of the floor plan of the building, the Cognitive Development Unit of the MRC in London, at which as I write this I am a visiting Fellow. Near the centre of this map is a conspicuous arrow to which is attached the caption "You are here." Like all successful maps it orients the viewer in the building.

But in a deep sense that usually goes unnoticed, the caption is anomalous. I don't need a map to tell me where I am; I know where I am, "I am here, right where I stand." The map, so to speak, contradicts me, insisting that I am at the point indicated by the arrow. The map undertakes to lift me from my firm stance on the floor and transpose me into this geometry of lines and angles.

Maps are perhaps the most conspicuous means for putting ourselves and the world on paper. We have not paid sufficient attention to the fact that our representations have a way of telling us, dictating to us, what and where we are. We are no where until our location is identified on the map. If we really want to know where we are we shall have to confront the map; it will tell us where we are. As if we didn't already know.

McLuhan told of some northern Inuit who were looking for a cache of supplies, the location of which was marked on a map. After some hours of fruitless search, their urban companions, unable to locate themselves on the map said "We are lost." The Inuit, on the other hand, insisted that they were not lost: "It is the cache which is lost."

It is not only our maps which put us and our world on paper. Our literature, our science, our philosophy, our law, our religion, are, in an important way, literate artifacts. We see ourselves, our ideas and our world in terms of these artifacts. As a result we live not in the world so much as in the world as it is represented to us in those artifacts.

The topic of literacy is all about the special, indeed peculiar properties of these artifacts, this paper world, about its strengths and limitations, its uses and abuses, its history and its mythology, and about the kinds of competence, the forms of thought and the modes of perception that are involved in coping with, indeed exploiting, this world on paper.

The specialist tools of science are not needed to show a reader that literacy is important and useful. But you do need such tools to bring into focus the set of assumptions about this paper world and about the nature of human cognitive competence called for in dealing with this paper world for these assumptions are deeply lodged in our conception of ourselves as "literate," "civilized" people. It is only recently that we have come to see these *as* assumptions, that is as beliefs that in large part are not warranted. Writing may be important but it may not be important for the reasons we have traditionally held. The specialist tools of science are required to determine the warrant for those beliefs.

Some have held that literacy, like circumcision, baptism or a private school education, is important for gaining access to a privileged elite. Others have held that literacy is not only useful but that it contributes directly to the growth of rationality and consciousness. Most believe that literacy does both. At least enough do to keep literacy high on the political and educational agenda as it has for well over a century. But only in the last three decades has the topic of literacy moved up to full respectability on the scholarly agenda. Classicists, historians, linguists, anthropologists, psychologists have joined educational theorists in the exploration of just what writing is, just what writing does, what people do with it, and how, precisely, those functions developed historically. The common goal is to determine all that is involved in our being and becoming literate.

And not only in what is involved in an individual's learning to read and write and exploit the resources of a literate culture but also to determine what happens to commercial, legal, religious, political, literary, and scientific activities and institutions when written documents come to play a central role. And to determine what happens when a significant number of people can read and write and so exploit these documents. Scholars are concerned with the social as well as the psychological implications of the invention of writing and the growth of a reading public.

The bold ideas of McLuhan, Havelock, and Goody and Watt opened up this field for study by contrasting literate with oral societies. Like most bold theory, little of the early enthusiasm stands unscathed. A recent careful review of this research tradition concluded:

> it is difficult to maintain any clear-cut and radical distinction between those cultures which employ the written word and those that do not.
> (Finnegan, 1973, p. 135; see also 1988, p. 178)

All cultures are, by definition, successful; if they were not they would not have survived. People of all cultures not only survive; ethnographers have shown the rich cultural practices and traditions that are part of every human group literate or not. The first lesson in anthropology, administered to me personally by Jack Goody, was "They are just the same as you and me, you know."

Consequently, explanations of cultural and historical change based on the notion of progress invite little enthusiasm. Indeed, accounts based on the notion of "primitive" thought or "primitive" language whether expressed in the classic work of Levy-Bruhl (1910/1926) or the more recent work of Hallpike (1979) seem crude and anachronistic. On the other hand cultural and historical differences in the ways in which people think about themselves and the world are becoming more and more conspicuous, and understanding them more and more urgent. Writing and literacy seem obvious candidate explanations.

While the earlier linguists' dismissive claim that "writing is not language; it is just a record of language" is no longer tenable, neither is the classification of people as primitive or modern, oral or literate, concrete or abstract, or as biased to the eye or the ear. We must go, it seems, back to the beginning.

The beginning is that at some point in the evolution of writing systems, writing came to preserve and thereby fix verbal form across space and through time. The magic of writing arises not so much from the fact that writing serves as a new mnemonic device, an aid to memory, as from the fact that writing may serve an important epistemological function. Writing not only helps us remember what was thought and said but also invites us to see what was thought and said in a new way. It is a cliché to say that there is more to writing than the abc's and more to literacy than the ability to decode words and sentences. Capturing that "more" is the problem. I have suggested that it is the ability to step into, and on occasion to step out again, from this new world, the world on paper. Just how that can occur is what I shall attempt to explain in this book.

Of course I am not alone in this enterprise. A number of scholars from a variety of disciplines are being led in the same direction by their own research. I mention, in particular, Michael Clanchy, Jack Goody, Brian Stock and Geoffrey Lloyd, all of whom argue that the important functions we are after are those which involve our means for thinking about the world; they vary in their assessment of how or why or how far literacy is implicated in these changes.

There are certain risks, grave risks some would say, of fraternizing with "other" disciplines. The problems are complex enough without amateurs high-jacking claims and evidence from specialist fields of research and perhaps misinterpreting them. However, Sir Ernst Gombrich in his *Art and illusion* approvingly cites Kohler's suggestion that we adopt "trespassing as a scientific technique" (1960, p. 26). It is particularly appropriate for a field of study such as literacy, for such trespassing is simply one of the uses of literacy. The fact is that the important work in history, philosophy, linguistics and anthropology is available to me as a reader; the authors will have to live with my inevitable misreadings. "No blunder could have been worse than that of confusing a reversion with an escheat," wrote Pollock and Maitland (1898) in their history of English law; I should say not!

I will say that the task is not easy. A book on literacy not written for the general reader really misses the point. One of the dramatic facts about Renaissance literacy was the impact writing had when texts came into the hands of the ordinary readers, the wrong people! Yet in attempting to write for the general reader, I have found myself veering from the commonsensically obvious to the technically abstruse. What I have to say is not complex but if it is oversimplified it will look boringly obvious and if its point is missed it may look profound. What is taken as profound is often not notably different from the merely obscure.

I have tried to set out a theory of literacy, that is to provide a way of interpreting a group of rather heterogeneous facts by means of a small number of principles. Further, those principles, ideally, should provide a possible cause of the facts in question. It would be simple minded indeed to believe that any small number of factors could explain major social or psychological transformations such as those associated with literacy. But if we think of a theory as a machine to think with, a device for organizing and interpreting events with the aim of bringing other questions and other forms of evidence into conjunction, then it is not at all unreasonable to aspire to a theory of how writing contributes not only to our understanding of the world but also of ourselves.

The theory I have tried to formulate was an outgrowth of two lines of interest which I began to think may be related. They were children's changing understandings of the relation between "what was said" and "what was meant" – changes I associated with reading and interpreting texts – and my interest in the possible relations between protestantism, early modern science and mentalistic psychology. Wouldn't it be interesting, I thought, if it could be shown that changes in the great social movements of the early modern period could be traced to altered practice and understanding of reading and interpretation. Perhaps Luther, Galileo and Descartes shared a common but new way of reading – of relating what was said to what was meant by it! But even to pose such questions required some analysis of just what scripts and writing systems are, how they relate to speech, how they are read, how those ways of reading changed, how ways of reading called for new distinctions, new awareness and new modes of thinking. And finally, the announced topic of this book, how the very structure of knowledge was altered by the attempts to represent the world on paper.

In Chapter 1 I review the vast array of beliefs about literacy and show that an enumeration of pros and cons does not yield much by way of theory. In Chapter 2 I review the classical problem of "primitive" modes of thought and the role that writing may have played in developing distinctive modes of thought. In Chapter 3 I review theories linking literacy to the conceptual revolutions in Classical Greece and in Renaissance Europe. Chapters 4, 5 and 6 set out the central claims of the theory of literacy and cognition by examining the relation between speech and writing – what writing represents as well as what it does not represent and what has therefore to be made up by the reader. Chapters 7, 8, and 9 interpret the history of reading in terms of that theory, showing that the history of reading is more-or-less a matter of coping with what scripts can't easily capture, namely, how texts are to be taken, their illocutionary force. Chapter 10 examines the ways in which visible artifacts including maps, drawings, paintings, diagrams, and mathematical representations came to serve as fundamental intellectual tools. Chapter 11 attempts to show that mentalism as expressed in Descartes and the British Empiricist philosophers was the by-product of a new understanding of what was in a text and what was contributed by a reader. Recognition of the reader's contribution to the interpretation of a text provided a model for the mind. Chapter 12 summarizes these arguments in terms of a set of principles and then concludes by showing how a revised conception of literacy contributes to a new understanding not only of reading, but more importantly, of thinking.

Readers of my earlier work on literacy (Bless them! as Nelson Goodman once said of his readers) deserve some added introduction to this volume. The closest I come to an explicit apology for my earlier over-simplifications is in Chapter 7. But the general orientation here is quite different. Rather than take as fundamental the autonomy of textual meaning, I now take as fundamental that the text provides a model for speech; we introspect our language in terms of the categories laid down by our script, to paraphrase Benjamin Whorf. This, of course, yields quite a different analysis of the conceptual implications of literacy; writing is largely responsible for bringing language into consciousness. My enthusiasm for diachronic accounts whether from the history of ideas or from developmental psychology has not diminished. Indeed, if I have a particular contribution to make it is to show that the concepts that children seem to acquire so naturally in the course of development in a literate society are concepts which were initially worked out in a particular historical, cultural context over two millennia.

Many people contributed importantly to this task. Conceptually, I am a child or at least a step-child of Jerome Bruner, Jack Goody, Marshall McLuhan and Eric Havelock. Others helped enormously by sympathetic and often critical readings of my earlier work on literacy and of drafts of parts of this volume. They include Janet Astington, Courtney Cazden, Michael Clanchy, Michael Cole, Carol Feldman,

Ernst Gombrich, Roy Harris, Frits van Holthoon, Geoffrey Lloyd, Christopher Olsen, Ragnar Rommetveit, Sylvia Scribner, Frank Smith, Keith Stanovich, Brian Stock and Gordon Wells. Others, whose work has strongly influenced me, are conspicuous in my citations.

The work was supported from beginning to end by personal encouragement and a generous grant from the Spencer Foundation, in particular two of its Presidents, Tom James and Larry Cremin and its Vice-President, Marion Faldet. In addition it was supported by a Fellowship to the Center for Advanced Study in the Behavioral Sciences, Stanford, California for the year 1983–84 and a Visiting Research Fellowship at the Child Development Unit of the Medical Research Council, John Morton, Director, and University College London for the year 1990–91. These Fellowships were made possible in part by paid leaves from my home institution, the Ontario Institute for Studies in Education. I am sincerely grateful for this support as it was these fellowships which made sustained thinking and writing on this topic possible. Research grants which supported the work on this topic were provided by the Transfer Grant from the Ontario Ministry of Education to the OISE, the Social Science and Humanities Research Council of Canada to Nancy Torrance and myself. Denese Coulbeck, Nancy Torrance and Marie McMullin assisted in the preparation of this manuscript. Judith Ayling of Cambridge University Press supervised the production.

If the thesis of this book is correct, books speak for themselves, even if they speak somewhat differently to each reader or group of readers. No amount of preparation either by hype or apology will compensate for what the book for its part, says or fails to say. I invite you to join me in reading it.

1 DEMYTHOLOGIZING LITERACY

There can be little doubt that a major feature of modern societies is the ubiquity of writing. Almost no event of significance, ranging from declarations of war to simple birthday greetings, passes without appropriate written documentation. Contracts are sealed by means of a written signature. Goods in a market, street names, gravestones – all bear written inscriptions. Complex activities are all scripted whether in knitting pattern books, computer program manuals, or in cooking recipe books. Credit for an invention depends upon filing a written patent while credit for a scientific achievement depends upon publication. And our place in heaven or hell, we are told, depends upon what is written in the Book of Life.

Correspondingly, among our most highly valued skills is our ability to make use of written texts, namely, our literacy. The primary function of the school is to impart what are called "basic skills," reading, writing and arithmetic, all of which involve competence with systems of notation. Public expenditure on education is rivalled only by defense and health and a major portion of children's formative years are spent in acquiring, first, some general literate competence and second, in using this competence to acquire such specialized bodies of knowledge as science and history.

Nor are the social concerns with literacy confined to a particular class or society. Free, universal public education has been government policy for well over a century in western democracies. Developing countries, too, frequently set the goal of a literate citizenry high in their priorities. Socialist movements of the twentieth century, whether in the Soviet Union, Cuba or Nicaragua, were accompanied by intensive programs to make everyone literate. An UNESCO policy document (1975) described literacy as crucial to "the liberation and advancement of man," and initiated a plan for the eradication of illiteracy by the year 2000. And demographers record, as part of the vital statistics for each nation, the percentage of persons who are illiterate. The figure given for Canada is fifteen percent, a figure which elicits both alarm and accusations in the popular media. Modern western democracies aspire to eradicate illiteracy as a means of solving a range of other social problems such as poverty and unemployment and the schools are routinely charged with upgrading the literacy standards of their students.

Where does this enthusiasm for literacy come from? For some three hundred years we in the West rested our beliefs in our cultural superiority over our pre-literate ancestors as well as over our non-Western neighbors, on our access to a simple technological artifact, an alphabetical writing system. Our social sciences tended to help us sustain that view. Theories of evolution, progress, and development all contributed to the comfortable view of our own superiority and the superiority of the means that allowed us to develop it.

In the past two decades this comfortable view has begun to come apart. Cultures with less literacy have come to see the value western cultures set on literacy as self-serving, as a form of arrogance (Pattanayak, 1991) and western scholars have found the rhetoric of literacy far exceeding the validity of the claims. Indeed, the evidence has begun to accumulate that our beliefs about literacy are a blend of fact and supposition, in a word a mythology, a selective way of viewing the facts that not only justifies the advantages of the literate but also assigns the failings of the society, indeed of the world, to the illiterate.

The situation in regard to literacy is not dissimilar to that faced a century ago by Christian theologians who began to cast a critical eye over the tradition that had come down to them and, recognizing certain archaic modes of thought and expression, adopted the task of "demythologizing" Christianity. The justification for this activity was not to undermine the hopes of the faithful but to put those hopes on a firmer, more truthful ground. Humble faith based on a secure foundation, they urged, was preferable to a robust faith based on surmise.

The faithful, of course, were not always willing to cash in the old for the new.

We are faced with a similar choice in regard to our beliefs and assumptions about literacy. The faithful need not be overly alarmed. The assumptions about literacy that we may have to abandon are not worth holding in any case. Indeed, they underwrite poor social policy and poor educational practice. And the new understanding of literacy that may emerge as we critically examine the facts, promises to have implications and uses far greater than those which the old dogma yielded. What we shall lose is the naive belief in the transformative powers of simply learning to read and write and calculate, the magical powers of the three Rs. More importantly for our purposes, we shall be able to move beyond the mere tabulation of pros and cons and set the stage for a new understanding of just what was involved in creating and now living in "a world on paper." That is the main purpose of this chapter.

There are six deeply held and widely shared beliefs or assumptions about literacy on which current scholarship has cast considerable doubt.

First the beliefs:

(1) Writing is the transcription of speech. The fact that almost anything we say can be readily transcribed into writing and that anything written can be read aloud makes irresistible the inference that writing is just speech "put down." Indeed, this is the traditional assumption dating back to Aristotle but explicitly expressed in the technical writings of Saussure (1916/1983) and Bloomfield (1933). Since readers are already speakers, learning how to read comes to be seen as a matter of learning how one's oral language (the known) is represented by visible marks (the unknown). Old wine, new wineskins.

(2) The superiority of writing to speech. Whereas speech is seen as a "loose and unruly" possession of the people, as Nebrija, the fifteenth-century grammarian, described oral Castellian to Queen Isabella (Illich & Sanders, 1989, p. 65), writing is thought of as an instrument of precision and power. Reading the transcription of one's oral discourse is a humbling experience, filled as it is with hesitations, false starts, ungrammaticalities and infelicities. Speech on important public

occasions is scripted – written, planned and corrected – to achieve the goals of saying precisely what is meant and yet appearing sincere and spontaneous. One learns to write, in part, as a means of learning to express oneself correctly and precisely in one's oral speech.

(3) The technological superiority of the alphabetic writing system. The invention of the alphabet by the Greeks is taken as one of the high points in cultural evolution, achieved only once in history and its presence serves, to this day, to distinguish alphabetic from non-alphabetic cultures. An early expression of this idea can be found in Rousseau's *Essay on the origin of language*:

These three ways of writing correspond almost exactly to three different stages according to which one can consider men gathered into a nation. The depicting of objects is appropriate to a savage people; signs of words and of propositions, to a barbaric people, and the alphabet to civilized peoples.

(1754–91/1966, p. 17)

Samuel Johnson, Boswell tells us, considered the Chinese to be barbarians because "they have not an alphabet" (cited by Havelock, 1982). To this day the French language makes no distinction between knowledge of writing generally and knowledge of the alphabet, both are "alphabétisme." Presumably other forms of writing are not "true" writing systems. The three classical theories of the invention of writing, those of Cohen (1958), Gelb (1963) and Diringer (1968) all treat the evolution of the alphabet as the progressive achievement of more and more precise visible means for representing sound patterns, the phonology of the language. The representation of ideas through pictures, the representation of words through logographic signs, the invention of syllabaries are all seen as failed attempts at or as halting steps towards the invention of the alphabet, it being the most highly evolved in this direction and therefore superior.

Havelock, perhaps the foremost authority on the uses and implications of the Greek alphabet, has written:

The invention of the Greek alphabet, as opposed to all previous systems, including the Phoenician [from which it was derived] constituted an event in the history of human culture, the importance of which has not as yet been fully grasped. Its appearance divides all pre-Greek civilizations from those that are post-Greek. On this facility were built the foundations of those twin forms of knowledge: literature in the post-Greek sense, and science, also in the post-Greek sense.

(1982, p. 185; see also 1991)

McLuhan (1962) was, of course, among the first to explore the relations between communication technologies, particularly the alphabet and the printing press, and the "galaxy" of intellectual, artistic and social changes that occurred with the Greeks and again at the end of the Middle Ages, a relation he summed up thus: "By the meaningless sign linked to the meaningless sound we have built the shape and meaning of Western man" (p. 50), thus tying intellectual progress to the alphabet.

(4) Literacy as the organ of social progress. One of the most conspicuous features of modern western democracies is their uniformly high levels of literacy. It is commonly held that it was the rise of popular literacy that led to rational, democratic social institutions as well as to industrial development and economic growth and that any decline in levels of literacy poses a threat to a progressive, democratic society.

Historians have attempted to specify the relation between literacy and social development in the West. Cipolla (1969, p. 8) found that although historical patterns were far from uniform "it appears that the art of writing is strictly and almost inevitably connected with the condition of urbanization and commercial intercourse." The correlation invites the inference that literacy is a cause of development, a view that underwrites the UNESCO's commitment to the "eradication of illiteracy" by the year 2000 as a means to modernization (Graff, 1986).

The perceived relation between literacy and social development has sometimes been expressed with considerable zeal. Luther, writing in the sixteenth century, urged the establishment of compulsory education arguing that a neglect of learning would result in "divine wrath, inflation, the plague and syphilis, bloodthirsty tyrants, wars and revolutions, the whole country laid to waste by Turks and Tartars, even the pope restored to power" (Strauss, 1978, p. 8). Gibbon, writing in the eighteenth century, claimed: "The use of letters is the principal circumstance that distinguishes a civilized people from a herd of savages, incapable of knowledge or reflection." He continued

"We may safely pronounce that, without some species of writing, no people has ever preserved the faithful annals of their history, ever made any considerable progress in the abstract sciences, or even possessed, in any tolerable degree of perfection, the useful and agreeable arts of life" (Gibbon, 1776/1896, p. 218).

An Ontario educator, writing in the last century but furnished with the new art of statistics, reported that "an uneducated person commits fifty-six times as many crimes as one with education" (cited by de Castell, Luke & Egan, 1986, p. 92)!

While we readily recognize some of these expressions as histrionic, it is generally granted that literacy has social and economic implications. These beliefs find expression in the policy documents and in the editorial pages of many, perhaps most, newspapers. Representative is that of "Canada's national newspaper" which recently asserted that "malnutrition, ill-health and illiteracy form a triple scourge for developing nations," that the illiterate are doomed to "lives of poverty and hopelessness" because they are "deprived of the fundamental tools to forge a better life," namely literacy, that "illiteracy is a $2-billion drag on the economy of Canada" and that "the social costs are enormous" (*Globe and Mail*, October 13, 14, 1987). Belief in the importance of literacy has come to so dominate our common consciousness that even a small decline in spelling-test scores is seen as a threat to the welfare of the society. We see literacy, as do most other literate peoples, as central to our conception of ourselves as cultured, indeed as civilized, people.

Three things "have changed the whole face and state of things throughout the world," wrote Francis Bacon (1620/1965, p. 373) in the seventeenth century: "printing, gunpowder, and the magnet." (*New Organon*, Aphorism 129). There seemed little reason to quibble.

(5) Literacy as an instrument of cultural and scientific development. We take it as going without saying that writing and literacy are in large part responsible for the rise of distinctively modern modes of thought such as philosophy, science, justice and medicine and conversely, that literacy is the enemy of superstition, myth and magic. Frazer (1911–1915/1976) in his compendium of myths and beliefs, *The golden bough*, argued for the progressive stages of mankind from magic to religion to science, a view he shared with such philosophers as Comte (1830–42)

and Hegel (1910/1967). In fact, it is usual to trace our modern forms of democratic social organization and our modern modes of thought to "the glory that was Greece." The Greek achievement has been credited, at least by some, to their alphabetic literacy:

The civilization created by the Greeks and Romans was the first on the earth's surface which was founded upon the activity of the common reader; the first to be equipped with the means of adequate expression in the inscribed word; the first to be able to place the inscribed word in general circulation; the first, in short, to become literate in the full meaning of that term, and to transmit its literacy to us.

(Havelock, 1982, p. 40)

The importance of writing to the advancement of philosophy and science has, in recent times been examined and defended in a series of major works by such writers as McLuhan (1962), Goody and Watt (1963/1968), Goody (1986), Ong (1982), works which trace a new orientation to language, the world and the mind, to changes in the technology of communication. To an important extent, it was this series of books that turned literacy into a research topic.

(6) Literacy as an instrument of cognitive development. As with cultural development, so too with cognitive development. Genuine knowledge, we assume, is identifiable with that which is learned in school and from books. Literacy skills provide the route of access to that knowledge. The primary concern of schooling is the acquisition of "basic skills," which for reading consists of "decoding," that is, learning what is called the alphabetic principle, and which for writing, consists of learning to spell. Literacy imparts a degree of abstraction to thought which is absent from oral discourse and from oral cultures. Important human abilities may be thought of as "literacies" and personal and social development may be reasonably represented by levels of literacy such as basic, functional or advanced levels.

Now the doubts:

(1) Writing as transcription. Writing systems capture only certain properties of what was said, namely, verbal form – phonemes, lexemes, and syntax – leaving how it was said or with what intention radically under-represented. The fact that visual signs can be routinely turned into verbal form obscures the fact that they can be verbalized

in several, perhaps many, different ways by varying the intonation and emphasis and give rise to radically different interpretations. Far from writing being mere transcription of speech, writing is coming to be seen as providing a model for speech itself; we introspect language in terms laid down by our writing systems. Learning to read in part is a matter of coming to hear, and think about, speech in a new way. This is the topic of Chapter 4.

(2) The power of writing. Rousseau raised the objection to claims about writing that has become the touchstone of modern linguistics. He wrote: "Writing is nothing but the representation of speech: it is bizarre that one gives more care to the determining of the image than to the object" (cited by Derrida, 1976, p. 27). That writing was simply transcription of speech was, as we have seen, first advanced by Aristotle but it was being used by Rousseau to criticize the lack of attention to speech. Saussure (1916/1983) for similar reasons, attacked "the tyranny of writing," the fact that linguistic theory took as its object written language rather than spoken: "The linguistic object is not defined by the combination of the written word and the spoken word: the spoken form alone constitutes the object" (pp. 23–24 or p. 45). So convinced are modern linguists of the derivative quality of writing that the study of writing has been largely neglected until very recently. Second, oral languages are not the "loose and unruly" possession of the people that the early grammarians took them to be; all human languages have a rich lexical and grammatical structure capable, at least potentially, of expressing the full range of meanings. Even sign-language, the language of the deaf, which for years was thought to be little more than gesture and pantomime, has been shown to be adequate in principle to the full expression of any meaning (Klima & Bellugi, 1979). And finally, oral discourse precedes and surrounds the preparation, interpretation, and analysis of written discourse (Finnegan, 1988; Heath, 1983). Writing is dependent in a fundamental way on speech. One's oral language, it is now recognized, is the fundamental possession and tool of mind; writing, though important, is always secondary.

(3) The superiority of alphabet. Only in the past decade has a clear case been made against the universal optimality of the alphabet as a representation of language (Gaur, 1984/1987; Harris, 1986; Sampson,

1985). First, counter to the received view, the alphabet was not a product of genius, that is, it was not the miracle of discovery of the phonology of language, but merely the adaptation of a syllabary designed for a Semitic language to the particularly complex syllable structure of the Greek language. Furthermore, an alphabet is of limited use in the representation of a monosyllabic language with many homophones as is the case in Chinese; a logographic system has many advantages for such a language. Nor is the simplicity of the alphabet the major cause of high levels of literacy; many other factors affect the degrees of literacy in a country or in an individual. Finally, our tardy recognition of the literacy levels of non-alphabetic cultures, especially the Japanese who routinely out-perform Western children in their literacy levels (Stevenson et al., 1982) has forced us to acknowledge that our view of the superiority of the alphabet is, at least in part, an aspect of our mythology.

(4) Literacy and social development. Some modern scholars have argued that literacy not only is not the royal route to liberation, but is as often a means of enslavement. Levi-Strauss (1961) wrote:

Writing is a strange thing. It would seem as if its appearance could not have failed to wreak profound changes in the living conditions of our race, and that these transformations must have been above all intellectual in character ... Yet nothing of what we know of writing, or of its role in evolution, can be said to justify this conception.

If we want to correlate the appearance of writing with certain other characteristics of civilization, we must look elsewhere. The one phenomenon which has invariably accompanied it is the formation of cities and empires: the integration into a political system, that is to say, of a considerable number of individuals, and the distribution of those individuals into a hierarchy of castes and classes ... It seems to favour rather the exploitation than the enlightenment of mankind. This exploitation made it possible to assemble workpeople by the thousand and set them tasks that taxed them to the limits of their strength. If my hypothesis is correct, the primary function of writing, as a means of communication, is to facilitate the enslavement of other human beings. The use of writing for disinterested ends, and with a view to satisfactions of the mind in the fields either of science or the arts, is a secondary result of its invention – and may even be no more than a way of reinforcing, justifying, or dissimulating its primary function.

                                                        (pp. 291–292)

While the contrast between enlightenment and enslavement may be overdrawn by Levi-Strauss, enlightenment is an effective means of ensuring the adoption of orderly conventional procedures. A number of historical studies have suggested that literacy is a means for establishing social control, for turning people into good citizens, productive workers, and if necessary, obedient soldiers (Aries, 1962). Strauss (1978, p. 306) concluded that the emphasis on literacy by the Protestant church in Reformation Germany could be seen as the attempt to convert the populace "from their ancient ways and habits to a bookish orthodoxy resting on the virtue of conformity." The rise of universal, compulsory education has rarely, if ever, been sought by the uneducated as a means of liberation but rather imposed on them by a well-meaning ruling class in the hope of turning them into productive workers and well-mannered citizens (de Castell, Luke & Egan, 1986; Graff, 1986; Katz, 1968; but see Tuman, 1987, chapter 5, for a critique of revisionist accounts). Recent calls for improvements in basic skills whether in Canada, the United States or Britain, come largely from employers in business and industry rather than from the workers themselves. And, with notable exceptions, the demand for evening, adult education courses, is a direct function of the amount of education people already have. So, is literacy an instrument of domination or an instrument of liberation? The impossibility of answering such a question has led such writers as Heath (1983) and Street (1984) to distinguish types of literacy, different ways of using and "taking from" texts, which are embedded in different social contexts; there may be no one literacy and no single set of implications.

Clanchy (1979) pointed out how the government policy of compulsory education as debated in Europe in the nineteenth century reflected not one literacy but two:

Opponents of government policy were worried that schools might succeed in educating people to a point where there would be a surplus of scholars and critics who might undermine the social hierarchy. Such fears were allayed by reformers emphasizing elementary practical literacy and numeracy (the three Rs of reading, writing and arithmetic) rather than a liberal education in the classical tradition, which remained as much the preserve of an elite of *litterati* in 1900 as it had been in 1200.

(1979, p. 263)

Similar complexities occur when we look more closely at industrial development. Simple claims regarding the relation between general levels of literacy of a population and economic development have not stood up to scrutiny. Cipolla (1969) and Graff (1979, 1986) have reviewed the disorderly relationship between popular literacy and economic development from the Middle Ages through the nineteenth century. They both noted that advances in trade, commerce, and industry sometimes occurred in contexts of low levels of literacy. Moreover, higher levels of literacy do not reliably presage economic development.

Kaestle, Damon-Moore, Stedman, Tinsley, and Trollinger's (1991) careful review of literacy in the US led them to conclude that literacy must be analyzed in specific historical circumstances and that "although for purposes of public policy, increased literacy is assumed to benefit both individuals and society as a whole, the association of literacy with progress has been challenged under certain circumstances" (p. 27).

The same point has been made in regard to the lack of scientific and economic development in other societies. In China the number of highly literate people always greatly exceeded the number of employment opportunities available (Rawski, 1978) and in Mexico while literacy levels have been found to be related to economic growth those effects were restricted largely to urban areas and to manufacturing activities (Fuller, Edwards, & Gorman, 1987).

Consequently, it is easy to overstate or misstate the functionality of literacy. Literacy is functional, indeed advantageous, in certain managerial, administrative and an increasing number of social roles. But the number of such positions which call for that level or kind of literacy is limited. Literacy is functional if one is fortunate enough to obtain such a position and not if not. Other, more general, functions served by literacy depend on the interests and goals of the individuals involved. The notion of "functional" literacy, unless one addresses the question "functional for what" or "functional for whom" is meaningless.

(5) Cultural development. Over the past two or three decades cultural historians and anthropologists have made us aware of the sophistication of "oral" cultures. Havelock (1963, 1982) provided evidence

that much of the "glory that was Greece" had evolved in an oral culture; writing had less to do with its invention than with its preservation. W. Harris (1989) showed that the degree of literacy in classical Greece, far from being universal, was quite limited. Probably no more than ten per cent of the Greeks in the era of Plato were literate. Thomas (1989) and Anderson (1989) have shown that classical Greek culture was primarily an "oral" culture, favoring the dialectic, that is discussion and argument, as instruments of knowledge and that writing played a small and relatively insignificant part. Consequently, it is unlikely that we can simply attribute the intellectual achievements of the Greeks to their literacy. Indeed, Lloyd (1990, p. 37) found that the discourse that gave rise to the distinctively Greek modes of thought "was mediated mainly in the *spoken* register." And anthropological studies of oral cultures, far from sustaining the earlier claims of Levy-Bruhl (1910/1926, 1923), have revealed both complex forms of discourse (Bloch, 1989; Feldman, 1991) and complex modes of thought which, for example, allowed Polynesian navigators to sail thousand-mile voyages without the aid of compass or chart (Gladwin, 1970; Hutchins, 1983; Oatley, 1977). Consequently, no direct causal links have been established between literacy and cultural development and current opinions run from the ecstatic "Literacy is of the highest importance to thought" (Baker, Barzun, & Richards, 1971, p. 7) to the dismissive "Writing something down cannot change in any significant way our mental representation of it" (Carruthers, 1990, p. 31).

(6) Literacy and cognitive development. It is simply a mistake, critics say, to identify the means of communication with the knowledge that is communicated. Knowledge can be communicated in a number of ways – by speech, writing, graphs, diagrams, audio tapes, video. The role of the school is not to displace children's pre-school perceptions and beliefs but to explicate and elaborate them, activities that depend as much or more on speech as on writing. Emphasis on the means may detract from the importance of the content being communicated. Furthermore it overlooks the significance of content in reading and learning to read. Reading ability depends upon not only letter and word recognition but in addition on the general knowledge of events that the text is *about*; consequently, a strict distinction between basic skills and specialized knowledge is indefensible.

Secondly, the use of literacy skills as a metric against which personal and social competence can be assessed is vastly oversimplified. Functional literacy, the form of competence required for one's daily life, far from being a universalizable commodity turns out on analysis to depend critically on the particular activities of the individual for whom literacy is to be functional. What is functional for an automated-factory worker may not be for a parent who wants to read to a child. The focus on literacy skills seriously underestimates the significance of both the implicit understandings that children bring to school and the importance of oral discourse in bringing those understandings into consciousness – in turning them into objects of knowledge. The vast amounts of time some children spend on remedial reading exercises may be more appropriately spent acquiring scientific and philosophical information. Indeed, some scholars find the concern with and emphasis on literacy puzzling. Bloch (in press) pointed out that even in the tiny remote village of rural Madagascar which he studied, in which literacy has essentially *no* functional or social significance, everyone, educated or not, is "absolutely convinced of the value of schooling and literacy" (p. 8). For the first time, many scholars are thinking the unthinkable: is it possible that literacy is over-rated?

Thus we see that all six of the major assumptions regarding the significance of literacy are currently under dispute. Yet despite the fact that virtually every claim regarding literacy has been shown to be problematic, literacy and its implications cannot be ignored. Derrida (1976, pp. 30–31) pointed out "this factum of phonetic writing is massive: it commands our entire culture and our entire science, and it is certainly not just one fact among others." Addressing this complexity by the enumeration of pros and cons, advantages and disadvantages of literacy – the so-called balanced perspective – is, as we have just seen, of limited use. What is required is a theory or set of theories of just how literacy relates to language, mind and culture. No such theory currently exists perhaps because the concepts of both literacy and thinking are too general and too vague to bear such theoretical burdens.

That is not to say that theories of great scope and influence have not been advanced. Although we shall consider these theories in detail in the next two chapters, it may be useful to indicate the general direction such theorizing has taken in the past. The great social theories of Durkheim (1948) and Weber (1905/1930) set out to relate cognitive change to social change but allowed no significant role to literacy in the transformations they described. Durkheim argued that cognitive structures are first social in nature; consequently, cognitive changes are by-products of social change; cognition was born out of coping with and rationalizing new social roles and relations. And Weber set out the possible relations between the "ethic" of Protestantism and the rise of capitalism, that ethic being centered on new forms of authority and an associated way of thinking. As Leach (1982) points out, only the sociological aspects of these theories have survived; the question as to how the culture could possibly affect cognition has been left aside.

This century has been witness to two grand psychological theories which have approached the question from the other end, namely, by attempting to explain social change on the basis of cognitive change, one tying cognitive change to the advance of science, the other to the advance of literacy.

The first of these theories was advanced by Levy-Bruhl (1910/1926; 1923) who proposed that the differences between traditional, oral cultures and modern ones was to be explained on the basis of differences in mental functioning:

The primitive's mind, oriented according to the law of participation, perceived no difficulty at all in statements which to us are absolutely contradictory. A person is himself and at the same time another being; he is in one place and he is also somewhere else; he is individual as well as collective, and so on ... The pre-logical mind ... by mystic symbiosis, felt and lived, the truth of them.

(p. 376)

The primitive mind constructed an "enchanted" world, a world inhabited by spirits and demons, influenced by incantations and omens, whereas the rational mind gave rise to a scientific conception of the world, a conception clearly based on evidence and on principles of causal and rational explanation.

Levy-Bruhl's writings continue to provide a fascinating introduction to all studies of the relation between culture and thought even if his conclusions are no longer considered defensible. He compared "their" religion with "our" science; he appeared to (but later denied it) equate primitive thought to childlike thought; he never raised the question of the appropriateness of using "our" conceptual categories for analyzing their statements, and he inferred patterns of thought from forms of expression when in fact the latter may have been little more than that (Sperber, 1975). Yet Levy-Bruhl's theory of mentalities remains not only one of the more readable but also more influential theories in the field. Although no one, these days, believes in the possibility of a non-rational mind, recent attempts are less matters of rejecting Levy-Bruhl outright than of explaining his observations in different ways (Goody & Watt, 1963/1968; Lloyd, 1990). Indeed, recent work on "styles" and "modes of reasoning" (Hacking, 1990; Tambiah, 1990) may be seen as an outgrowth of Levy-Bruhl's concern with distinctive ways of thinking and knowing.

The second of the great theories sometimes referred to (by others) as that of the Toronto School (Goody, 1987) because of the convergence there of McLuhan, Havelock and Innis, is the theory that the cultural differences described by Levy-Bruhl and others could be accounted for in terms of specific technologies of communication, first the alphabet and later, print. Although some versions of this theory are alive and well (indeed, I consider this volume to be part of that tradition), early formulations of that view have come in for severe criticism if not outright rejection. I have already mentioned some of these arguments: writing did not always and everywhere lead to democracy, science and logic; some non-alphabetic cultures evolved abstract sciences and philosophies; the evolution of Greek classical culture evolved from particular forms of political debate rather than from poring over written documents; different communities of readers may treat the same written documents in vastly different ways, and so on.

Furthermore, McLuhan's speculations regarding "eye" for "ear" or "oral" man versus "visual" man or "left-hemisphere" versus "right-hemisphere" seem to me merely metaphors for referring to the properties of literate cultures he so brilliantly collected and discussed, and fall far short of offering an explanation of those properties. In fact, McLuhan appeared to despair of making a general theory suggesting instead that the very attempt to synthesize a theory was a throwback to an obsolete literate culture and that one would do better in an eclectic culture to concern oneself with percepts rather than concepts. Goody and Watt's (1963/1968) proposal for relating literacy to the rise of syllogistic reasoning was criticized by Scribner and Cole (1981) who, when they distinguished literacy from schooling, found little evidence for a general effect of writing on reasoning. Goody (1987) in his most recent work tempers his original claims regarding the distinctiveness of the alphabet and remedies his under-emphasis of the social conditions in which writing is used, but holds fast to the notion that a written record has decisive practical advantages for carrying out a variety of cognitive functions. Ong's (1982) claim that "writing raises consciousness" held as plausible by some is flatly denied by others, most recently, as mentioned, by Carruthers (1990) who asserted that writing something down cannot change our mental representation of it. And Havelock's (1982) argument connecting the Greek invention of science and philosophy to the availability of a writing system is at least suspect in view of Lloyd's (1979) findings regarding the importance of oral political debate for that development. Suffice it to say, at this point, that the simple theory relating the availability of an alphabet or the availability of the printing press to altered patterns of speech or thought is at best a conjecture and at worst simply false (Finnegan, 1988; Halverson, 1992; Smith, 1989).

Although the resolution of this problem is the concern of this whole book we may note that while writing and literacy can be shown to serve certain important utilitarian functions such as making possible an "archival research tradition" (Eisenstein, 1979) and making possible the comparison and criticism of various versions of events (Goody, 1987, p. 237), no clear logical or empirical arguments have established any direct causal linkages between writing with thinking, partly as mentioned, because of the absence of a clear notion of either literacy or thinking. Indeed, such evidence as there is points in the opposite direction. A number of recent writers provide evidence that the cognitive processes thought by many to be dependent upon writing, such as memorization, reflection and composition of texts (Carruthers, 1990) or scientific thinking (Lloyd, 1990) were in fact invented for oral discourse. Even Aquinas' magisterial *Summa theo-*

logica (1267–73/1964–81), we are told, was dictated rather than written, from memory rather than from written notes.

Yet, it is undeniable that the invention and use of writing systems were instrumental, indeed essential, to the formation of modern bureaucratic societies. And although clearly not undeniable, it is at least plausible that literacy contributes in particular ways to the development of distinctive modes of thought that are conveyed through systematic education. But to make that case will require a much more nuanced account of the nature and implications of writing, an account that distinguishes the social from the psychological implications of literacy, the uses of basic skills from the more advanced literary skills, the relevance of literacy to particular groups from relevance to the general reading public. And to do that we require a more careful analysis of just what writing and literacy are, how language functions in various literate and oral contexts, what distinctive modes of thought and specialized forms of discourse are involved, what interpretive skills are called upon by each, and the particular picture of language, the self and the world that results from these activities.

Earlier attempts at a general theory failed, I suggest, because of a series of oversimplifications. For one, literacy was tied to alphabetization rather than to notations generally. For another, writing was seen as embodying grammar and logic rather than as providing a representation of the grammar and logic of ordinary speech. Correspondingly, metalinguistic knowledge and awareness was seen as all or none, either as a product of writing or as independent of writing. For another, literacy was seen as a direct function of a written text rather than as a way of taking texts by a group of readers. Finally, writing was seen as either superior to or as inferior to speech.

If literacy is thought of as simply the basic skill of recognizing emblems or of decoding letters to sound or words to meanings, the implications of literacy, while important, are bound to be limited. But if we regard literacy in the classical sense, as the ability to understand and use the intellectual resources provided by some three thousand years of diverse literate traditions, the implications of learning to exploit these resources may be enormous. Enormous not only in that literacy has permitted the accumulation of treasures which are stored in texts but also in that it involves a diverse set of procedures for acting on and thinking about language, the world and ourselves. That is the main concern of this book.

What could we expect from a theory of literacy and mind? It should address the relations between speech and writing, specifically, the lexical, grammatical, speech act and discourse properties of both speech and writing and the role that transcription plays in their divergence. It should offer an account of how the evolution of scripts altered the practices of reading. In turn, it should suggest how changes in reading and writing practices contributed to the distinctive shifts in conceptual orientation that were associated with significant cultural changes. It should indicate the ways in which learning to read and criticize texts contributes to the development of critical thought generally. It should contribute to our understanding of the intellectual development of children from the pre-school to the more advanced levels of schooling. And it should provide us with an enlightened attitude as to why literacy and written texts came to hold the position of prominence and authority they do in modern bureaucratic societies. But most importantly, it should contribute to a clear and defensible notion of the overused but little understood notions of reading, literacy and thinking.

But at the same time such a theory should help to disabuse us of our simple prejudices regarding literacy. It should offer an alternative to the superficial understanding of literacy which allows the perpetuation of the view that people who cannot read are pathetic and deprived, that illiteracy is a social problem comparable to poverty, malnutrition and disease with which it is commonly grouped, that members of non-literate societies are ignorant savages, that children who fail to learn to read are ineducable, and that those who have not gone to school know little of value.

To provide a general hint as to the line of argument I shall develop, it is that the failure of earlier theories of the implications of literacy comes from their assumption that literacy has its effects through advances *in ways of writing*, that is, the form of the script; in contrast I shall argue that conceptual implications arise from the *ways of reading*, for it is the art of reading which allows a text to be taken as a model for verbal form, that is, for "what is said." These models of what is said, whether as sounds, words or sentences, are always incomplete, giving rise to problems of interpretation. Whereas scripts provide reasonably adequate models for what is said, they provide less adequate models for how what is said is *to be taken*, what in modern parlance we describe as illocutionary force. The problems of reading/interpretation, then, arise not from what texts represent – sounds, words and sentences – so much as from what they fail to represent, the manner or attitude of the speaker or writer to what is said. I trace the history of solutions to the reading/interpretive problem, showing how ways of writing and ways of reading yield a set of beliefs and assumptions, a "logocentrism," which pervades readers' understanding of language, the world and themselves. I focus on the new way of reading scripture – for its intended meaning – that evolved in the late Middle Ages and that gave rise to the Reformation, and the corresponding new way of reading the "Book of Nature" that gave rise to early modern science. My goal is to show how our understanding of the world, that is our science, and our understanding of ourselves, that is, our psychology, are by-products of our ways of interpreting and creating written texts, of living in a world on paper.

THEORIES OF LITERACY AND MIND
FROM LEVY-BRUHL TO SCRIBNER
AND COLE

••

> The external world they perceive differs from that which we
> apprehend.
>
> (Levy-Bruhl, 1910/1926)

With the publication of Scribner and Cole's (1981), *The psychology of literacy*, the theory that literacy could account for the broad-based social and psychological changes set out in the revolutionary writings of Havelock, McLuhan, Goody and Watt, and Ong, was, at least in many people's eyes, laid to rest. The introduction of a script into a traditional society, they found, produced no general cognitive effects such as the ability to memorize, to classify, or to draw logical inferences. The source of significant cognitive change, if indeed such changes occurred, had to be sought elsewhere such as in altered social conditions or in the processes of schooling. Patricia Greenfield (1983) expressed the general view by saying that the Scribner and Cole volume "should rid us once and for all of the ethnocentric and arrogant view that a single technology suffices to create in its users a distinct, let alone superior, set of cognitive processes" (p. 219). To see how theories of literacy and mind that began the century with such promise could have fallen to such low estate by the end of the century is the purpose of this chapter. Its second purpose is to set the stage for a new beginning: Minerva's owl takes flight only in the gathering dusk.

Does cognition have a history?

Either to assert or deny a relation between literacy and thought requires that we have some working conception of both. Literacy is, of course, a historical achievement; we can track both the evolution of the technology of writing and the spread of readership. But it is not at all certain that thinking – forms of rationality – has any such history. We begin, therefore, with the question: Does rationality have a history?

Clearly, thinking has a developmental history; children's thinking is demonstrably different from that of adults. Piaget's legacy is the idea that not only the quantity of children's knowledge grows but that their *epistemology* develops; development involves both learning more and thinking about it differently. To cite a simple example: When children are still infants they acquire a huge store of knowledge about themselves and their world. But when they are four or five years of age they begin to understand *how they know* about the world. This is not merely another piece of knowledge; it is a matter of developing an entirely new stance to their prior knowledge. They acquire an epistemology, a new understanding of the conditions of knowledge (Wimmer, Hogrefe, & Sodian, 1988). This is, of course, only a first stage of a series of transformations. Much later they learn that not only is there a distinction between what they know and what they believe but also that what they know is a species of what they believe – that even knowledge is revisable. At that point we could say that they begin to think theoretically.

Some writers have been tempted to take Piagetian stages as a model for cultural states, suggesting that some cultures are concrete, others formal in their modes of thought (Hallpike, 1979). While the parallel is suggestive it is also misleading. The fact that cognition develops through a series of transformations in childhood is no argument for the hypothesis that the cognition of adults has a history. For one thing, while children's development is usefully viewed as progressive, cultural differences do not represent stages on a universal scale with Western culture at the top. Stable cultures are all "mature." For another the metaphor offers nothing that would causally explain the parallel. While it is obvious that different people and different cultures hold different beliefs, it is not obvious that they have different ways of thinking about their beliefs, that is, that they hold different epistemologies. But if they do not, if human cognition, human rationality, is always and everywhere much the same, then cognition does not have a history and we can make short work of the theory connecting cognition with literacy.

We can approach the same point from another angle. Some disciplines, notably history, attempt to describe particular modes of thought and forms of discourse that characterize particular historical periods and particular social groups. Thus, we have an account of the legal or religious or scientific thinking of Socratic Greece, Medieval England or Puritan New England or the Zafimaniry of Madagascar. More generally, and perhaps less defensibly, we may characterize thought as magical, that is, "enchanted," or fundamentalist or critical, each of which would seem to imply not only different levels of sophistication but also different ways of generalizing, using evidence, or justifying inferences. We are back to the same question: Are there in fact such things as modes of thought and do they have a history? If thinking is always and everywhere the same we can again make short work of the theory relating literacy to cognition.

Of course all people are rational; it is part of the definition of a human being. One of the more obvious achievements of a century of anthropological research is the discovery that people are remarkably similar in forms of talk and thought and that there are deep commonalities in the ways they assign privilege, mete out justice, worship their gods, bury their dead, and so on. While in Marco Polo's day (twelfth century) informed people could believe in the possibility that there existed, somewhere, dog-headed people and in Daniel Defoe's day (seventeenth century) that there were truly uncivilized people such as the boy "Friday," those days are gone forever. "They're the same as you and me, you know" or should know. Only in time of war do we allow ourselves the liberty of thinking that other societies are composed of or led by "madmen."

Non-literate cognition: Neolithic thinking

In what ways are we all cognitively the same? Although this is an important question, good answers are not yet available. The "psychic unity of mankind" is not adequately characterized by listing the chapter headings in any introductory psychology book: sensation, perception, thinking, memory, language. You could not have a human being without these. We gain a new respect for the cognitive powers of our Neolithic forebears by considering Levi-Strauss' (1966) account:

To transform a weed into a cultivated plant, a wild beast into a domestic animal, to produce, in either of these, nutritious or technologically useful properties which were originally completely absent or could only be guessed at; to make stout, water-tight pottery out of clay which is friable and unstable, liable to pulverize or crack (which, however, is possible only if from a large number of organic and inorganic materials, the one most suitable for refining it is selected, and also the appropriate fuel, the temperature and duration of firing and the effective degree of oxidation); to work out techniques, often long and complex, which permit cultivation without soil or alternatively without water; to change toxic roots or seeds into foodstuffs or again to use their poison for hunting, war or ritual – there is no doubt that all these achievements required a genuinely scientific attitude, sustained and watchful interest and a desire for knowledge for its own sake. For only a small proportion of observations and experiments (which must be assumed to have been primarily inspired by a desire for knowledge) could have yielded practical and immediately useful results . . . Neolithic, or early historical, man was therefore the heir of a long scientific tradition.

(1966, pp. 14–15)

We would be misguided if we looked to literacy for an explanation of the evolution of Neolithic thought although there is some evidence that pre-writing in the form of tokens may date back to Paleolithic times as do the impressive cave drawings at Altamira and Lascaux. Levi-Strauss does contrast such concrete science with the more abstract, symbol-based scientific thought more characteristic of Western science. It is not unreasonable to expect that just as practical "science" has a history, such symbol-based thought has a history as well. And it is a proper task of psychology, along with its allied disciplines, to attempt to characterize those symbolic developments, developments in which literacy may play a critical part. We shall consider those related to writing in Chapter 4.

Thus, while it is unreasonable to expect that there is a history of the basic cognitive processes such as perception and inference – no one expects brain function to change notably in a mere twenty or even two hundred generations – it is not unreasonable to expect that the techniques, technologies, systems, schemes, forms and formats for managing these processes would have changed and, indeed, would have a history. Memory has a history in the sense that some cultures evolved particular mnemonic systems for preserving significant cultural and verbal information. Thinking has a history in the sense that cultures have evolved and accumulated both practices, concepts and categories for thinking about language, the world and the self. These practices and associated concepts are what give thinking a history. And although cognition in each human culture may have a distinctive history, it is important that we begin to understand something of the forces that gave rise to our "modern" or privileged modes of thought.

Histories of thinking

If literacy did play a role in such a history, what concept of literacy are we to adopt in formulating this role: the invention of a script? of an alphabetic script? of scripting a particular form of discourse, such as literature or law? of reading (interpreting) a script in a particular way? of talking about the things that were scripted? of the democratization of a script? of the invention of specialized written genres? Any explanatory theory will have to state just how writing and literacy altered rational activities.

Certainly it does not seem unreasonable to narrow our focus to a concern with the evolution of particular forms of thought, in particular, ways of thinking about nature, about scripture, about law and life, and about the role that writing played in that evolution. Different disciplines formulate their theories at different levels of generality. Some theories may be satisfied to show a general correlation between writing and cultural change or between degree of literacy and social development. But we (I invite you the reader to join in this enquiry) are after something more precise. What we seek is an explanation which would indicate just how reading and writing could contribute to that effect. Consequently, we cannot appeal to some general notion as "visual bias" or "visual abilities" or "levels of consciousness" or "analytic skill" or "abstraction ability" – concepts of dubious explanatory value – but rather we must indicate just what thinkers were attending to, looking for, representing, and remembering about what they said, did, wrote, drafted and drew. We seek, in a word, the evolution of a new set of concepts, concepts brought into focus in the attempt to use writing for a variety of social purposes such as science, law, literature, history, philosophy and religion; indeed to the differentiation and specialization of these activities.

Even if we grant that thinking indeed has a history and that literacy could have played a part in it we still may have to assign a priority to social changes as opposed to psychological changes. Social theorists have always argued that social changes, urbanization for example, bring cognitive changes in their wake. Cognitive theorists argue that need alone never gives rise to concepts; concepts, and not just institutions, are invented by people and have a history. Conceptual changes, on this latter view, set the stage for social ones. Social conditions, rather, may determine which concepts are adopted and which rejected. This issue sets the stage for our review, for in fact, the first modern theories of the rise of modern thought were in fact social theories, namely, those of Marx, Durkheim and Weber. Let us begin there.

Social histories of thinking: Marx, Durkheim and Weber

There is a strand in the social sciences leading from Marx and Durkheim to Weber and later to Vygotsky and Luria which allots primacy to social conditions over psychological structures. Marx (1906) had argued in *Capital* that human nature and human abilities were always secondary to modes of production; what you did determined how you thought. Durkheim, too, argued that logical life was rooted in social life (Lukes, 1973, p. 441). Concepts, what he called *collective representations*, are not just ideas held for their truth, they are the glue which binds a society together. To be a person in a society you have to adopt the concepts of the culture; such concepts are binding and have a sacred, that is, religious status. Durkheim argued, however, that social change could bring about, indeed had brought about, a shift from religious to scientific concepts, the latter marking progress not only in social organization but also in modes of thinking. As we noted, only the sociological aspects of Durkheim have survived, leaving little room for attention to the cognitive processes of individuals. The strength of the theory, for our purposes, is that it did offer a possible explanation for the Reformation, the rise of Early Modern Science and mentalistic psychology; all were manifestations of social changes associated with the decline of feudalism and the rise of individualism, capitalism and democratic political organizations.

This theme was picked up more explicitly by Max Weber (1905/1930), who advanced the idea of a link between the Reformation and the rise of capitalism; both were seen as manifestations of a formal logic of the rationality of means and ends. Logical analysis of means – ends relations, a sort of assembly line form of thought, contributed to a disenchanted view of nature, that is science, and a methodical form of religion, Protestantism. Neither Durkheim nor Weber had much to offer by way of psychological theory and, as mentioned, their influence today is primarily in sociology and anthropology, although Latour and Woolgar (1986) have shown the usefulness of the Durkheimian per-spective in understanding the sociology of scientific discovery.

The Merton (1970) thesis, a refinement on Weber's thesis, again attempted to explain the relation between religious and scientific thought, specifically, to explain just why so many of the Early Modern scientists were also Puritans. Merton offered the view that Puritan communities offered an "ethic" of utilitarianism, hard work and personal responsibility, each man being his own interpreter of scrip-ture and nature, which was conducive to the development of experi-mental science. Kuhn (1977) has criticized proponents of the Merton thesis for assuming that the critical factor in the scientific revolution was the development of the experimental method. In Kuhn's view experimentalism was secondary; what was required was "putting on a different kind of thinking cap," a notion he borrowed from Butterfield (1965). Kuhn concludes that "it has yet to be shown that the ideology which a number of them embraced had a major effect, substantive or methodological, on their central contributions to science" (p. 117). Just where that new thinking cap came from remains unclear. Could a theory of reading help fill that gap?

The Marxist view took a more specifically psychological form in the writings of Vygotsky and Luria. Both adopted the view that the "higher mental processes" always involve the use of socially invented signs such as language, writing, numerals, and depictions which are culturally diverse, and which, to return to an earlier point, have a history. The means by which these cultural resources come to be psychological resources is described as "internalization," a concept which I shall argue later is irredeemably vague. Yet they offered specific proposals as to just how writing and literacy could influence cognitive operations and activities and offered these proposals as candidate explanations of the development from primitive to modern forms of thinking, a development they both associate with literacy. To understand their proposals we will have to return to the anthropological work of Levy-Bruhl (1910/1926, 1923) where the concept of "primitive thought" was first elaborated.

Primitive thinking

The notion of a "primitive" mind, one bereft of the benefits of culture, and indicative of the first age or stage of mankind, the natural or the "savage" mind, dates from the age of discovery. Explorers such as Columbus in the fifteenth century and Cook in the eighteenth produced extensive accounts of the thought and actions of so-called primitive people, not only their apparent savagery – Cook was appalled by the cannibalism he encountered in Van Daiman's Land (Tasmania) – but also their sensitivities – Cook noted that the cannibals who 'relished' their enemies were equally appalled at Cook's suggestion that they might also eat one of their own slain tribesmen (Beaglehole, 1955/1967, p. 71). Belief in magic and witchcraft, in supernatural explanations for what appeared to be ordinary events, and in the perception of writing as a magic art was frequently documented by early explorers.

Systematic attempts to work out the properties of primitive thought took a modern form with Levy-Bruhl's systematic anthropological studies as reported in his first volume, *How natives think* (1926), first published in French in 1910. In fact his book is a charming tabulation of observations and anecdotes of events deemed magical by traditional non-literate, unschooled subjects. The cases Levy-Bruhl discusses can be shown to have a similar underlying form. I will describe one such case in detail, namely, the belief held by the Huichol of Mexico that "Corn, deer, and hikuli (a sacred plant) are, in a way, one and the same thing." Levy-Bruhl points out that all three are associated with intense religious emotions because of their significance, and for this reason are referred to by the Huichol as "the same thing" or again as "identical." In addition their mythology claims that corn was once a deer, and so on. Levy-Bruhl offers and abandons several explanatory hypotheses: they are all necessary for life and therefore "the same"; they are all "analogies," that is figures or models of each other, and so on. He points out that "from the standpoint of logical thought, such 'identities' are, and remain, unintelligible." His preferred hypothesis is a cognitive one; such beliefs arise from a pre-logical mode of thought, a logic of participation, which allows that some spiritual quality connects these diverse objects, and allows the primitive mind to affirm at the same time "This is a deer" and "This is corn" (1923, pp. 122–125). Modern anthropologists continue to debate the meaning of such expressions which have been reported in many traditional cultures. The Nuer of Sudan claim that "Twins are birds" (Beattie, 1970), the Zafimaniry claim that "The centre post (of the clan's chief's house) is an ancestor" (Bloch, in press), and the Puluwat Islander navigators claim that "East is a big bird" (Gladwin, 1970), all of which are similar in form to that of the Huichol.

Levy-Bruhl explained such thoughts by appeal to Durkheim's notion of collective representations:

... primitives perceive nothing in the same way as we do. The social milieu which surrounds them differs from ours, and precisely because it is different, the external world they perceive differs from that which we apprehend. Undoubtedly they have the same senses as ours ... and their cerebral structure is like our own. But we have to bear in mind that which their collective representations instil into all their perceptions ... [For them] all things have an invisible existence as well as a visible one.

(1910/1926, p. 43)

Although many critics have ridiculed Levy-Bruhl's notion of primitive thought – in fact he later abandoned the notion because it tended to represent such thought as childish – others (Tambiah, 1990), I among them, believe that Levy-Bruhl was very close to the correct explanation. Levy-Bruhl (1923, p. 43) traced these magical beliefs to the fact that "the mind does not differentiate between sign and cause." Natural signs such as tracks cause no problem. But when signs "manifest the presence of mystic forces, it is no longer possible to distinguish 'sign' and 'cause'." Stated in a modern argot, Levy-Bruhl was claiming that traditional thought had difficulty managing the relation between thing and representation of a thing, believing that the representation carried some of the properties of the thing represented, a relation which is technically referred to as metonymy.

This suggestion gains plausibility when we note that metaphor and metonymy have not always been distinguished. Lloyd (personal communication, 1993) has suggested that the distinction between the two is unique to the traditions that stem from Aristotle. In the Middle Ages many people believed in the efficacy of relics and to this day we are tempted to believe in the efficacy of charms, curses, blessings and well-wishings. As we shall see, the issue of determining precisely how to take such biblical statements as "The kingdom of heaven is within you" or "This is my body," continued to puzzle scholars throughout the Middle Ages just as they continue to puzzle many of us to this day.

Metonymy, taking signs, especially images, as somehow embodying the things they are signs of is deeply rooted in all of us, primitive or modern. The ancient stricture on "graven images" implies a concern with the possibility of confusing the image with the thing it is an image of. Gombrich (1950) reminds us that even the most civilized among us would still feel a twinge if we were to poke a pin through the eye of a photograph of a friend. Revolutionaries topple statues of deposed despots and we do not allow our children to mutilate their dolls.

The gulf, therefore, between primitive and modern is a subtle one. But it is nonetheless a significant one. Although we may be squeamish about poking a pin through the photograph of a friend's eye, most of us do not believe that harm to a photograph or a doll would adversely affect the person represented; we do not believe in voodoo magic. We consent, grudgingly perhaps, to Magritte's caption "Ceci n'est pas une pipe" lettered underneath a painting of a pipe (see Figure 2.1). And we do our sciences by exploring alternative models or representations of things – a form of activity which presupposes a radical discontinuity between a thing and a representation of a thing. For now it is sufficient to suggest that changing notions of representation may indeed be an area in which understanding has evolved. Just how that shift in understanding occurred is the subject of Chapter 5.

If we are correct in diagnosing the principal feature of "primitive" thought as, at base, one of understanding the relation between representations and reality, we will not be surprised to find that members of traditional societies unfamiliar with writing also hold views, which to us are extravagant, about writing. In fact, Levy-Bruhl found that writing was treated by his "natives" as magical: "Even when the native

Figure 2.1   *Ceci n'est pas une pipe* by René Magritte

appears to have learnt what writing is, even if he can read and write, he never loses the feeling that a mystical force is at work" (p. 430). Again, "For the savages, books and writing are no less an object of astonishment than firearms ... They see them at once as an instrument of divination" (1923, p. 424). Thus Levy-Bruhl reports a man from Bechuanaland as saying "I will not carry letters any more. If this letter had talked to me on my way, I would have been so scared" (p. 427). Others pierced the paper with a spear to prevent it from doing any harm by suddenly speaking up. Wundt (1916) in his *Elements of folk psychology (Volkerpsychologie)* extensively discussed the relation between writing and magic suggesting that even the newly literate treat writing as having magical powers. W. Harris (1989) provides a photograph of an ancient Greek curse-tablet which reads: "Earth, Hermes, Gods of the Underworld, accept Venusta the slave of Rufus." The written version was felt to add strength to the curse; perhaps it can keep uttering the curse relentlessly, without stopping for breath!

Blixen in her book *Out of Africa* gives a kindly portrayal of the mixture of astonishment and hilarity which greeted her oral reading of the personal letters received by non-literate Kikuyu written in their own language but which they could not read and which she could read but not understand:

> I learned that the effect of a piece of news was many times magnified when it was imparted by writing. The messages that would have been received with doubt and scorn if they had been given by word of mouth – for all Natives are great sceptics – were now taken as gospel truth. Natives are, in the same way, extremely quick of hearing towards any confounding of a word in speech; such a mistake gives them a great malicious pleasure, and they will never forget it, and may name a white man for his lifetime after a slip of his tongue; but if a mistake was made in writing, which was often the case, as the Scribes were ignorant people, they would insist on construing it into some sense, they might wonder over it and discuss it, but they would believe the most absurd things rather than find fault with the written word.
>
> In one of the letters that I read out to a boy on the farm, the writer, amongst other news, gave the laconic message: 'I have cooked a baboon.' I explained that he must have meant that he had caught a baboon, since also in Swahili the two words are somewhat alike. But the receiver of the letter would by no means consent to it.
>
> 'No, Msabu, no,' he said, 'what has he written in my letter? What is written down?'
>
> 'He has written,' I said, 'that he has cooked a baboon, but how would he cook a baboon? And if he had really done so he would write more to tell you of why and how he did it.'
>
> The young Kikuyu grew very ill at ease at such criticism of the scriptural word; he asked to have his letter back, folded it up carefully and walked away with it.
>
> (1972, pp. 93–94)

No one doubts the veracity of these accounts but no one finds it useful, that is explanatory, to label such episodes as "primitive thinking." But if we see them as examples of cases in which signs or symbols not only stand for an object or event, but, in fact, carry or convey some of the properties of the referent, that is, of cases in which a strict boundary is not enforced between representation and represented especially in dealing with sacred symbols, we will no longer find such behavior simply incomprehensible. Further, we will have set the stage for asking the question as to the conditions under which such distinctions come to be made systematically. For when honored systematically, I suggest, we see if not the end at least the beginning of the end of magical thinking.

We should be sympathetic to the possibility that the problem is one of sorting out distinctions between representations and things represented when we realize that contemporary philosophy continues to grapple with just that problem. We don't know, for example, whether Artificial Intelligence systems, implemented on computers, simulate, that is represent thought, or actually think. That is not so much different than the Huichol not being sure whether "Corn is deer" or only that "Corn stands for deer."

Harbsmeier (1988) has examined the reported cases of "primitive" attitudes to writing and finds little difference between non-literates' attitude to written texts and that of the literates with which they dealt. The writing to which they had been exposed, he notes, was principally the Bible: "Learning to read for him therefore is tantamount to changing religion" (Levy-Bruhl, 1923, p. 425). Thus when a missionary questioned a man from Transvaal about his practice of rolling "bones" as a divinatory practice, he replied "For us, this is our book; you are reading the Bible all day, and you believe in it; we are reading ours" (p. 425).

Evans-Pritchard (1937), too, reported that the Azande often say: "'The poison oracle does not err, it is our paper. What your paper is to you, the poison oracle is to us,' for they see in the art of writing the source of a European's knowledge, accuracy, memory of events, and predictions of the future" (p. 263). Harbsmeier (1988) notes that these informants grasped the equivalence between their "writing" and the western missionary's Bible in a way that the missionaries and anthropologists themselves had failed to. Both are equally magical; they can safeguard the present and foretell the future.

In my view, the perspectives on writing taken by non-literate peoples are not dissimilar from those which literates, on occasion, take to sacred documents, our holy books or personal documents. Yet as with the totemic beliefs discussed earlier, attitudes to writing do suggest that a conceptual boundary between the words and their meanings or texts and their messages has been redrawn under the impact of a literate tradition. That boundary, again, is between the representation and what is represented or, more precisely, between metonymy and metaphor. In metonymy a *part* stands for the whole; the symbol is a part of the thing symbolized; in metaphor it merely stands for something. To modern literates the boundary is a rather strict one; to traditional subjects, at least in sacred contexts, it is not strict if it exists at all. The result is a magical orientation to texts as well as to nature.

Psychological perspectives

It is one thing to try to characterize the mode of thought of a people and quite another to attempt to determine just how any one individual thinks. We must allow for diversity and we must make allowance for the possibility that there is not a close match between the popular, public view and the actual beliefs and feelings of individuals. So even if someone claims that "Corn is deer" it is not clear what inferences they will draw from a neutral statement such as "All the bears in Novaya Zemlya are white." That requires experimental test. In fact the first systematic tests of the logical reasoning of members of traditional societies were carried out by Vygotsky and his colleague Luria in the mid-1930s.

As mentioned, Vygotsky and Luria worked from the Marxist perspective which claimed that cognition and consciousness were the products of human activity, rather than the cause. Vygotsky (1962, 1978), for example, suggested that human memory takes alternative forms depending upon cultural resources. While all humans remember by virtue of "natural memory," that is memory called up on the basis of the direct influence of external stimuli, cultures differ in their evolution of mnemonics, devices to artificially enhance remembering including notched sticks, knotted strings, memory aids and writing: "even at early stages of historical development humans went beyond the limits of the psychological functions given to them by nature and proceeded to a new, culturally-elaborated organization of their behavior" (1978, p. 39).

The way that cultural technology was thought to affect cognitive process was both through allowing a new level of activity, and more importantly, through making the primary activity conscious. Thus, both Vygotsky (1962, p. 99; 1978, Ch. 7) and Luria (1946; cited by

Downing, 1987, p. 36) suggested that writing not only allowed one to do new things but, more importantly, turned speech and language into objects of reflection and analysis. The beginning reader, Luria suggested:

> is still not able to make the word and verbal relations an object of his consciousness. In this period a word may be used but not noticed by the child, and it frequently seems like a glass window through which the child looks at the surrounding world without making the word itself an object of his consciousness and without suspecting that it has its own existence, its own structural features.
>
> (p. 61)

Although this is an extremely important claim, it should be noted that it is not obvious why a secondary activity makes the primary activity conscious, that is, why writing makes language into an object of consciousness. Nor does it indicate what particular features of language become such objects of thought, nor whether writing itself is essential or merely useful for this new consciousness. But we do have the feeling that this hypothesis is pointing in the right direction.

In cooperation with Vygotsky, Luria conducted a series of psychological studies in Central Asia, an area then undergoing rapid social change under the collectivization programs of the government. Luria was able to give a series of psychological tests, including classification and reasoning tasks, to a group of traditional non-literate farmers and to a comparable group from the same villages who had some exposure to literacy and to a third group that had some teacher training experience. Those least literate were more likely to treat tasks in a concrete, context-bound way while the more literate took an abstract, principled approach to the series of tasks. Those with a low degree of literacy fell between these groups.

Most interesting for our purposes were subjects' performance on tasks designated as "formal reasoning tasks," basically syllogisms. Here is a typical, widely cited example:

> In the far North, where there is snow, all bears are white. Novaya Zemlya is in the Far North and there is always snow there. What color are the bears there?

To which a non-literate subject, not untypically responded:

"I don't know ... There are different sorts of bears."

(Luria, 1976, pp. 108–109)

Luria called such responses failures to infer from the syllogism. In general, when subjects had no knowledge of the facts alleged in the premises they were unwilling to draw any inferences from them; if the alleged facts contradicted their beliefs, they based their conclusions on what they knew rather than on the premises.

Both Vygotsky and Luria concluded from such findings that advancing technical change and urbanization brought on by collectivization did lead individual subjects to reason more formally, to confine their inferences to the stated premises. I have always felt that they should have adhered to their original theory which suggested that the main role of literacy and urbanization was not so much that it developed new resources such as logical thinking so much as it brought the old resources into consciousness. Surely we must agree with John Locke who said "God has not been so sparing to men to make them barely two-legged creatures, and left it to Aristotle to make them rational" (quoted by Goody & Watt, 1963/1968, p. 65). But it is completely reasonable to expect that literacy, schooling, and perhaps public discourse (in the forum) would bring those logical resources into consciousness. Humans could always reason but they did not always reason about reason. They did not always recognize that sound reasoning could be characterized by a set of rules which could be used to judge the validity of reasoning. Those rules make up logic. Concepts and consciousness may have a history. It seems necessary to conclude that the distinction between representation and metarepresentation, between reasoning and logic, was not consistently honored even in the salutary work of Vygotsky and Luria.

The studies of Vygotsky and Luria on the cognitive effects of literacy and culture have been pursued by Scribner and Cole recently with the pessimistic conclusions mentioned at the beginning of this chapter. But before we explore those findings it is necessary to point out the important theoretical developments that occurred in the 1960s which informed the more recent work. I refer to the remarkable, contemporaneous publications of McLuhan, *The Gutenberg Galaxy* (1962), Goody and Watt, "The consequences of literacy" (1963/1968), and Havelock, *Preface to Plato* (1963).

All three of these texts reversed the conventional assumption about media, namely, that they passively represent their subject. Harold Innis (1950) had somewhat earlier suggested that media of communication each had a "bias." Writing on stone, he suggested, organized societies through time as in Egypt. Writing on papyrus, on the other hand, organized societies across space as in Rome. But in the 1960s the hypothesis was pushed forward that the major features that characterize our own "modern" societies, our sciences, and our psychology are simply by-products first of alphabetic writing and later of printing.

Goody and Watt pointed out that the study of logic and of grammar always followed the invention of a writing system. They argued that writing made it possible to set pieces of text side by side and check them for identity or to look for relations between them. This resource, when applied to accounts of the past, would permit the differentiation between myth and history, when applied to arguments would permit the differentiation between rhetoric and logic, when applied to nature would permit the differentiation between science and magic. Writing, they suggested, preserves statements and thereby opens them up to critical inquiry. In this way they suggested one might account for the dramatic changes that occurred in Classical Greek times after the invention of alphabetic writing in about 750 BC.

Havelock, relying on the work of Milman Parry on Homeric verse, developed the argument that the use of writing to preserve information permitted a radical discontinuity with the oral poetry which had been used for that purpose. He saw Plato's attacks on the poets in the Classical Greek period as a manifestation of the rivalry between these competing traditions. Oral tradition depends upon rhyme and rhythm as well as dramatic deeds of gods and heroes if it is to be memorable and serve as the base of a culture. Writing relaxed these constraints on memorability. Equipped with an optimal writing system, that is, one capable of preserving in writing everything that could be said orally, the stage was set for the evolution of a new, now literate, form of discourse and hence of thought. The literate mode depended not on memorability but on stated principles, on explicit definitions of terms, on logical analysis and detailed proofs. The result was the end of enchantment and the beginning of the modern conception of the world.

McLuhan was more concerned with the impact of the printing press. Some of his conjectures have been fully established by the thorough work of Eisenstein (1979, 1985). The manufacture of identical copies of texts, maps, charts and diagrams and their simultaneous distribution to hundreds of readers, contributed enormously to the establishment of an archival research tradition. As McLuhan mentioned, the average seventeenth-century scientist had access to more medieval writers than any medieval scholar ever did. Clanchy (1979) noted that Rochester Cathedral library in 1202, for example had only 241 items; Durham Cathedral had 490. McLuhan pointed out that reading in the Middle Ages tended to be oral; printing brought silent reading and so to "divorce eye and speech in the act of reading" (1962, p. 83), a point which has been examined and verified, by Saenger (1982, 1991). I (Olson, 1977) attributed my own hypothesis that writing permitted the distinction between "sentence meaning" and "intended meaning" to McLuhan, but in my more recent rereading I failed to find him actually making that specific claim.

The excitement of McLuhan's writing springs from its sheer scope; the particulars of his hypotheses regarding oral man, literate man, electronic man and so on continue to be apt metaphors but have limited theoretical use. They fail, I believe, not because they are false but because they do not indicate precisely how writing or printing could actually have produced those effects. To appeal to the visual sense modality as providing linearity of thought is good metaphor but poor science.

Walter Ong's writings on the shift from medieval to renaissance thought are perhaps the clearest extension of McLuhan's theory. In a series of books, represented by *The presence of the word* (1976) and *Orality and literacy* (1982), Ong explored the idea that writing and particularly printing was responsible for the death of rhetoric and dialectic as instruments of thought. Following Descartes, Ong examined the displacement of the logic of disputation by a logic of inquiry – "which is not the art of discourse but the art of thinking," as the Port Royal grammarians put it (Hacking, 1975a). The transformation comes about, Ong argued, by the substitution of reading for listening, the shift from an acoustic image to a visual one. Ong charts the development of "the self-conscious individual" (1976, p. 134) and the "shift in human consciousness" (1982, p. 78) by showing how writing lifts speech out of its context and turns it into an object of thought and interpretation. But he prefers to explain these shifts by appeal to the sense modalities employed, as did McLuhan; the ear tribalizes, the eye analyzes. As metaphor, that is apt, but it detracts, I believe, from the search for a causal explanation. Explanation by appeal to eye versus ear or to left and right brain as McLuhan did in his later years may ultimately be relevant but so far it has mostly been co-opted by pop psychology.

It was these four writers who gave new impetus and perspective to the serious study of literacy. Scholars in a variety of disciplines realized, many for the first time, that literacy may matter. I (Olson, 1977) began to wonder if learning to read and write would help children to distinguish what was said by a speaker or a text from what was intended by it; Clanchy (1979) began to examine in detail just what happened to legal thinking as legal practice began to rely more systematically upon written laws, writs and evidence; Eisenstein (1979) examined how the printing press influenced how post-reformation religion and science were conducted; Stock (1983) began to examine how "textual communities" organized around a text, an interpretation and an interpreter, gave rise to the groups of heretics frequently appearing just prior to the Reformation.

All of these theories were offered as explanations of historical changes in cognition associated with the exploitation of literate technologies. None of them were guilty of "technological determinism," that is, of advancing a monocausal account of social and cognitive change, but all contributed to the current intellectual scene which is characterized by an interest in the implications and uses of literacy. In my view, all of these theories are largely correct; but they all fail to show precisely how writing could bring about cognitive change, that is, how they could permit the generation of new concepts, for it is the new concepts that produce new consciousness. In fairness, it should be mentioned that some of these theories do not argue that writing alters one's stock of concepts; it simply makes it easier, they say, to use the concepts you already have. In Goody's view, for example, you don't need new concepts such as myth and history, you just need better records and the divergence will tend to appear.

Such hypotheses, being ,historical ones, are not readily put to psychological test. As Goody points out (1987, p. 221), his analysis was concerned with the question of what writing made possible, and which of those things the cultures he had studied had, in fact, seized upon. His was *not* work in the Vygotsky tradition which compared people in the same culture, some of whom could read and others not.

On the other hand, if access to a written code does alter one's perception of linguistic form, of phonemes, of words, of sentences, and perhaps, of arguments, then it is not unreasonable to expect that literate subjects will be more skilled at such tasks than non-literate ones. This was the hypothesis of Vygotsky and Luria and the one taken up by Scribner and Cole (1981), who put these ideas together and subjected them to empirical test. They found themselves in a natural laboratory for examining various literacy hypotheses for they located a traditional society, the Vai of Liberia, who had available an indigenous syllabic script which was used primarily for writing letters and which was mastered by a sizable percentage of adult males in a non-school context. In the same society they found a sufficient number of individuals who were schooled-literate in English, as well as a group which was literate in Arabic and a group of individuals who could not read at all. These groups permitted them to examine the ways that Vai literacy or illiteracy as well as schooling influenced subjects' orientation to language and their solution of logical tasks.

While this work benefitted from the historical arguments, it falls more directly within the research tradition begun by Vygotsky and Luria. A number of studies by Scribner (1975), Scribner and Cole (1981) and others (Cole, Gay, Glick, & Sharp, 1971) have followed up and extended the Luria findings on the particular difficulties non-literate subjects are reported to have in dealing with syllogistic reasoning tasks. Representative of this work is Scribner and Cole's (1981, p. 127) finding of an increase in premise-based reasoning as a function of schooling. Here is a sample from the syllogism task:

All women who live in Monrovia are married.
Kemu is not married.
Does Kemu live in Monrovia?

(1981, p. 127)

First, many of the non-schooled subjects rejected the first premise because they knew it to be false, consequently, it "created considerable controversy both in individual administration and in group discussion." When subjects' answers were followed up by a request to justify their answer, unschooled subjects tended to give an empirical explanation, that is, they appealed to real world knowledge, thus: "I don't know Kemu" or "Kemu could live with her mother in Monrovia." Schooled children tended to provide theoretical, premise-based explanations: "That is what you said." Neither Vai literacy nor Qur'anic literacy had any influence on such reasoning. Indeed, such logical reasoning tasks showed the strongest effect of schooling of any that were administered.

Scribner and Cole (1981) point out that "most psychologists would agree that the tendency to respond empirically to syllogisms is not so much a sign of inability to reason logically as it is an indication of how people understand this particular verbal form" (p. 155). To illustrate that logical competence was not exclusive to schooled or literate subjects, they devised analogous tasks which took for major premises such pretended, fantastic notions as the following:

All stones on the moon are blue.
The man who went to the moon saw a stone.
Was the stone he saw blue?

In such cases, performance, including justifications, went almost, but not quite, to the levels achieved by schooled children and was quite amenable to training. They concluded that such studies "cast doubt on hypotheses that implicate literacy directly in the acquisition of metalinguistic knowledge about the properties of propositions" (p. 156) and they favor the hypothesis that such competence has more to do with learning a particular school-related mode of discourse.

But suppose that the mode of discourse in question is, in fact, a literate mode of discourse, a way of setting out arguments to make their logic particularly visible and explicit primarily but not exclusively in writing. To illustrate, suppose that couplets are a written poetic form; someone who is familiar with couplets then teaches someone else to do the same without using writing. Would that prove that formulating couplets is not a literate activity? I would suggest not.

This is the line of argument Goody (1987) has recently taken in his critique of the Scribner and Cole research program and which leads him to reassert vigorously his earlier view, namely, that "Cognitively as well as sociologically, writing underpins 'civilization,' the culture of cities" (p. 300). Goody's critique rests on two main points. First, Scribner and Cole, following Vygotsky, take a narrow view of adopting a basically "mentalistic view of intellectual operations or cognitive skills" (p. 216) and, second, they adopt a too narrow view of literacy. What he means by the former is that one cannot determine the implications of a resource such as writing by looking only at the effect that learning to write has on an individual. Writing is a cultural resource and its implications have to unfold in historical time. Writing may permit the listing of the laws of the culture, for example, but merely teaching someone to read and write is not going to make them immediately better at drafting law codes. A historical process must intervene.

So Goody rejects as naive the hypotheses regarding the consequences of literacy which Scribner and Cole test and subsequently refute. Scribner and Cole looked for, but failed to find, that literacy has "general cognitive effects as we have defined them" (1981, p. 132); that it has "set off a dramatic modernizing sequence [or] led to the growth of new intellectual disciplines" (1981, p. 239), that it "profoundly change[s] what people know about their language and how they think about it" (1981, p. 134), or affects "the process of thinking – how we classify, reason, remember" (1981, p. 5). Their mistaken expectations, he suggests, come from the inappropriate notion that the cognitive implications of literacy can be determined by examining the direct impact on the individual who learns to read and write. Learning to read and write is at best a mere introduction to the world of literacy. It is not appropriate to assume that all of the things that could ever be done with literacy will immediately come into learners' minds when they first learn to read. Consider another example: Literacy, let us say, facilitates the writing of dictionaries. But it would be wrong to think that just because one learned to read and write one could give better definitions. That would depend upon learning to use a dictionary. Goody puts it this way:

> It is the written 'tradition', the accumulated knowledge stored in documents as well as in the mind, whether over a few years ... or over a millennium ..., that provides an intervening variable between mastery of a skill and cognitive operations.

(1987, p. 222)

For the same reason Goody also rejects Scribner and Cole's (1981) strict distinction between schooling and literacy; schooling as we know it, says Goody, is a literate institution. To study the implications of literacy one will have to examine what can be done and what has been done with literacy especially in its institutional contexts.

In fact, at the midpoint of their research program, Scribner and Cole recognized the fact that their original hypotheses had been too general and they reoriented their perspective in order to determine what exactly their subjects had learned in the course of becoming literate in the Vai script. In the second half of their report they examine the specific functions involved in reading the Vai script and those involved in schooling, what I think of as schooled literacy, and the relation of those functions to the knowledge and competencies acquired. These findings are particularly interesting.

First, subjects literate in English, unlike non-literate subjects and those literate in Vai, had little difficulty in engaging in discourse involving metarepresentational concepts. While the non-schooled literate could distinguish things and names for things, the discourse about the relation was problematic (p. 141). Second, in the Vai language there was no lexical item which referred exclusively to what "word" does in English; a word was essentially a piece of speech. As the Vai script does not mark lexical units by means of spaces, being literate in the Vai script had little clear influence on the ability to segment discourse into word-like units; the basic units for them continued to be such meaning-carrying phrases as "my big brother" (p. 149). Third, Vai script, being a syllabary, enabled readers to be significantly more competent in comprehending speech which was presented as strings of segmented syllables (p. 165). Fourth, those familiar with writing personal letters in Vai were more skilled in organizing information in an informative way than those unfamiliar (p. 219). And finally, spelling patterns tended to influence the pronunciation of the Vai literates; an "l" in the script tended to preserve the /l/ in the pronunciation of those who could read. Schooled literacy, on the other hand, tended to influence performance on all of the tasks, and in particular the ability to "talk about" and justify answers to various questions, the kind of talk that often requires metalinguistic reference to what was said, meant, intended and implied.

As mentioned, Scribner and Cole distinguish schooling from literacy suggesting that some of the effects of schooling are discourse related, for example, treating a sentence as a premise in an inference task, rather than literacy related. Others, including Goody, have argued that what matters is literate discourse; whether spoken or written is of less significance.

My own view is that Western literacy can no more be separated from schooling than Vai literacy can be distinguished from letter writing. Literacy in Western cultures is not just learning the abc's; it is learning to use the resources of writing for a culturally defined set of tasks and procedures. All writers agree on this point. Literacy is not just a basic set of mental skills isolated from everything else. It is the competence to exploit a particular set of cultural resources. It is the evolution of those resources in conjunction with the knowledge and skill to exploit those resources for particular purposes that makes up literacy. That is why literacy and literate competence can have a history. But it does mean that we cannot grasp the full implications of literacy by means of research which simply compares readers and non-readers. We require a richer more diversified notion of literacy.

Scribner and Cole's work is significant in helping to reconceptualize literacy in these more specific terms: What does one learn when one learns to read a syllabary as opposed to an alphabet? How do the activities of reading and writing affect the understanding of language and discourse? What are the conditions under which one composes or appeals to writing? How does the *form* of knowledge change when it is set out and accumulated in writing? What is the metalanguage that is used in discussing written texts? These are all open, perhaps urgent, questions and they are much more precise than any general hypotheses linking writing, literacy and thinking. In fact, more specific research directed to the problem of the role that literacy has played in the evolution of particular cultural activities such as law, science, literature, religion and philosophy has now begun and we shall examine these lines of research in the next chapter.

3 LITERACY AND THE CONCEPTUAL REVOLUTIONS OF CLASSICAL GREECE AND RENAISSANCE EUROPE

....

> By the meaningless sign linked to the meaningless sound we
> have built the shape and meaning of Western man.
>
> (McLuhan, 1962, p. 50)

Two of the most noteworthy and certainly most studied intellectual revolutions, that of classical Greece in the fifth, fourth and third centuries BC, and that of the European Renaissance, roughly the period from the twelfth to the seventeenth centuries AD were accompanied by dramatic changes in the type and extent of reading and writing, that is, in the nature and extent of literacy. Such eminent historians of science as Marie Boas and George Sarton, and more recently Elizabeth Eisenstein, have argued that increased availability of documents that accompanied the invention of printing were critical to the European developments just as the celebrated theories of writing of Ignace Gelb and David Diringer, and more recently Eric Havelock, tied the Greek achievement to the invention of the alphabet. Yet the most recent analyses by Geoffrey Lloyd, Rosalind Thomas, Mary Carruthers and others have claimed that the transformations may not be as abrupt or categorical as had been thought and that writing may have played a less critical role than we had been led to believe. While writing may be useful in preserving intellectual gains it may not have played any causal role in producing them. To evaluate the traditional emphasis on the role of writing and reading in these intellectual achievements is the purpose of this chapter.

While anthropologists and psychologists can compare the mental activities of contemporary cultures with and without writing, one of the virtues of writing is that written records permit historians to examine what changes occurred within a social group as it came to depend more and more on writing. The distinction is what linguists call *synchronic* versus *diachronic* descriptions. As mentioned, the two periods of radical cultural change in which writing and literacy have been implicated are, first, the evolution of classical Greek culture and, second, the European Renaissance culminating with the Protestant Reformation and the beginnings of Early Modern Science. Our questions are: What role, if any, did writing and literacy play in these cultural transformations? What is there about writing and literacy that could contribute to those changes? And finally, did writing contribute to those conceptual changes or was it merely responsible for the dissemination and preservation of those changes?

In the preceding chapters I set out the alphabetic hypothesis as advanced by McLuhan, Havelock, Goody and Watt, and Ong. And in the next chapter we will examine specifically what scripts, in particular, what alphabets "represent." But while the alphabetic hypothesis may plausibly be connected to the Greek revolution it has little to contribute to the changes which occurred in the Early Modern period; the alphabet had been available for almost two thousand years by the sixteenth century. McLuhan believed that these changes were brought about by the printing press; print was a new technology that heightened the effects of the alphabet. But the printing press was invented only at the end of the fifteenth century and most of the conceptual changes of concern, those underlying the Reformation for example, had already occurred by then. Others have suggested that the changes associated with printing were the product, not of printing specifically, but of the rise of literacy, a major increase in the number of people who could read and write and whose social activities were regulated in part by written documents. Both the printing press and the growth of literacy were undoubtedly important, but just how they played a role remains uncertain. Research in the past decade alone has thrown important light on this question.

Greek literacy

Havelock (1963, 1982) provided a detailed argument to show that the primary shift from the Homeric epic tradition to the Socratic tradition was associated with a decline in the social uses of poetically based oral tradition, with a correspondingly increasing reliance upon written records and explicit prose argument, a literate tradition. The shift was from an account featuring "the panorama of doings and happenings" to "a program of principles," the latter featuring precise definition and logical argument. Havelock pinned this change to the invention of the alphabet because the alphabet, he claimed, was the first writing system which was capable of recording completely novel utterances which could be read and re-read without ambiguity and because it was simple, learnable and hence readily democratized. The argument is compelling but is it true?

Two recent accounts have been provided on the literacy of the classical Greeks. W. Harris (1989) has attempted to answer such questions as who was literate in classical times? what percentage of Greeks were literate? what were their attitudes to literacy? for what was it used? Harris examined all of the evidence on this question: existing documents, references to documents which no longer exist, graffiti, accounts of cultural life and of public education in ancient Greece, classical Greece, Hellenistic Greece through to the decline of the Roman Empire, the period from seventh century BC through to the second century AD. On the basis of this evidence Harris concluded that there was no mass literacy in Greek or Roman societies although by 70 AD perhaps twenty per cent of males in urban settings may have been literate. Degree of literacy was influenced by the availability of a simple script, in this case the alphabet, the variety of functions writing served, degree of urbanization, the availability of leisure, and the availability of schooling.

Written laws first appeared about 620 BC and writing proliferated in the fifth century BC. Literacy facilitated "a sort of canonization of discourse" (Harris, p. 39) in which there came to be a body of fixed texts that served as objects of admiration, quotation and study. Writing established new standards of quotation; precisely what was said became increasingly important (p. 32). Written contracts and written evidence came to be valued over oral reports and by the fourth century BC a remarkable Athenian law required the use of written evidence (p. 71). Texts "became fixed and solemn through being written" (p. 72) and there was a "growing belief in the authority of the written word" (p. 73).

Harris is not sanguine about the role of literacy in the Greek "miracle." While widespread literacy was not essential for Greek democracy, writing did play an important part in civic affairs in recording laws, records and contracts. The elite often maintained its power over others and over empires "partly by its superior command of written texts" (p. 333).

But did literacy alter their ways of thinking? "What little is known about the cognitive effects of literacy" he writes, "does not support any facile conclusions" (p. 41). Harris suggests that so far as one can tell the ancient Greeks were always curious and argumentative but what they argued about may have been influenced by the accumulating written records: "the material which Greek and Roman minds worked on partly consisted of written texts, and this permitted the development of refined systems of philosophy and the accumulation of information" (p. 336).

In the Preface to that book, Harris mentions that partway through the writing of the book a colleague suggested that he was not even asking the most interesting questions. The evidence indicates that he has attempted to answer some of them but several remain unasked let alone answered. Harris cites the trust ascribed to the written version, the new attention to the precise wording of a statement and to the correctness of quotation. Why these concerns? Does it indicate a new attention to issues of texts and interpretation, to the distinction between what was said and what was meant? Does it indicate the evolution of new concepts such as evidence, proof, literal meaning, and metaphor? And why literacy rather than just writing? Why should or could we expect that a sizable population of readers mattered rather than availability of writing for oneself or to a small elite? Does a popular audience or a reading public alter forms of discourse in some as yet unspecified way? Harris' conservative conclusion that literacy accompanies social change without putting a decisive stamp on that change puts a useful constraint on current enthusiasms but leaves open the question of how writing and literacy modify or erode oral, rhetorical discourse.

R. Thomas (1989) is less concerned with the degree of popular literacy in Classical Greece and more concerned with challenging the general hypothesis that the Greek revolution was a literate one. She examines the interaction between the spoken and the written word, the relation between oral memory and written record, and the authority of the spoken and written word, and shows the degree to which oral activities permeated literate ones. She points out that many early Greek philosophers, including Plato, distrusted writing and how oral argument and testimony were trusted over written forms. She points out that although Herodotus, the great historian of the fifth century BC characterized the Greek "stories" as ridiculous, he worked primarily with oral sources rather than written records. Consequently, she concludes that not only should oral not be seen as antonymous to literate but also that writing was less critical to the Greek achievement than is usually assumed.

This question about the relation between literacy and thought takes a new and somewhat more specific form in Lloyd's (1979, 1983, 1990) sustained examination of the rise of a scientific tradition in classical Greek thought and the origins of the rejection of non-scientific explanations as magical and metaphorical.

Lloyd (1979) examined, among other documents, an early treatise *On the sacred disease* which was directed to showing that the sacred disease, namely epilepsy, is no more sacred than any other disease and that those who claim it is and treat it by ritual, that is, religious means, are frauds. The Greek account provides a factual description in naturalistic terms as to what brings it about: "The brain is responsible for the disease." The "veins" which carry air to the brain and thereby give the brain sensation and consciousness may become blocked by phlegm, the account continues. "This blockage causes loss of voice, choking, foaming at the mouth, eyes roll, the patient becomes unconscious and, in some cases, passes a stool." Then the treatment: "The majority of maladies may be cured by the same things as causes them." And the proof of the theory that the disease is caused by phlegm, especially when the wind is southerly, is then offered: "This observation results especially from a study of animals, particularly of goats which are liable to this disease ... If you cut open the head to look at it, you will find that the brain is wet, full of fluid and foul-smelling, convincing proof that disease and not the deity is harming the body" (pp. 20–23).

We scarcely need point out that the theory is wrong and the evidence adduced is feeble, yet the argument is scientific in the modern sense in that it contrasts rational explanation with magical ones and it advances a theory testable by appeal to the empirical facts.

Case histories of patients "were carried out with great care and thoroughness, and they contain few interpretive comments and no explicit overall theory of disease" (Lloyd, 1979, p. 154).

Thus distinctions were drawn between the theory (logoi) and the evidence for the theory (phenomena), between appearance and reality, between science and magic. In a footnote Lloyd adds that talk about evidence in scientific inquiry is the same as that used in legal proceedings and historical research (p. 129), a relation earlier noted by Robert Boyle (see Chapter 9).

In a later work, Lloyd (1983) enlarged on the distinctions between pre-Greek and post-Greek science. Hesiod, for example, classified animals not only in relation to other animals but also in terms of mythical and non-mythical beings. By Aristotle's time, completely naturalistic categories were used in which animals were classified exclusively in terms of physical characteristics. Mythologies no longer had anything to do with scientific accounts. As we shall see later, these developments reoccurred in the seventeenth century as well.

In his most recent work, Lloyd (1990) is even more guarded both about the extent of the Greek achievement and about the role that literacy played in it. Differences between pre-classical Greek and post-classical Greek cultures are perhaps not as dramatic as usually claimed. Yet, Lloyd is convinced that a shift in understanding did occur. The altered understanding achieved in such sciences as medicine and astronomy were related, he suggests, to the developments in the uses of evidence and of methods of proof. But he traces this development not to the availability of the alphabet and writing, but to the forms of sceptical argument that had evolved in judicial and political contexts. He concluded:

[The Greeks] were certainly not the first to develop a complex mathematics – only the first to use, and then also to give a formal analysis of, a concept of rigorous mathematical demonstration. They were not the first to carry out careful observations in astronomy and medicine, only the first – eventually – to develop an explicit notion of empirical research and to debate its role in natural science. They were not the first to diagnose and treat some medical cases without reference to the postulated divine or daemonic agencies, only the first to express a category of the 'magical' and to attempt to exclude it from medicine.

(1979, p. 232)

The critical notions here are those marked by the terms "concept," "explicit notion" and "category." What the Greeks invented was not argument but ideas about argument; not so much knowledge as an epistemology involving a set of categories or concepts for "representing" forms of argument – the concepts of logic, proof, research, and magic. Thus the Hippocratic writer writing on the sacred disease "rejects the notion of supernatural intervention in natural phenomena as a whole, as what might even be called a category mistake" (Lloyd, 1979, p. 26). Magic belongs to a different category from natural causes. The concepts in question have taken on an oppositional quality, logos as opposed to muthos, natural as opposed to magical, literal as opposed to metaphorical. Thus the achievement is less a matter of research, proof or magic than an oppositional set of concepts that allow these things to be seen as proof, research or magic. They allow these things to become objects of further discourse: What is a proof? What is research? What is magic? What is knowledge?

Lloyd (1990) examines the generality of his theory by comparing the evolution of ancient Greek science with ancient Chinese science. Both, he found, were concerned with ethics, natural philosophy, medicine, astronomy, metallurgy and epistemology, especially on the reliability of perception and reason. Yet Lloyd finds striking differences. Whereas ancient Chinese science explored correlations, parallelisms and complementarities, the Greeks seem preoccupied with proof, contrasting proof with persuasion, and seeking for incontrovertibility. Whereas the Chinese were sophisticated in the use and criticism of metaphor, the Greeks thought that metaphor was in principle a deviant form of expression. Again, Lloyd traces these differences to social organization and to the availability of a general audience which was free to judge the plausibility of an argument. In such contexts, the balance may shift from authority to evidence in sustaining a conclusion. Secondly, Lloyd points out that writing cannot be the causal factor as the Chinese were as literate as the Greeks. In fact China is "very much a culture mediated by the written, more than the spoken word" (p. 112) and yet only Greek science took the particular direction we recognize as the route to an empirical scientific tradition.

Bloch (1989) has recently made a similar argument in his criticism of Goody. He points out that writing can play vastly different roles in different cultures, a point also developed by Heath (1983) and Street (1984). In Chinese culture, Bloch points out, the written word is taken as the standard while the oral forms are considered derivative; in India just the opposite holds – the oral is sacred, writing is not trusted. Any understanding of literacy will have to pay attention to the structure of the culture into which it is introduced.

Thus while Lloyd concedes that writing may have increased the availability of certain arguments and may have served as an archive, he rejects the Goody hypothesis that writing could have in any way caused the Greek revolution in thinking. Goody (1987) had argued that literacy played an important role in the evolution of science in two ways. First, scepticism can arise because writing allows the accumulation of evidence. Goody writes: "In oral memory the many misses tend to get forgotten in favour of the occasional hits; this is the memory of the gambler who recalls his wins more frequently than his losses. It is the systematic recording (or even the possibility of so doing) rather than an initial attitude of mind that allows us to be 'generally sceptical'" (p. 69). Lloyd, on the other hand, argued that the general scepticism developed in the public forum, through oral argument before an unbiased audience.

Secondly, Goody had argued that the critical concepts of evidence and proof are present in oral societies but they may become more "formalized" by virtue of writing which "operating in a single communicative channel, necessarily introduced a tighter formulation" (Goody, 1987, p. 72). Lloyd acknowledges that writing may have permitted the tightening up, the editing, of arguments but denies that it could have altered their basic form. Goody, too, lacks critical evidence for his claim and he attempts to secure his point by a series of "dares": "Try under oral conditions to formalize a general proposition; try expressing ideas in the form of a syllogism; try formulating opposition and analogy" (p. 72). Clearly Goody is correct in pointing out that writing facilitates formation of lists, tables, classifications and the like but whether the degree of formalization achieved by the Greeks developed "because the Greek versions were developed in a written tradition" (p. 72) as Goody claims, is at best a hypothesis, lacking convincing evidence. It seems we must look elsewhere for an explanation of how the Pre-Socratics came to develop their particular concepts of proof, evidence, research, magic and metaphor.

Lloyd locates the origins of these concepts in public debate conducted before unbiased audiences. He writes (G. E. R. Lloyd, personal communication, April 1990): "It's not because words get to be written down that the question as to whether they are used literally or metaphorically comes to be put." I am less convinced. Conceptualizing the distinction between literal meaning and metaphor depends, I would think, upon a scrutinizable text. Literal meanings can be determined only by close attention to the very wording, properties difficult to analyze if exclusively spoken, especially since, as we saw earlier, oral cultures tend to have a less stringent notion of "the very words." How, one could ask, could one have a stringent notion of literal meaning if one had a lax criterion for the very words? Similarly, the contrast between proof and persuasion depends upon an understanding of the relation between propositions expressed by statements, for example, that one proposition follows logically from another. Literal meaning and logic are complementary notions. The possibility of distinguishing these and operating on them would at least seem to be enhanced by the availability of a written record. Admittedly, new concepts must be built upon old ones so we cannot expect completely new ones to arise because of writing, but as we shall see later, problems in interpreting written texts could provide an occasion for their elaboration, refinement and systematic application.

My own view is that Goody is right but has not gone far enough. Writing and increasing literacy were undoubtedly instrumental in the development of a sceptical, scientific tradition as Goody has argued. But the reasons are to be sought not merely in the evolution of record keeping but the ways of reading texts and in a new attitude to language fostered by reading, interpreting and writing those texts. That is a link I can trace only in the medieval and early modern period, a topic I take up more fully in Chapter 7.

Renaissance literacy

The conceptual revolutions associated with the Renaissance – the re-birth – bear important similarities to those of the Greek revolution. In fact, the Medieval period is distinguished by its renewed interest in the translation, study and application of the classical Greek texts.

McLuhan (1962) provided an exotic tabulation of the differences in

attitudes to and uses of texts between the later Middle Ages and the
Renaissance. Sworn testimony was replaced by written documents,
private study replaced public performance, silent reading replaced oral
reading, religious icons gave way to religious representational paintings, a rhetorical persuasive style gave way to a modern prose style,
and so on. McLuhan explained these changes by appeal to a general
principle that each medium altered one's perception of the content; in
the McLuhan argot "The medium is the message." The principle
applied equally to the alphabet, to printing, to television and to the
computer. Just exactly how these changes in media produced their
effects was less clear; he appealed, as I mentioned earlier, to notions of
altered sense ratios, an idea McLuhan took from William Blake. But
McLuhan was a literary critic and while his theme was irresistible, his
theories were not.

The general theme has been given precise form in the historical
research of Clanchy (1979), McKitterick (1990) and Eisenstein (1979),
the former two on the increasing use of writing in the later Middle
Ages, eleventh to fourteenth centuries, the latter on the implications of
the printing press for the rise of Early Modern Science and for
Protestantism.

Clanchy (1979) charts in patient detail the increasing use of written
records in the administration of justice in England from the time of
the Norman Conquest (1066) to the death of Edward I (1307). The
period is noteworthy for the changing conceptions of justice, evidence
and proof, for the increasing use of documentation and documentary
evidence and also for the domestication of vernacular languages,
French and English, as languages of the court. By the end of the
thirteenth century, for example, a legal "charter" or "deed" was no
longer an oral ceremony accompanied by the conveyance of, for
example, a piece of turf from the deeded land; instead it was a sealed
document (p. 36).

Similarly the notion of a jury changed. Clanchy cites a case in 1297
in which *jurors* from Norfolk came to the King's Bench to provide
"sworn testimony" that a certain person had reached the age of
majority (1979, p. 175). In the pre-documentary period jurors were
witnesses, people who could swear to the truth of a claim; by the
fourteenth century they were unbiased persons who could carry out a

critical assessment of testimony (Pollock & Maitland, 1898, p. 622).
Similarly, proof changed from being an act carried out by the accused
whether proof by battle, ordeal, or oath to a mode of proof called "trial
by jury." Clanchy points out that writing played an increasingly
important role in this changing form of proof in that writing "seemed
to be more durable and reliable than the spoken word" (p. 150).

Legal "writs," explicitly stated complaints which had to be
answered, came to dominate the administration of justice. They
provided a canonical form for the presentation of complaints and
allowed standardized procedures to evolve for dealing with them. "In
Glanville's day ... English law is already taking the form of a
commentary upon writs" as Pollock and Maitland (1898, p. 151) put it
in their authoritative account of the history of English law.

In matters of justice the increasing use of written documents rather
than oral testimony may have contributed to the development of more
precise methods of examining evidence and forming judgments. Yet
the increasing use of written records for surveys, court roles, year-
books and chronicles "was more of an indication of governmental
efficiency rather than its cause" (Clanchy, 1979, p. 50). Although
Clanchy describes this increasing use of written records as an indication of a "literate mentality," he points out that what changed was
the language of record more so than the language of the courts
themselves. Thus, he leaves more or less open the question as to
whether writing was instrumental in these changes in thinking about
justice or whether it merely accompanied those changes.

Street (1984) suggests that these legal changes had much less to do
with efficiency and effectiveness of the written record than with the
political changes that were taking place. Written records, he suggests,
were a device employed by the French Normans after the invasion in
1066 to establish and legitimate control of a conquered people and had
little to do with their putative superiority to traditional oral forms.

Yet literacy did have its uses. McKitterick (1990) documented the
uses of literacy in early medieval Europe. Writing was useful as an
instrument for the kingly exercise of power, for controlling markets,
collecting taxes, controlling bureaucracies, and promoting one's prestige in the present and for posterity. She concludes "Literacy was
perceived as a practical tool and a potent instrument of power ... Side

by side with the exploitation of literal modes of government are royal initiatives for the promotion of literacy" (p. 324).

Eisenstein (1979) adopts an exclusively instrumental view of literacy and its role in those changes that characterize the rise of modernism, in particular, the Reformation and Early Modern Science. She summarizes her view thus: "Intellectual and spiritual life were profoundly transformed by the multiplication of new tools for duplicating books in fifteenth-century Europe. The communications shift altered the way Western Christians viewed their sacred book and the natural world" (p. 704). For Reformation theology, the printing press placed a copy of Scripture in the hands of every reader and thereby circumvented the role of the Church; one could encounter God through the simple practice of reading for oneself without the mediation of the priest. Furthermore, the printing press provided an important means for spreading the gospel to a rapidly growing reading public.

As for Early Modern Science, Eisenstein suggests that printing was primarily responsible for placing an "original" copy of a text, map, chart or diagram, free from copyist errors, into the hands of hundreds of scholars who could study them, compare them, criticize and update them. New discoveries could be incorporated into newer editions. In this way printing contributed to the development of an accumulative research tradition. Hence, the developments in both science and religion were produced more by exploiting the new opportunities afforded by printed materials than by any particular alteration in modes of thought.

However, because Eisenstein focuses her attention on printing and on the different roles played by printing in science and religion, she overlooks, I believe, an important aspect of the relation between the Reformation and the rise of Modern Science. The relation she over-looks, I suggest, may be crucial to detecting a way in which the increased use of writing could produce a genuine change in the structure of cognition. She argues that until the Reformation, science and religion were closely related, whereas after the rise of Modern Science, they went their separate ways. They did so because "the effect of printing on Bible study was in marked contrast with its effect on nature study" (p. 701). Science, she suggests, used printing for the consensual validation of observations, that is, the rise of objectivity, whereas religion used it primarily for the spread of glad tidings. Because of their different uses, "The changes wrought by printing provide the most plausible point of departure for explaining how confidence shifted from divine revelation to mathematical reasoning and man-made maps" (p. 701).

Indeed, the apparently different ways that religious and scientific traditions were affected by the communications revolution, suggested to Eisenstein the "futility of trying to encapsulate its consequences in any one formula." Printing sometimes led from words to images – McLuhan's eye for ear formula – as when geographic and botanical information was printed in exactly repeatable pictorial representations, but it equally often went from images to words as when stone and stained glass images gave way to personal bible study. The effects call for "a multivariable explanation even while stressing the significance of the single innovation" (pp. 701–702).

Admittedly, Eisenstein provides abundant evidence that printing (and writing) did serve different purposes in religion and in science, yet a second look reveals a deeper relation between them than Eisenstein allows. To see this we must distinguish ways of reading, that is literacy, from the technology of printing. Printing was indeed used in quite different ways in science and religion as Eisenstein showed and yet new ways of reading and writing may have played much the same fundamental role in the Reformation as it did in the rise of Modern Science. As we shall see in Chapter 7, both cases reflect a changing assessment of what was "given" both in a text and in nature and what came to been seen as accretion, interpolation and personal interpretation of those "texts." Changing attitudes to texts, that is new ways of reading, allowed a sharp contrast between what the text meant and what readers traditionally had thought that it meant. Writing created a fixed original objective "text" with a putative literal meaning – a meaning which came to be seen as determinable by systematic, scholarly methods – against which more imaginative and deviant interpretations could be recognized and excluded. Furthermore, especially after the invention of printing, the ability to read put that text into the hands of thousands of people who could see for themselves what it said. By following along in a text, readers could become

"virtual witnesses" to the truth of the interpretation offered by priest
or teacher. The notion of virtual witness is borrowed from Shapin's
(1984) discussion of the use of empirical observation in the scientific
writings of Robert Boyle (see Chapter 8). Eisenstein quotes Sprat as
making precisely this point in his joint defense of the Church of
England, of which he was a bishop, and the Royal Society, of which he
was the historian. Both, he claimed, had achieved a Reformation:

> ... both have taken a like course to bring this [reformation] about; each of
> them passing by the corrupt copies and referring themselves to the perfect
> originals for instruction; the one to Scripture, the other to the huge Volume of
> Creatures. They are both accused unjustly by their enemies of the same
> crimes, of having forsaken the Ancient Traditions and ventured on Novelties.
> They both suppose alike that their Ancestors might err; and yet retain a
> sufficient reverence for them.
> (Sprat, 1667/1966, part 3, sect. 23, p. 371; cited by Eisenstein, 1979, p. 668)

Why this search for the perfect originals? The Renaissance writer
Barbaro claimed to have found five thousand errors in copies of Pliny's
Latin text, errors of both transcription and of fact, which led him to
publish a book entitled *Castigations of Pliny* (Boas, 1962, p. 53). My
suggestion, which I develop in Chapter 7 on a history of reading, is
that a correct original would help to fix a reading against which any
novel interpretation could be assessed. The fixed text of nature was
God's creation; the fixed text of scripture was a carefully translated
Bible. This distinction was to lie at the basis of both Reformation
hermeneutics and Early Modern Science. Both made a sharp conceptual distinction between the given, whether in scripture or nature, and
those interpretations fabricated by men. The printing press was
extremely important in making this practicable as it was the printing
press that made it possible for a multitude of readers actually to look at
the same text at the same time and thereby see for themselves – to be
virtual witnesses to the correctness of an interpretation. This common
shift in modes of interpretation seems to have been overlooked by
Eisenstein.

Perhaps it is appropriate that she do so. She has since suggested
(E. Eisenstein, personal communication, August 1986) that the
distinction between text and interpretation pre-dates the communi-

cations revolution of primary concern to her. The conceptual changes common to the Reformation and with Modern Science, lay in an earlier period, just prior to the printing press. The printing press, as Eisenstein correctly noted, was primarily an instrument of standardization, accumulation and dissemination more than an instrument of conceptual change.

The origin of the concepts in question have been examined by Stock (1983, 1990) in his examination of the implications of literacy in the late Middle Ages. Stock reviews much of the evidence examined by Clanchy, pointing out how legal practices changed to reflect the growing reliance on written records and systematic examination of evidence in deciding on the innocence or guilt of the accused. But he also shows that there was a parallel shift in theological discussions as they came to depend increasingly on written records. Hagiographic judgments, that is, judgments regarding sainthood, were increasingly based on written records rather than oral testimony, religious services increasingly combined reading from texts along with oral rituals, saints' lives were put into written form, and written records were put into more readily consultable form through improved indexing, improved page layout, marking of chapter headings, uses of different forms of script and the like. Perhaps more significant was the fact that new methods for organizing knowledge appeared, as for example in Abelard's *Sic et non* and Lombard's *Sentences*, which involved systematic methods for classifying, encoding, and retrieving written information: "People began to think of facts not as recorded by texts but as embodied in texts, a change in mentality of major importance" (Stock, 1990, p. 126).

Literacy, for Stock, had its impact, particularly in pre-Reformation times, through the formation of a textual community, a group of believers at the centre of which was a leader who was the reader/interpreter, a sacred text or fragment of such a text and a fervently held if somewhat idiosyncratic view of the meaning of that text. It was not unusual for this textual community to find itself at odds with the views of the established church. Stock provides, as illustration, an account of the heretics of Orleans, who were burned on the Feast of Holy Innocents in 1022 AD. The accounts of the heresy, the first of which was written some forty years after the event, tells of the heretics' rejection of church dogma pertaining to the Mass and the Trinity, explains their heresy as the work of the devil, recounts their unwillingness to recant from their heresy, and their sentence to death.

Stock shows how their heresy was related to their literacy. The heretics were asked whether they believed in the virgin birth, incarnation and resurrection. They had replied: "'We ourselves were not present and therefore cannot believe such events took place'; [They] reject[ed] traditional interpretation which they did not think out for themselves in favor of an actual, historical and thereby sensible reality" (p. 114).

Heresy, then, involved a changing attitude to religious texts. Heretics, Stock points out, had a "highly developed if somewhat personal style of 'rationality' which depended on the individual interpretation of theological texts ... For the heretics, the hidden meaning emerged as they themselves interpreted Biblical text, patristic writings, and their own maxims" (pp. 110–120). And these interpretations were seen both as inherent in the text and as flatly contradictory to the teachings of the church. Ginzburg (1982, see also 1986) has given a similar account of a sixteenth century miller who was tried and found guilty for claiming that all the sacraments, including baptism, were "human inventions" (1982, p. 10), claims he based on his personal, if somewhat superficial, reading of scripture (1982, p. 36).

The strength of Stock's account is that he studies the implications of literacy through altered forms of *reading* and interpreting texts rather than on the simple technology for disseminating them. For as I shall argue later it is the fact that writing represents only some aspects of what a speaker has said that makes reading such a sticky interpretive problem. Second, Stock provides an account of the changing style of reading, namely, a new concern with the surface, sensible, actual properties of the text at the expense of putative underlying, mystical or deep aspects of meaning. As Stock points out, a developing principle of the later Middle Ages was the "identification of objectivity with a text" (1984–85, p. 24). Documents in courts were seen as providing that objectivity just as were the very words, the surface or determinable meanings of scripture.

This theme comes up again when we examine in more detail the history of reading in Chapter 7. For now, we can conclude our review of theories of literacy and cognition by restating the main points. First, all of the accounts we examined note the increasing reliance upon written records, whether in written or printed forms beginning in the twelfth century. All have noted the increasing trust in written forms and the assumptions of objectivity regarding those forms. All point out how new types of documents came into existence often with the effect of simplifying both claims and interpretations of those claims. And all note how those written forms came to serve archival functions which in some cases surpassed the authority given to oral, traditional ones.

The more controversial issue is whether writing and literacy actually caused, or at least affected, the development of new ways of thinking about scripture, nature, and the self. Eisenstein emphasized how new devices served existing functions on such a dramatic scale that they in effect change those functions. Clanchy suggested that a new literate mentality did develop in the period in question, a mentality that consisted at base of a new attitude to texts rather than new cognitive processes. Stock, by suggesting that what is at stake is a new way of reading and interpreting texts, clearly aligns himself with the hypothesis that literacy may actually contribute to the evolution of a new mode of thought. Yet the burden of proof lies on anyone making that claim.

Perhaps the most remarkable recent work on this topic and certainly the most frustrating for students of literacy is Carruthers' (1990) detailed analysis of the uses of memory and the conceptions of memory in the Middle Ages. Building upon the earlier work of Yates (1966) on the Medieval arts of memory, Carruthers shows convincingly that Medieval writers never thought of writing as a substitute for memory but rather as an aid to memory. Writing was thought of and used merely as a mnemonic device, a system of visible marks that could be used to check memory. Memory was thought of as "writing" on the mind and memory was the primary instrument of thought. No medieval text, she points out, makes any distinction between the act of writing on the memory and writing on some surface; both involved the use of devices, the method of "loci" – locating items of interest in known locations – or making marks on paper. Writing in itself was of no particular significance; significance

was attached to important teaching or "texts" which had been preserved in memory, thought about and commented on, and which
thereby had become an important cultural resource. The way to use a
text was to "ingest" it and "digest" it thoroughly, to extract its juices
and to internalize its meaning, its *res*. And composing a text was not
writing at all but composing mentally and performing orally and, on
occasion, dictating from memory. Indeed, Carruthers argues that
Aquinas' multi-volume *Summa theologica* was produced in just this
way:

Thomas's flow to his secretaries was unceasing: it 'ran so clearly that it was as
if the master were reading aloud from a book under his eyes'. He dictated 'as
if a great torrent of truth were pouring into him from God. Nor did he seem
to be searching for things as yet unknown to him: he seemed simply to let his
memory pour out its treasures'.

(Carruthers, 1990, p. 6)

Carruthers' major contribution is to show the extent to which these
highly literate medieval churchmen did their work orally, relying on
memory for examining, criticizing and developing ideas rather than
relying, as is usually assumed, on the written text. Sermons were
composed in the mind and sometimes written down later. Texts were
not scrutinized so much as used as a record against which to check
memory. Reading was not so much a matter of studying a text as
ingesting or internalizing it. Once ingested, it could become the object
of meditation and reflection. The scrutinized object was in the mind
not in the text.

The Medieval attitude to and use of texts is the subject of a later
chapter; at this point we are concerned with Carruthers' critique of
the significance of literacy in late Medieval thought. This is the aspect
that is somewhat frustrating: for the historian of literature it may be
appropriate to distinguish literature from literacy, for the literacy
theorist the relation is critical. Her assumption that "writing something down cannot change in any significant way our mental representation of it" (Carruthers, p. 31) is simply false. By adopting the view
that mental representations are independent of the activity of organizing them into a form appropriate to putting them down on some
surface (p. 32) she is led to conclude that "neither the prevalence nor

the form of written materials in a culture should ... be taken as any sure indication of those people's ability to think in rational categories or of the structures those categories may take" (p. 32). Not as a sure indication, admittedly, but writing is a particular form of representation and, as a general principle, a representation is never equivalent to the thing represented. If so, it is a serious mistake to think of written representations as transparent or neutral.

Carruthers, like the Medievals she discusses, assumes that the arts of memory, mnemonic schemes of various sorts, are identical to the mental representations which are a product of ordinary verbalized experience. However, mnemonics, as she points out are "arts"; they are devices for ordering, classifying, judging and interpreting that are only indirectly related to the mental representations that naturally accrue from experience. These arts are not neutral in their effects any more than writing is; both provide categories and forms for the re-representation of experience. They both facilitate certain kinds of mental activity while inhibiting others. Consequently it is inconsistent to celebrate the significance of mnemonics while disparaging the significance of writing.

There is a more serious problem. By playing down the significance of writing she does not do justice to the fact that the mnemonic devices she describes are devised to deal *with written texts*; memory arts are not devised for remembering just what someone says but primarily for preserving written documents in memory. And they died out when printed books became plentiful. So convinced is Carruthers that these "arts" are not dependent upon literacy that in her long description of Luria's account of the mind of a mnemonist, a person capable of prodigious feats of memory, she does not even tell us if the Mnemonist was literate. I infer he was from the fact that he carried out his mental activities on the basis of words rather than things – a point we shall examine in the next chapter.

On the other hand, Carruthers is completely convincing in her argument that in Medieval culture, the oral and the literate are not contrastive categories. The most highly literate were also the most highly oral, hence, the appositeness of her title *The book of memory*.

Perhaps these differences in estimates of the significance of writing and literacy arise from the different conceptions of literacy. Carruthers uses a rather strict definition, the ability to read and write with an alphabet, whereas I am using as a working definition the ability to exploit the resources of a written tradition – not just the ability to read and write but to think about texts in particular ways. My definition therefore goes over into Carruthers' idea of literature. Carruthers contrasts two attitudes to texts, fundamentalism and textualism, the former assuming that texts do not require interpretation, the latter that they do, suggesting that "the distinction has to do with a view of literature which can exist among either oral or literate groups" (pp. 20, 290). For myself I cannot imagine fundamentalism or textualism creating schisms within an oral culture. Attitudes to texts are ways of reading and those ways of reading constitute a part of the history of literacy, a history which differs in important ways from one culture to another (Tambiah, 1990).

Just how ways of writing could affect ways of reading requires that we examine just what a writing system represents, or more precisely, what writing systems can be taken as representing. As we shall see in the next chapter, different scripts may be seen as representing different things. What writing systems represent depends not only on the invention of more analytic scripts but also on the structure of the language being represented. More fundamentally, what writing systems represent determines what tasks are left to the discretion of the reader. Consequently, in the chapter following the next we shall turn to the question of what writing systems *do not* represent.

4 WHAT WRITING REPRESENTS: A REVISIONIST HISTORY OF WRITING

··

Written words are the signs of words spoken.

(Aristotle, *De interpretatione*)

At least since Aristotle's time it has been assumed that writing is a graphic device for transcribing speech. This assumption provides the basis for both early and recent theories of the evolution of writing systems, theories which claim a linear ascent from early pictorial systems to later phonological ones culminating in the alphabet. Compared with other writing systems, the alphabet is seen as uniquely successful in representing anything that can be said. It does this by capturing the elementary constituents of the sound system of speech, namely, the phonemes of the language. The history of writing then can be, indeed has been, seen as a series of failed attempts at or faltering steps towards the representation of those phonological elements. Neither of these assumptions, that writing is transcription, nor that the history of the alphabet is strictly an evolutionary one, is currently seen as defensible. In this chapter we consider how the history of writing can be rewritten without these flawed assumptions. The purpose of this chapter is to show that the relation between speech and writing may be just the opposite of that traditionally assumed. Revising our notion of the relation between speech and writing will turn out to be just the clue we require to approach, in a new way, the relation between writing and cognition.

Making marks which can serve mnemonic and communicative purposes is as old as human culture itself. What such marks may be taken as representing by those who make and those who read those marks is the critical question. A glimpse at our own writing systems suggests that what a writing system represents is what is said – an ideal writing system is a fully explicit representation of oral language. Indeed, this is the classical view developed by Aristotle and seconded in our own time by de Saussure and Bloomfield. Aristotle wrote in

De interpretatione (l.4–6): "Words spoken are symbols or signs of affections or impressions of the soul; written words are the signs of words spoken" (b. 384 BC, 1938, p. 115). Saussure (1916/1983) attacked as the "tyranny of writing" the fact that linguistic theory took as its object written language rather than spoken: "The sole reason for the existence of [writing] is to represent [speech]. The linguistic object is not defined by the combination of the written word and the spoken word: The spoken form alone constitutes the object" (pp. 23–24). And Bloomfield identified speech with language and saw writing as "a way of recording language" (Bloomfield, 1933, p. 21). More recently, Mattingly (1972) expressed the same view, namely that writing is "a simple cipher" on speech.

One advantage of such an assumption is that it allows for a fairly straightforward account of the history of writing. Writing systems evolved, on this account, in the attempt to make a writing system which adequately and explicitly represents one's speech practices. Historical developments in the evolution of writing systems – from idea-writing, to whole words, to syllables, to consonants, and finally to consonants and vowels – may be seen as progressive achievements towards the goal of representing the ultimate units of speech, phonemes. Rousseau's famous claim, mentioned earlier, that a savage people wrote by depicting objects, barbarians wrote by means of word signs and civilized people wrote by means of an alphabet was among the first expressions of this evolutionary perspective (1754–91/1966, p. 17).

The orderliness of this development has led most modern theorists to see a single evolutionary achievement with the alphabet at the pinnacle. Gelb (1963) distinguished four stages in this evolution beginning with picture writing which expressed ideas directly, followed by word-based writing systems, then by sound-based syllabic writing systems including unvocalized syllabaries or consonantal systems, and terminating with the Greek invention of the alphabet. And Diringer (1962) saw in the evolution of the alphabet the "history of mankind." As Havelock (1982, p. 11) put it: "At a stroke the Greeks provided a table of elements of linguistic sound not only manageable because of economy, but for the first time in the history of *homo sapiens*, also accurate." Thus, the achievement is seen as one of a series of successes in representing more fundamental aspects of the linguistic system, ultimately phonemes, to make a system which is both economical – employs a small number of signs – , and complete – capable of representing anything that can be said. Writing, on this view, is the attempt to represent the sound patterns of speech.

Such accounts, which we shall examine more carefully presently, suffer from what I take to be a critical flaw. They assume what they need to explain. Specifically, they assume that the inventors of writing systems *already knew* about language and its structure – words, phonemes and the like, and progress came from finding ways to represent those structures unambiguously. As Harris (1986) points out such descriptions are misleading in that they take a characterization of the current state (or at least a part of that state) as if it were the goal towards which writing was evolving, that is, as if all attempts at writing, always and everywhere were crude attempts at the transcription of the sound patterns of speech. On the contrary it may be argued, as Harris (1986) and Gaur (1984/1987) have done, that writing systems were created not to represent speech, but to communicate information. The relation to speech is at best indirect.

The evolutionary story is misleading in two other ways. If it is assumed that writing systems represent different levels of structure of language – ideas, words, syllables, phonemes – it follows that writing systems can be classified as to their type. This is the typical portrayal of writing systems and their history (Gelb, 1963; Sampson, 1985). However, if writing systems are communicational systems in their own right which are then taken as models of speech – inadequate models at that – it follows that these classifications are at best rough descriptions and not clearly different types. DeFrancis (1989) has recently made this point, emphasizing the essential oneness of writing systems.

Secondly, the traditional assumption that the history of writing is the progressive evolution culminating in the alphabet is misleading in the ethnocentrism implicit in such a view (Coulmas, 1989; DeFrancis, 1989; Keightley, 1989). The limitation of the evolutionary theory is that it leads to an underestimation of the optimality of alternative writing systems, such as the *logographic script* employed in China and the mixed logographic and syllabic script employed in Japan. At the end of World War II, Douglas MacArthur, commander of the allied forces, was urged by a panel of western educationists to completely revise the educational system of Japan and abolish "Chinese derived ideograms" if he wanted to help Japan develop technological parity with the west (Gaur, in press)! They needn't have worried. Furthermore, an authority on Chinese science, J. Needham (1954–59, 1969) has concluded that the Chinese script was neither a significant inhibitory factor in the development of modern science in China nor an impediment to scientists in contemporary China.

The view I shall elaborate in this chapter is that writing systems provide the concepts and categories for thinking about the structure of spoken language rather than the reverse. Awareness of linguistic structure is a product of a writing system not a precondition for its development. If that is so it will not do to explain the evolution of writing as the attempt to represent linguistic structures such as sentences, words or phonemes for the simple reason that pre-writers had no such concepts. The explanation for evolutionary changes in the writing systems of the world will have to be found elsewhere. The hypotheses I shall examine then are, first, that writing systems are developed for mnemonic and communicative purposes but because they are "read" they provide a model for language and thought. We introspect on language and mind in terms of the categories prescribed by our writing systems. And second, the evolutionary development of scripts, including the alphabet, is the simple consequence of attempting to use a graphic system invented to be "read" in one language, for which it is thereby reasonably suited, to convey messages to be "read" in another language for which it is not well suited. In each case the development of a functional way of communicating with visible marks was, simultaneously, a discovery of the representable structures of speech. This, I believe, is the sense in which some radical writers have talked about writing being prior to speech (Derrida, 1976; Householder, 1971).

The history of writing

Let us examine these hypotheses in the light of the available evidence on the history of writing. It is, of course, impossible to know with certainty what the earliest graphic representations represented. The

Neolithic revolution beginning some ten thousand years ago was marked by the beginnings of pottery making, food preparation, and domestic agriculture, as well as the psychological developments involved in the ornamentation and burial of the dead. Those developments are more or less contemporaneous with the beginnings of drawing and the use of tallies (Goody, 1987, p. 10; Schmandt-Besserat, 1986, 1987). Our question is how such representational systems developed and how they were "read." For how they are read will determine how they come to serve as models of speaking. My account is based largely on the analyses provided by Gelb (1963), Diringer (1968) and the more recent writings of Goody (1987), Gaur (1984/1987), Sampson (1985), Schmandt-Besserat (1986), Harris (1986), and Senner (1989). My hypothesis linking speech and writing borrows heavily from Harris (1986).

Although tallies and drawings are both graphic representations and may serve similar functions, historically those functions and structures have tended to diverge, drawings remaining iconic and tallies becoming arbitrary and conventional. But attempts to account for or correctly describe that divergence have remained a major theoretical puzzle. It is an anachronism to attempt to explain the evolution of graphic signs as the attempt to express ideas via *ideographs* for there is no reason to believe that early writers had any clear notion of ideas prior to the invention of writing either (Snell, 1960).

The earliest writing systems as well as many contemporary ones exhibit these diverse properties and functions. Geometrical signs were used to indicate ownership in Mesopotamia four millennia ago in ways analogous to the crests and cattle-brands used to this day; tally sticks were used in Ancient China to keep records of debts or other data and tallies were used in Britain by the Royal Treasury until 1826; knotted cords were used for keeping records in Ancient China and elsewhere and reached an extremely high level of complexity in the *quipu* of pre-colonial Peru; and *emblems*, that is, seals, totem poles, coats of arms, hallmarks, banners, and religious signs made up a part of graphic codes in ancient times just as they do today (Gaur, 1984/1987, pp. 18–25).

Some of these graphic devices not only symbolized objects or events but also represented a sequence of events which could be narrated,

that is, told rather than just named. Best known is the so-called
picture writing of the type developed by the aboriginal peoples of
North America. The Ojibway employed a series of depictions
inscribed on birch-bark scrolls to represent the rituals of the culture
including the creation of the world and of the Ojibway people. Such
scrolls could be interpreted only by the shaman and could be
described in quite different ways depending on the narrator's purpose.
The Iroquois Confederacy used a series of wampum belts to symbol-
ize treaties pertaining to land claims, the interpretation of which is
currently the object of a Canadian Royal Commission on Aboriginal
Peoples. "The two-row wampum, the best-known treaty belt,
symbolizes the conditions under which the Iroquois welcomed white
people to Turtle Island (North America). The belt features a canoe for
aboriginal people and a ship for non-native people, travelling side by
side down the river of life.

The two-row wampum is often cited as proof that the Mohawks
never surrendered their land and self-government rights" (Globe and
Mail, April, 1993). Similar graphic representational systems were
employed in ancient southern Mexico (Smith, 1973) and are employed
to this day by story-tellers in India (Gaur, 1984/1987, p. 55) and in
Ethiopia (Goody, 1987, p. 9).

Such visual graphic systems served as mnemonics by means of
which a suitably trained expert could recover important cultural
information. To describe the use of such systems as "reading" perhaps
stretches the modern meaning of that term unduly; certainly, in such
cases no clear distinction is made between *reading a text* and *describing a
picture*. What such graphic systems do is bring the cultural meanings
or interpretations of symbols into memory and consciousness but do
little to contribute to such notions as language, word or phoneme.
Specifically, while a graphic device would be taken as saying "the same
thing" on each occasion of reading, it would not bring such linguistic
notions as a "word," or "the same words" into consciousness, for there
is nothing in the graphic form that can be taken as a model for such
linguistic constituents; a picture of a dog is simultaneously a picture of
a domesticated quadruped, a collie, a pet, man's best friend, and so on.
There is no one-to-one mapping between linguistic element and sign.

We may note that emblematic forms of "writing" such as that

Figure 4.1   North American Indian pictorial
representation of an expedition

involved in the use of visual signs to indicate one's totem or one's
tribe, do not create a distinction between the name and the thing; the
emblem simultaneously stands for the totem and the name of the
totem. Similarly, one may have a concept of a name without having the
concept of a word; a word is a linguistic unit, a name is a property of
an object. Emblems represent names not words. Harris has suggested
that the failure to distinguish words from names produces a form of
emblematic symbolism which may extend to various gods and spirits
and "is often bound up in various ways with word magic and practices
of name-giving. It reflects, fundamentally, a mentality for which
reality is still not clearly divisible into language and non-language,
any more than it is divisible into the physical and the metaphysical, or
into the moral and the practical" (1986, pp. 131–132). Of course, a
little of that word magic exists in all of us; if not a crime it is at least a
sin to desecrate a prayer book.

Similarly, when pre-reading children "read" logos such as "Coke"
or take the inescapable golden arches as "McDonalds" it is unlikely
that they take the emblem as a representation of a word rather than as
an emblem of the thing. Consequently, there is no reason to suppose
that recognizing such logos contributes to children's understanding of
what a word is or to their reading skills more generally (Masonheimer,
Drum, & Ehri, 1984). Note, too, that this is not a claim about
understanding the arbitrariness of names, an understanding which has
been examined in children by Piagetian scholars, Sinclair (1978) and
Berthoud-Papandropoulou (1978). The concept which can plausibly
be linked to writing is that of word not that of name. Karmiloff-Smith

(1992) reports that only around age 6 do children begin to recognize that "of" and "the" are words as well.

But the puzzle remains as to how such tokens and emblems which represent things ever turn into signs which represent words and consequently how their recognition could ever turn into reading as we know it. Historical evidence may help to provide the needed clue. One extremely important graphic form from which most western writing systems may have evolved is the token system developed for accounting purposes in Mesopotamia beginning in the ninth millennium BC. The system, developed by the ancient Sumerians living in what is now southern Iraq, about the time that hunter-gatherer societies were giving way to an agricultural way of life, consisted of a set of clay tokens of distinctive shapes and markings, used to keep records of sheep, cattle and other animals, and goods of various kinds such as oil and grain.

About the fourth millennium BC, roughly at the time of the growth of cities, the variety of tokens increased greatly, presumably because of the increasing number of types of items to be inventoried, and the tokens began to be pierced in such a way that they could be strung together. Shortly thereafter they were placed in envelopes or *bullae* which, like the string, could mark off a single transaction. Schmandt-Besserat (1986, 1987, 1992) has suggested that the markings on these bullae constitute the first true writing. The connection between the tokens and the writing comes from the fact that the contents of the bullae were indicated on the surface of the bullae itself by impressing the token in the soft clay before baking it. But once the contents are marked on the envelope, there is no need for enclosing the actual tokens. The envelope has become a writing surface, and the shapes of the tokens when inscribed on to the surface become the earliest written texts. The tokens which represented units of goods are the origin of the Sumerian signs representing units of goods. All of the eighteen signs denoting commodities such as grain, animals and oil which appear on the earliest tablets derive from tokens.

But were such tokens taken as representing words or things? Have we here taken the critical step towards what we now consider writing to be? Harris (1986) has argued that the decisive step from tokens to scripts occurs when symbols shift from token-iterative to emblem-

Figure 4.2   Clay tokens from Tello, Iraq (some of which correspond to inscriptions on tablets from Uruk) circa 3200 BC

slotting systems, or what I prefer to think of as acquiring a syntax. A system which represents *three sheep* by three symbols for a sheep (i.e., sheep, sheep, sheep) is categorically different, he suggests, from one which represents the same three sheep by two tokens, one representing sheep, the other the number. Just as syntax is what makes a language a language, it is the syntax which makes a graphic system "generative" for it permits the combination and recombination of symbols to express a broad range of meanings.

An example of such a script is that from Ur, dated some 2900 BC and now filed as 10496 in the British Museum, which inventories the contents of a storehouse. The tablet is squared off into cells, each of which lists a product and an amount. The symbol for a jar resting on a pointed base stands for beer while the round impressions stand for quantities. Quantity is represented by two shapes, one produced by the end of a round stylus, perhaps representing ten, and the other produced by the edge of the stylus, perhaps representing units. Although much uncertainty as to just what various marks indicate, the cell in question could presumably be read as "twenty-three vats of beer." Thus this elementary script has a syntax and could be taken as a

Figure 4.3   Syntactic writing. Tablet from Ur,
2960 BC itemizing contents of a storehouse

precise model for an oral utterance. But there is no reason for
believing that such graphic signs yet represent a particular word or
words in a natural language. The tablet described above could be read
out in any language much as the Arabic numeral, *4* can be read out as
"four" or "quatre." It is not essential to claim, as do most theorists,
that syntactical scripts now represent speech; it is equally true that
such a script is now a language. That is to say we need not assume that
these early writers were conscious of or had a model of language as
consisting of words ordered by a syntax which they tried to get their
script to represent. Rather we can explain the relation between
language and script by saying that a script with a syntax provides, for
the first time, a suitable model for speech.

Two developments suggest that syntactic scripts are now taken as a
model for speech. The first is that the signs now come to be seen as
representing words rather than things. Paleographers (Gaur, 1984/
1987; Nissen, 1986) note that by the third millennium (2900 BC) the
earliest literary texts written in cuneiform appeared and such scripts
give clear indications of reflecting the linguistic knowledge of the
writer. That is, the script allows the reader to infer the language of the
writer; early tablets, as we have seen, do not. But what, exactly, is
involved in this achievement?

The first is the introduction of word signs. The sign for *beer* in the cuneiform tablet in Figure 4.3 represents beer not the word "beer." Nor does the sign for a *bee* necessarily represent the word "bee"; it may just represent the object, a bee. But if the sign is now appropriated to represent the verb "be," the sign has become a word sign, a *logograph*. The principle involved in this case is that of the *rebus*, the use of a sign which normally represents one thing to represent a linguistic entity that sounds the same; this entity is a word. What needs emphasis is that the rebus principle does not merely play upon pre-existing word knowledge; the substitution of the signs on the basis of their sound is what brings words into consciousness. A script which can be taken as representing both syntax and the words combined by the syntax produces a canonical writing system, one which is capable in principle of representing everything that can be said.

Even new words may enter the lexicon this way. Schmandt-Besserat (1986) has noted that the invention of abstract numbers coincides with the invention of such "syntactic" writing. Early tallies and tokens, as mentioned earlier, represent number by simple one-to-one correspondence – one token for each object. Four sheep could be represented by four marks on a stick, four pebbles in a pouch or by four sheep-shaped tokens on a string. The ancient Sumerians, with their system of tokens, had distinctive tokens for sheep, cows and the like. But when four sheep tokens are replaced by two tokens, one representing sheep and one representing the number of tallies, that token may be read as a word for an integer, "four," so the invention of syntactic writing would have allowed the invention of the abstract number!

Such scripts provide a model for the language which may now be seen as language independently of the things the language is about. But a new understanding of language as consisting of words also has conceptual implications. It spells the death of "word" magic or more precisely, "name" magic. Words are no longer emblems; words are now distinguished from both things and from names of things; words as linguistic entities come into consciousness. It becomes feasible to think of the meanings of words independently from the things they designate simply because the written form provides a model, the concept or categories for thinking about the constituents of spoken form. To elaborate, when the word is thought of as representing a thing rather than as an intrinsic property of the thing, word magic loses its power. An action on the name, as in a *hex*, does not affect the named because the word, unlike the name, is not a part of the thing; it is, as we say, just a word.

Such a writing system, independently of whether or not it was an alphabet, could have been instrumental in assisting the ancient Greeks in advancing a new and important set of concepts into consciousness. Havelock (1982) and Snell (1960) noted the ways that notions like *idea*, *mind*, and *word* developed and the ways in which words from the common vocabulary suddenly became the subject of analysis and reflection in classical Greek culture. Whereas for the Homeric Greeks notions like *justice* and *courage* were exemplified in the deeds of gods and heroes, for the literate Greeks they became philosophical concepts. The writing system, Havelock argued, was partly responsible. More recent studies have cast doubt on the abruptness, significance and permanence of that development (Padel, 1992). My suggestion is that the graphic system may play such a role by providing a model for language in a way that emblematic symbols never could. Rather than viewing writing as the attempt to capture the existing knowledge of syntax, writing provided a model for speech, thereby making the language available for analysis into syntactic constituents, the primary ones being words which then became subjects of philosophical reflection as well as objects of definition. Words became things.

It is interesting to note that in learning to read and write children go through just such a shift in understanding. If non-reading pre-school children are given a pencil and asked to write "cat" they may write a short string of letter-like forms. If then asked to write "three cats" they repeat the same initial string three times. Conversely, if such pre-reading children are shown a text which reads, "Three little pigs" and the text is then read to them while the words are pointed out they tend to take each of the words as a representation, an emblem, of a pig. Consequently, if the final word is erased and children are asked, "Now what does it say?" they may reply "Two little pigs." Alternatively, if each of the three words is pointed to in turn and the child is asked what each says, they reply, "One little pig; another little pig; and another little pig." That is, signs are seen as emblems rather than as words (Berthoud-Papandropoulou, 1978; Ferreiro, 1985, 1991;

Ferreiro & Teberosky, 1979/1982; Serra, 1992). Even when they begin to distinguish a word from a thing, their first notions of a word are tied to the written rather than to the spoken form (Downing, 1987; Reid, 1966). Francis (1975) for example, found that children's acquisition of the concepts of *letter*, *word*, and *sentence* were closely tied to their learning to read.

Once a writing system has a syntax, the emblems or tokens can now be seen as words rather than as emblems and the construction can be seen as a proposition rather than as a list. The structures present in the *script* now provide the categories needed for introspecting the implicit structures of language. Such scripts are logographic in that the tokens now represent the major grammatical constituents of the language, namely, words. But, to repeat, it does not follow that the inventors of such a script already knew about words and then sought to represent them in the script. The opposite may be true. The scribal inventions dictated a kind of reading which *allowed language to be seen as composed of words related by means of a syntax*. Writing thereby provides the model for the production of speech (in reading) and for the introspective awareness of speech as composed of grammatical constituents, namely, words.

The possibility that graphic systems with a syntax can be read as expressions in a natural language is what makes the written form a model for the spoken. Of course graphic schemes can always be verbalized or talked about; but only when it becomes possible to differentiate the activity of describing what a picture shows from reading what a text says, can the graphic structure be seen as a model for the syntactical properties of language.

Not all graphic features need be verbalized and not all verbalized differences need appear in the script. The decisive factor in the elaboration of the script will not be the verbal models (for as we have noted such models are not available prior to writing) but rather the attempt at a functional, unambiguous representation (Gaur, 1984/1987; Harris, 1986). In English script, a word beginning with a capital letter is not read any differently than one beginning with a lower case letter; the convention facilitates interpretation not pronunciation; it does not follow a verbal model. Conversely, English script does not employ different graphic signs for long and short vowels; both long and short /a/ are written *a*. Hence a script is not initially or primarily an attempt at a complete linguistic representation.

A further indication that writing, rather than being an attempt to represent speech, provides a model for that speech comes from the work of Larsen (1989), who pointed out that Sumerian texts fail to represent many morphological elements and the script offered information which could not be lexicalized. There was no attempt to record verbal statements but rather to fill administrative needs. When literary texts were written, beginning about 2600 BC, they were written in that "administrative script" and were, therefore, not complete renderings of a text but rather "an aid for someone who was to give an oral performance" (p. 130).

Is every script with a syntax a writing system? In terms of the history of writing it seems necessary to conclude that when signs acquired a syntax they were writing systems. On that basis we would say that the set of signs for Arabic numerals and operators is a writing system. But is it a logographic script as usually claimed? Not really, for as mentioned the signs do not represent words in any particular language. Such a script can be verbalized in more than one way: $3 \times 4 = 12$, can be read as three fours make twelve and so on and they can be lexicalized in any oral language. The way out of our dilemma is to recall that scripts are not primarily attempts to represent "what is said" but to represent events, and some of those representations can be taken as a model of speech. Numerical notations provide one kind of model; logographic scripts another and so on.

To conclude this discussion we may say that the evidence here examined tends to sustain our first hypothesis, namely, that writing far from transcribing speech tends to provide a model for that speech. To invent a writing system is, in part, to discover something about speech; to learn to read is, similarly, to discover something about one's speech, and ultimately, about "what is said." The script provides the model, however distorted, of one's speech.

The history of the alphabet

Next, let us turn to the hypothesis regarding the historical changes in scripts that led eventually to the alphabet. General purpose logographic scripts can represent anything that can be said. But the device of one token for each expressible semantic difference (essentially one sign for one word or morpheme) would require an extremely large set of tokens. Indeed, modern dictionaries of Chinese, the best exemplar of a so-called logographic script (but see Unger & deFrancis (in press) for a critique of this classification) list some 50,000 characters. Three principles of character or graphic formation appear to have been involved. First, ease of recognition is increased by employing iconic representations of objects – the sun being represented by a circle or waves by a wavy line, second, on economy – borrowing the sign for an object to represent another word or part of a word with a similar sound, the so-called *acrophonic* or *phonographic* principle employed in the rebus, and third, on unambiguity – distinguishing homophones, words that sound the same but mean different things, by an unverbalized *determinative* which indicates the semantic class to which the word belongs. A logographic script such as Chinese, while cumbersome to Western eyes, is no longer thought of as primitive or limited as it was even two decades ago (Unger & deFrancis, in press). Why then did some logographic scripts give way to the syllabaries and alphabets? Before we attempt to answer that question it is worth noting the clear shift in that direction in the evolution of scripts.

The ancient Sumerian script remained primarily logographic and rarely resorted to phonographic, that is sound-based, signs. When adopted by the Akkadians in the third millennium BC to represent a somewhat different language, the phonographic properties of the script were greatly expanded, giving rise to the Babylonian and Canaanite cuneiform, the best known of such scripts.

Egyptian hieroglyphic script, which developed around 3100 BC, employed a system similar to that of cuneiform although there is no evidence that the script was borrowed from the Babylonians. Simple signs were logographs, the drawing of a leg representing the word "leg," two legs meaning "to go" and so on. Complex signs were made by combining simple signs, each of which represented a sound drawn from a simple sign, along with an indicator specifying the domain to which the word belonged. Thus the sign for *sun* may be borrowed to represent "son" on the basis of their similar sound, the latter being turned into a complex sign by the addition of an indicator sign or

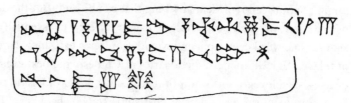

Figure 4.4   Canaanite cuneiform: thirteenth century BC

determinative, say, that of a man (Gaur, 1984/1987, p. 63). The Egyptian hieroglyphic inscriptions on the Rosetta stone which allowed the decipherment of the hieroglyphic code early in the nineteenth century provide a clear illustration of how such a script works. Many of the signs were found to represent semantic values such as the *cartouche* or oval around the royal names including Ptolemy and Cleopatra. Other signs represent sound values corresponding to syllables and to the letters of an alphabet. The first sign in the name Ptolemy is identical to the fifth sign in the name Cleopatra and must, therefore, represent a sound similar to that represented by our letter "p." The bird sign in the sixth and ninth position in Cleopatra represents the sound similar to that represented by our letter "a." The two symbols after the final bird sign are "determinatives" indicating that this is a feminine name.

Subsequent developments which gave rise, eventually, to the alphabet may be traced in large part to the consequences of borrowing. A shift in what a script "represents" is a consequence of adapting a script to a language other than that for which it was originally developed, an activity that led logographs to be taken as representations of syllables and later for syllables to be taken as representations of phonemes. Let us explore this hypothesis in detail.

The first syllabary was the result of using Sumerian logographs to represent a Semitic language, Akkadian (Larsen, 1989, p. 131). To represent an Akkadian word such as "a-wi-lu-um," *man*, with Sumerian logographs, the Akkadians simply took the Sumerian graphs which could be read as "a," "wi," "lu," and "um," ignoring the fact that in Sumerian each graph represented a separate word: "a" would mean *water*, "wi" would mean something else and so on. Reading Akkadian would then be a matter of pronouncing this series and the graphs

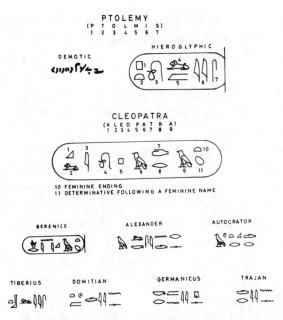

Figure 4.5 Ancient Egyptian hieroglyphs representing the Imperial names

would now be taken to represent syllables of Akkadian rather than words as they had done in Sumerian. Logographs have become syllabics. Note that the argument is not that this use was the product of the application of the acrophonic principle of using signs to represent syllables but rather that the new use of old graphs for a new language produced a script in which the constituents *could be seen* as representing syllables. The syllable is as much a product of the graphic system as a prerequisite for it. To state this point as neutrally as I can, for it remains an open question, the old script is fitted to the new language as a model is fitted to data; the data are then seen in terms of that model. In this case, the model is that of audible constituents and the flow of speech is heard, perhaps for the first time, as a string of separable, itemizable, syllables. Recent research has shown that the Mayan script of ancient southern Mexico was indeed a fully developed syllabary (Coe, 1992).

Psychological evidence is also relevant to this point. First, sensitivity to some syllabic constituents, especially those relevant to rhyme and alliteration, pre-date literacy. On the basis of their comprehensive review, Goswami and Bryant (1990) concluded that although young children are not aware of phonemes, they are sensitive to the initial and final sounds of words and phrases, what they refer to as "onsets" and "rimes," and this sensitivity may be relevant to early word recognition (see also Treiman, 1991). Consequently, early readers may take even alphabetic signs as if they are representations of syllables and read them as such.

Secondly, syllabic scripts are easily acquired. Scribner and Cole (1981) noted that the Vai learned to read their syllabaries in a matter of weeks and Bennett and Berry (1991) noted that Cree syllabics could be acquired in a few days. McCarthy (1991) noted that the whole Cree nation became literate in a mere ten-year span in the 1840s. She goes on to suggest that the ease with which such learning takes place suggests that not much has in fact been learned about the structure of language in this case; the mapping from script to syllable is relatively straightforward.

But it does not follow that awareness of language as a string of syllables is completely independent of knowledge of a script. Scribner and Cole (1981) found that Vai literates, familiar with a syllabic script, were much more skilled in integrating separate syllables into phrases and decomposing phrases into such syllables than were non-literates. This suggests that the learning of a syllabary is a matter of coming to hear one's continuous speech *as if* it were composed of segmentable constituents. Yet it is a surprisingly easy task for even quite young children (Fox & Routh, 1975; Karpova, 1977).

The first writing system based exclusively on such principles was *Linear B*, a Mycenaean Greek script developed around 1600 BC and deciphered only in modern times by an English architect, Michael Ventris, in 1952. The script is strictly syllabic, each syllable employing a distinctive graph. The script was apparently abandoned because the Greek language has complex syllable structures (e.g., C-V-C) in addition to those simple syllables (C-V) represented by the script; consequently the script is thought to have been seriously deficient, that is, it allowed an unacceptable level of ambiguity.

The immediate ancestor of the Greek alphabet has been viewed by some as a simplified form of syllabary (Havelock, 1982) and by others as an abstraction from a syllabary (Gelb, 1963). The script was invented by speakers of some Semitic language, possibly Phoenician, who lived in the northern part of the Fertile Crescent, that area of arable land connecting Babylonian and Egyptian civilizations. Modern versions of Semitic script include the Hebrew script and the Arabic script.

Semitic languages, however, have the interesting property of carrying the lexical identities of the language in what we think of as consonants; what we think of as vowels were used only for inflections. To illustrate, the string of sounds /k/, /t/, /b/ vocalized in somewhat different ways all convey the basic lexeme *write* with vocalic differences marking grammatical subject, tense and aspect: *katab* 'he wrote,' *katabi* 'I wrote,' *katebu* 'they wrote,' *ketob* 'write,' *koteb* 'writing,' *katub* 'being written.' All can be written simply *ktb*.

Because the vowels provide only grammatical rather than lexical or morphemic information, some Semitic writing systems never developed any device for representing them. This is not necessarily a flaw in the script because inserting vowels would make morpheme and word identification more difficult. Obviously, some semantic distinctions are not marked in the script and must be inferred from context. Some scripts, such as Hebrew, add *matres lectionis*, literally, mothers of reading, a pointing system to distinguish vocalic sounds especially for sacred texts in which proper articulation is important as well as in books written to be read by children. Whether such additions in fact facilitate reading remains an open question.

The major achievement of such scripts, from an evolutionary perspective, is the representation of a group of syllables such as the English *pa*, *pe*, *pi*, *po*, *pu*, by a single graphic sign, say, *p*. If the discovery of the common property of such different syllables is the product of abstraction it is a remarkable intellectual achievement; that, in fact, is the traditional view. But if it is simply the failure to discriminate them, treating the vocalic variants as of little or no significance and hence disregarding them, then it is the simple product of borrowing, that is, of applying a script to a language for which it was important to mark vocalic differences (different vowels make different syllables) to a language for which it was not important to mark such differences. In fact, both Gelb (1963) and Havelock (1982) deny that such a script represents consonants, rather, they claim, it constitutes an unvocalized syllabary, a syllabary which simply does not distinguish vocalic differences. Others such as Sampson (1985) refer to it as a consonantal writing system. In my view, the script is a simplification, a discarding of characters thought to be redundant just as "going to" gets attenuated to "gonna" to form "I'm gonna go home" in vernacular speech. But once so attenuated, the graphic system *can be seen as* a representation of consonants, particularly when, as we shall see, it was borrowed by the Greeks to represent yet another different language.

Regardless of how it was arrived at, the Phoenician's new set of twenty-two graphic signs with a memorized order beginning *aleph*, *bet*, *gemel*, was adequate for representing a full range of meanings and the graphs can be seen as representing not only syllables but the consonantal sounds of the language.

The "final" transition from consonantal to *alphabetic writing* occurred, uniquely in the history of the world, when the Semitic script was adapted to a non-Semitic language, Greek. The application, bypassing Linear B, occurred about 750 BC. Scholars have traditionally considered the Greek invention to be the stroke of genius. While not minimizing the significance of the Greek achievement, it is now recognized that the development of the alphabet, like the development of the syllabary, was a rather straightforward consequence of applying a script which was suitable for one language, to a second language for which it was not, namely, of applying a script for a Semitic language in which vocalic differences were relatively insignificant to the Greek language in which they were highly significant (Sampson, 1985; Harris, 1986).

Many of the syllable signs from the Semitic alphabet fitted and could be utilized directly for representing Greek; these came to be the consonants. But unlike a Semitic language, Greek, like English, is an Indo-European language in which vowel differences make lexical contrasts – "bad" is different from "bed." Moreover, words may consist simply of vowels, words may begin with vowels, and words with pairs of vowels are not uncommon. To fill the gap, six Semitic characters which represented sounds unknown in Greek, were borrowed to represent these isolated vowel sounds. But equipped with such signs representing vowel sounds, the Greeks were in a position to "hear," perhaps for the first time, that those sounds also occurred within the syllables represented by the Semitic consonant signs. In this way syllables were dissolved into consonant-vowel pairings and the alphabet was born.

Again, the point to note is that such a theory does not require the assumption that the Greeks attempted to represent phonemes; it does not assume the availability to consciousness of the phonological structure of language. Rather, the script can be seen as a model for that structure. That is, phonological categories such as consonants and vowels need not exist in consciousness to be captured by writing. Rather writing provides a model for speech; all that is required is that speech be seen, that is, heard in terms of that model. This point is relevant to current discussions of dyslexia and learning to read; those who assume that reading is decoding assume, erroneously, that the phonology is available to consciousness; those who assume that reading is meaning detection assume, erroneously, that sound-symbol mapping is either irrelevant or impossible. The way between these extremes is to note that scripts provide a model for speech; learning to read is precisely learning that model. Ironically, learning to read is learning to hear speech in a new way!

Such a roundabout explanation of the relation between script and awareness of language is required to explain several facts. First, the alphabet in fact does not constitute a phonological theory. Harris (1986) points out that the Greeks, the inventors of the alphabet, never developed an adequate theory of phonology. The sound patterns they described were a direct reflection of the Greek alphabet; "consequently, the Greeks were led to ignore phonetic differences which were not reflected in Greek orthography" (p. 86). In this the Greek linguists were not different from children who are exposed to the alphabet. Ehri (1985) has shown that children think there are more "sounds" in the word *pitch* than in the word *rich* even if phonologists inform us that they are equivalent. Obviously, children, like the classical Greeks, introspect their language in terms of their alphabet.

Secondly, that the alphabet serves as a model for speech, rather than as a representation of pre-existing knowledge, is shown by the elegant studies on "phonological" awareness in speakers who are not readers. The studies of people's awareness of sub-syllabic constituents have established that familiarity with an alphabetic writing system is critical to one's awareness of the segmental structure of language. People familiar with an alphabet *hear* words as composed of the sounds represented by the letters of the alphabet; those not familiar do not. To illustrate, those familiar with an alphabet are able to delete the sound /s/ from the word "spit" to yield /pit/ or to add an /s/ to /pit/ to make "spit" while those not so familiar are not. Morais, Bertelson, Cary, and Alegria (1986) and Morais, Alegria, and Content (1987) found that Portuguese fishermen living in a remote area who had received even minimal reading instruction some forty years earlier and who had done little or no reading since, were still able to carry out such segmentation tasks while those who had never been to school could not. Similar findings have been reported for Brazilian non-literate adults by Bertelson, de Gelder, Tfouni, and Morais (1989). Scholes and Willis (1991) found that non readers in rural parts of the American Southeast had grave difficulties with a large variety of such metalinguistic tasks. Even more impressive is the finding by Read, Zhang, Nie, and Ding (1986) who found that Chinese readers of traditional character scripts could not detect phonemic segments whereas those who could read Pinyin, an alphabetic script representing the same language, could do so. To learn to read any script is to find or detect aspects of one's own implicit linguistic structure that can map onto or be represented by that script.

This point is nicely exploited in Frith's (1985) three-stage model of learning to read. Frith suggests that early readers treat an alphabet as if it were a logograph, each letter string as a whole representing a word. As they begin to attempt to spell words, they decompose those logographs into alphabetic constituents, each representing a phoneme. At a third stage they begin to see relations between letters and therefore detect morphemes, seeing the "boy" in "cowboy" for example.

I have been suggesting that the invention of a writing system does two things at once. It provides a graphic means of communication but, because it is then verbalized, that is, read, it comes to be seen as a model of that verbalization. As scripts became more elaborate they provided increasingly precise models of speech, of "what was said." Thus cultures developed a more precise criterion used for deciding whether or not two utterances were "the same words." Traditional cultures treat alternative expressions of the same sense as being "the same"; literate ones using the stricter criterion of verbatim repetition as "the same" (Finnegan, 1977; Goody, 1987).

This shift in criterion in judging "the same words" can be seen as well in children as they become more literate (Hedelin & Hjelmquist, 1988). In our recent work on children's understanding of the fixity of text, to be discussed more fully in Chapter 6, we (Torrance, Lee, & Olson, 1992) examined young children's ability to distinguish between verbatim repetitions and paraphrases of an utterance. A series of stories were presented in which a puppet was to produce either an exact repetition of what a character in a story had said or a paraphrase of what the person in the story wanted. Needless to say, the experimenter "spoke" for the puppet while the children judged the adequacy of the response. Whereas they could readily reject incorrect paraphrases, children under six found it impossible to reject a paraphrase when they were asked to accept only "exactly what was said." We inferred that they could not systematically distinguish between a verbatim repetition and a paraphrase of that utterance. This is just what one would expect on the basis of the theory that writing is an important factor in "fixing a text." If the analysis I have proposed is correct, these are the products of learning certain graphic conventions.

Once a script is taken as a model for speech it becomes possible to increase the mapping between the two, to allow a relatively close transcription of speech and conversely, to speak like a book. As scripts became more elaborate, their lexicalization or "reading" became more constrained. In fact, no script ever succeeds in completely determining the reading – any actor can read a simple statement in many different ways. The script merely determines which variants will be treated as equivalent, as "the same words." It seems clear that any phonographically based text, whether syllabary or alphabet, determines in large measure the lexical and grammatical properties of a reading. It is less certain for a logographic script such as Chinese which is designed to be read in quite different dialects and may, I am told, allow some variability in lexical and grammatical rendering even within a single community of readers.

How scripts control the reading is nicely illustrated by Boorman (1986) in his discussion of the history of musical scores. In the sixteenth century, composers began to add notations to their scores to restrict performers' autonomy in realizing a musical composition. As a consequence the language of music became more complex. The trend was part of a general reaction against the ambiguity of scribal and early printed forms. Parallel developments occurred in the development of conventions for punctuation of texts (Morrison, 1987).

A second advantage that resulted from taking the script as a model for language, was that it allowed the formation of explicit logics, grammars and dictionaries (Goody, 1987). Alphabetic scripts are taken, somewhat mistakenly, as models of phonology (Harris, 1986). In all cases, the script became a useful model for the language, turning some structural aspects of speech into objects of reflection, planning and analysis.

But the fact that alphabetic scripts can be lexicalized in only one way creates a blind spot that we have only recently come to recognize. Because an alphabetic script can transcribe anything that can be said, it is tempting to take it as a complete representation of a speaker's utterance. Just as the readers of a logographic script or a syllabic script may be unaware of what their script does not represent, namely, the phonological properties of their language, so we, alphabetics, may be unaware of what our writing system does not explicitly represent. In fact, our writing system, too, represents only part of the meaning; it is a simple illusion that it is a full model of what is said. An utterance spoken with an ironic tone is represented in writing the same way as the same utterance spoken with a serious tone. Again, a skilled actor can read the same text in many different ways. So the graphic form does not completely determine the reading.

The blind spot which our alphabetic script continues to impart leads us into two kinds of errors. It invites the inference that any meaning we personally see in a text is actually there and is completely determined by the wording – the problem of literalism. Conversely any other "reading" of that text is seen as the product of ignorance or "hardness of heart." How to cope with this interpretive problem attracted the best minds of Europe for a millennium giving rise ultimately to the new way of reading we associate with the Reformation. Secondly, it leads literate people to an oversimplified notion of what "to read" means. Does "read" mean to lexicalize or "decode" a text or does "read" mean to construct a meaning? Is it decoding or interpretation? Battles over the verb "read" are usually non-productive; what is critical is understanding what a script represents and what it fails to represent.

So what aspects of speech are not represented in a writing system? This too, has many classical answers. Plato thought that writing represented the words but not the author. Rousseau (1754–91/1966) thought it represented the words but not the voice. Some say that it represents the form but not the meaning. I suggest that while writing provides a reasonable model for what the speaker said, it does not provide much of a model for what the speaker meant by it, or more precisely how the speaker or writer intended the utterance to be taken. It does not well represent what is technically known as illocutionary force. Writing systems by representing the former have left us more or less blind to the latter.

I have tried to establish four points. First, writing is not the transcription of speech but rather provides a conceptual model for that speech. It is for this reason that typologies of scripts – as logographic, syllabic and alphabetic – are at best rough descriptions rather than types; there never was an attempt to represent such structural features of language. Second, the history of scripts is not, contrary to the common view, the history of failed attempts and partial successes towards the invention of the alphabet, but rather the by-product of attempts to use a script for a language for which it is ill-suited. Third, the models of language provided by our scripts are both what is acquired in the process of learning to read and write and what is employed in thinking about language; writing is in principle meta-linguistics. Thus, our intellectual debt to our scripts for those aspects of linguistic structure for which they do provide a model and about which they permit us to think, is enormous. And finally, the models provided by our script tend to blind us toward other features of language which are equally important to human communication. That is the topic of the next chapter.

Writing systems, then, do represent speech. But not in the way that is conventionally held. Writing systems create the categories in terms of which we become conscious of speech. To paraphrase Whorf (1956), we introspect our language along lines laid down by our scripts. We have seen what our scripts reveal to us; we turn now to what they may conceal.

5 WHAT WRITING DOESN'T REPRESENT: HOW TEXTS ARE TO BE TAKEN

....

"Smile when you say that"; how do you smile in writing?

You attribute to letters a fortune that they cannot possess.
(Plato, *Phaedrus*)

In the preceding chapter we concluded that because writing is "read," it comes to be taken as a model for speech; whatever is represented in the script becomes an object of knowledge or awareness to the person literate in that script. Thus, to the alphabetically literate person, speech is seen as composed of a string of phonemes represented by the letters of the alphabet. Furthermore, the model provided by the script tends to be seen as a complete representation of what is said. The alphabet in particular is usually celebrated for its ability to transcribe anything that can be said and to represent any speaker's or writer's intention. That, as we saw, is what misleads many writers to think of the alphabet as a simple cipher.

In this chapter we reverse the ground by focusing on aspects of meaning that writing systems fail to represent and which consequently are difficult to bring into consciousness. I refer, not to what is said but rather to the indications provided by a speaker and by the shared context as to how what is said is to be taken by the listener or audience. The hypothesis we consider in this chapter is that whereas spoken utterances tend to indicate both what is said and how it is to be taken, written ones tend to specify only the former. In subsequent chapters we shall examine the ways in which attempts to cope with the limitations of scripts contributed to the conceptual revolutions associated with literate culture.

Two simple illustrations may help to indicate what scripts fail to represent. If one says, as Eeyore did to Pooh: "You're a real friend," tone of voice and context may indicate whether it is said sincerely or ironically. A writing system which simply transcribed what was said would capture neither tone nor context. Yet the tone and context convey part of the meaning of an utterance. In fact, it is well known that young children are more sensitive to the tone and context of an utterance than to its precise verbal form.

A second type of illustration. Herbert Simon is reported to have said (and written) that the mind is a computer. That expression, however, gives no indication of how it is to be taken; was it intended to be taken literally or metaphorically? Similarly, when the pre-Socratic philosopher Empedocles said that the salt sea was the sweat of the earth, was he being scientific or poetic? There is nothing in the transcription of what was said that indicates how the author intended it to be taken. Sincerity, seriousness and commitment are aspects of what is said which are not represented by a script which transcribes (or is taken as representing) phonemes, words and sentences.

Halliday (1985) points out that these omissions are the result of the difficulty writing systems have in capturing prosodic features of speech, such as the rising intonation in a question, and paralinguistic features such as volume and voice quality – ironic tone among them. It is difficult to represent stress and intonation in a script because such features are spread out over an utterance. Rather than represent such features directly, many scripts have turned to representations of what those prosodic and paralinguistic features signify either through meta-linguistic commentary (Tannen, 1985) or through punctuation marks. The earliest Greek texts consist of strings of letters without word spaces or punctuation. Vai texts are strings of syllables. Modern scripts represent some of the prosodic features of speech by punctuation marks which are not "read" but indicate how what is written is to be read; "Bob!" is to be read differently from "Bob?"

While the linguistic features that writing fails to capture are by now reasonably well known, their contribution to meaning is both more complex and less well known. In the theory of Speech Acts (Austin, 1962) a distinction is drawn between the locutionary act – what is said or asserted – and the illocutionary force – how the speaker intended what was said to be taken – as a statement, a promise, a command, a declaration or an expression of feeling. Illocutionary force, ordinarily, is not lexicalized: We say "I'll get it" rather than "I promise that I'll get it," we say "Sit down" rather than "I order you to sit down" and we say "Hydrogen is a chemical element" rather than "I assert that hydrogen is a chemical element" and so on. Lyons (1977, Vol. 2, p. 731) notes that "illocutionary uptake is a necessary ... condition of ... understanding an utterance." Consequently, listeners have little difficulty recognizing a command when they hear one even if it is disguised as a simple prediction such as "Candidates will provide their own drawing equipment." All oral utterances are composed of both what is said and some indication of how they are to be taken – as statement, question, command, promise or whatever; writing, capturing only what was said, represents only the former. How it is to be taken is underspecified and hence becomes the central problem in interpreting written texts and a critical problem in composing them.

The first argument of this chapter, then, is that the illocutionary force is an aspect of an utterance which in oral discourse is, by and large, detectable by a listener. A written transcription, on the other hand, captures only a privileged aspect of the utterance, namely, "what is said" and not "how it is to be taken." Oversimplifying somewhat, writing readily represents the locutionary act, leaving illocutionary force underspecified. Recovering that force becomes a fundamental problem in reading and specifying it a central problem in writing.

Worse still, because illocutionary force is not indicated in the transcription of what is said, and because what is transcribed tends to be taken as a completely adequate representation of what is meant, naive readers often fail to see that there is any problem. Indeed, the discovery and then the management of illocutionary force make up a fundamental part of the history of literacy. The history of reading may be seen, in part, as a series of attempts to recognize and to cope with what is *not* represented in a script.

The significance of a text is perhaps the easiest aspect of illocutionary force to detect and to represent graphically. Among the treasures of many museums and rare book collections are the illuminated manuscripts of the later Middle Ages – Bibles and Books of Hours – elaborated and adorned with beautiful illustrations in reds, blues and golds, and written in an ornate script. They are rightly regarded as objects of art. Could not the illuminations, in addition, be seen as an attempt to compensate for what was lost in simple tran-

Figure 5.1   From *Liturgy and ritual horae, ca 1425*

scription of the words of the text? The illuminations tell the reader that these are not mere or ordinary words but sacred texts. The manuscripts are icons as much as texts. In fact, the illuminations changed importantly in the later Middle Ages, a point to which we shall return.

Figure 5.2   POGO

A more homely example comes from the comic strip *Pogo* in which
the speech of the Deacon is printed in Gothic script with the result
that what he says "sounds" ponderous. The typographic choice in this
case represents an aspect of the Deacon's speech which is otherwise
unrepresented.

For literate people, that is, people who take written language as the
standard and the norm, it is difficult to imagine that writing is a
representation of only a part of speech, namely, phonemes, words, and
sentences. It takes a special effort to see that the written version is not
a complete representation of the speaker's or writer's intention. As
mentioned, most readers are afflicted by the notion that texts mean
just what they say. The inferred communicative intention is taken as
much as given as the verbal form. Texts provide a representation of
what was said but not of how the speaker intended it to be taken. The
clues indicating the latter – prosodic and paralinguistic clues including
intonation, stress and voice qualities which indicate "speakers' state of
mind, the reservations and doubts, ... the weight given to different
parts of an argument" are lost in the act of transcribing what a speaker
may say (Halliday, 1985, p. 32). To make a written text clear this
information must be "edited in" by descriptive commentary and by
elaboration of a metalanguage indicating how the text is to be taken
(Traugott & Pratt, 1980, p. 42). In the absence of such commentary,
the reader is faced with the task of determining how the text is to be
taken. A naive reader, faced with a text, may be tempted, indeed was

tempted as we shall see later, to ascribe whatever effect the text had on him or her as being the meaning intended by the writer.[1]

Of course, such problems can occur also in speech. Shakespeare in *Richard II* (V, iv), has Bolingbroke moan under his breath "Have I no friend will rid me of this living fear [the King at Pomfret]?" which when overheard by his followers was interpreted as warrant for murder, much to the anguish of Bolingbroke. The point is that this is generally the case with written texts and suitable interpretive procedures have to be developed to deal with them. Hermeneutics, the science of interpretation, is a science for interpreting just such written texts. Oral expressions require interpretation, of course, but they do not require a science, or at least the same science, of interpretation; interpretation can ordinarily take place unreflectively.

Conceptual advance, I shall argue, comes first from inventing means for rationally and methodologically assigning interpretations to texts and second from inventing linguistic or other resources for controlling how a reader would take a text. Interpretation, we may say, becomes conscious.

The second argument of this chapter, then, is that the reader's attempts to compensate for what had been lost in the act of writing a text is one of the means by which literacy imparts its conceptual advantages.

But to say this may seem to imply a certain weakness or inadequacy or limitation in those who rely exclusively on oral speech. A fundamental assumption in anthropological linguistics is that all human languages are capable in *principle* of expressing any thought. This is not to say that all languages are elaborated or specialized to the same degree in every domain but rather that if people fail to come to an agreement in face-to-face contexts, even people from different cultures, that failure is unlikely to be due to the limitations of language. Ordinary oral language is completely adequate for the representation of a full range of meanings, including direct expressions of truth.

[1] Justice Blenus Wright informs me that Appeal Courts adjudicate on matters of law rather than matters of credibility of evidence. They have access only to the written transcript of the proceedings rather than the actual oral statements presented in court. Hence they lack knowledge of "how" the recorded statements were expressed, an important part of their meaning.

Writing can scarcely improve on these basic resources, although as we shall see, by bringing these resources into consciousness, it may allow them to be systematically distinguished and exploited in somewhat different ways.

Reported speech, the use of one person's speech by another person, presents many of the same problems that written texts do. Upon analysis reported speech presents three unique problems for which solutions must be sought by a speaker. First, the speaker requires some device to mark off quoted from direct speech. Second, the speaker may have to indicate whether this is a direct quotation, indirect quotation or mere paraphrase or gist of what is said. And third, the speaker must find some means of expressing not just the content quoted but the manner in which it was expressed. How is one, for example, to express whether the cited utterance was a threat, a comment, an order, a suggestion or a guess? Or, to allude to the epigram at the beginning of this chapter, how do you report that something was said with a smile? Clearly a direct quotation of only the speaker's words will not capture *how* it was said nor consequently how the speaker intended it to be taken – a metalinguistic commentary has to be added. Thus in the management of reported speech – preserved expressions, speech divorced from context – speech and writing tend to diverge.

In speech, brief quotation appears to be a relatively simple matter which is universally exploited. All languages, including languages without writing, have some metalinguistic terms, technically speech act verbs such as "say," "ask," "speak," and "tell" to distinguish direct from reported speech (Feld & Schieffelin, 1982; E. Goody, 1978; Leech, 1983; McCormick, 1989; Rosaldo, 1982). Furthermore, at least some traditional cultures, such as the Eipo of West New Guinea (Heeschen, 1978) and the Limba of Sierra Leone, have a particular inflection to mark a quotation (Finnegan, 1988, p. 50). Quotation may turn a piece of speech into the object of discussion (Feldman, 1991). And Chafe (1985) and Sperber (1975, p. 148) note that many non-literate cultures employ evidential markers, such as, *it is the custom*, or *I saw with my own eyes*, or *it is said*, some of which appear to have the effect of putting the statement in quotes. And capturing the attitude of the original speaker to the text being quoted can be solved by imitating or describing the manner of speech – a sneering comment reported in a sneering intonation, a question with a question intonation and so on.

Even then, there are limitations in the management of quotation in situations and cultures without writing. Distinctions between precise and approximate quotation may be vague or absent given the latitude involved in determining what is meant by "the very words" (Goody, 1987, p. 168). Quotation or citation of longer pieces of discourse and quoting discourse from earlier periods in time, present additional difficulties – difficulties sufficiently severe that in traditional oral societies such tasks tend to be managed primarily by experts. First, there is the obvious problem of remembering the content and especially remembering the exact wording. And second, there is the matter of preserving and reporting not just what was said, whether word or content, but also the original speaker's attitude to that content, that is, the speech act or illocutionary force involved. In this case simple imitation may be difficult or impossible. How then is one to express whether an utterance was originally made as a threat or a prediction, or whether it was a guess or an assertion, or whether it was a literal claim or a loose metaphor? And thirdly, a refinement of the second, how was one to capture the degree or intensity of speaker's attitude to the utterance. Commands have a certain kind of illocutionary force but, within that category, how is one to convey whether it was an order or merely a suggestion? When Jesus told the rich man to sell all that he had, was that an order or a suggestion? How is one to characterize and convey the intensity of the speaker's original attitude to the expression. Let us examine these in turn.

First, the memory problem. We who are immersed in literacy may find it difficult to imagine that extended discourse, especially discourse from an earlier period could be quoted and thereby preserved without writing. But, in fact it can. There is now a flourishing branch of literary theory devoted to the topic of oral tradition, a sub-discipline that has convincingly shown that cultural traditions and specialized knowledge can be preserved and transmitted without the archival means that we literates rely on. Even the highly literate medieval scholars have been shown to rely primarily on memory rather than on written documents in most of their scholarly activities (Carruthers,

1990). It remains to be seen if the information intrusted to living memories is stored and interpreted in the same ways as that intrusted to written record.

Vansina (1961/1965) who made extensive studies of African oral traditions pointed out that there are numerous special forms of discourse including slogans, proverbs, stories, poems, prayers which fall roughly into two classes, those that preserve the wording, primarily poetry, and those that preserve the content, primarily narrative. The recall of important content information was facilitated by mnemonic devices; some of these involved specific memorial devices similar to the *quipu* employed in Peru, others involved a traditional, ritualized performance which would facilitate recall, and still others involved the use of professional remembrancers such as bards, poets and rhapsodists. Through such means, remarkable storage of specialized knowledge may be achieved and passed on. Since such speech is reported by rather than originated by the speaker, special marking such as the physical stance of the speaker, the vocal properties of the speech, and lexical markings such as "it is said" distinguish such speech (Bloch, 1975; Feldman, 1991).

The Ashanti, Vansina (1961/1965, pp. 37–38) informs us, had a royal employee who served as the keeper of the king's stool who not only preserved the physical object but also the history of the stool, that is, the history of the kingdom. Another group, the people of Luapula, have a number of traditions that are recited only when passing the places mentioned in the tales; the places served as mnemonics.

Thus oral cultures do not rely only upon oral memory. The *quipu*, the mnemonic system developed in Peru, is perhaps best known and certainly one of the most impressive, so much so that some have considered it as a writing system (Gaur, 1984/1987). Quipu were knotted cords of variable colour and length tied together and attached to a head-dress so as to make a fringe. Colour, length, type of knot all had a meaning. The quipu were borrowed by the Inca to preserve oral traditions, including names and chronologies. Vansina relates that on some occasions penitents at confession may "read" off their sins from quipu specially constructed for that purpose.

The line between a mnemonic device such as the quipu, and a writing system is not a technically defensible one. As we saw in the preceding chapter no writing system is pure linguistic transcription. Writing systems differ in their methods of reading and interpreting, and more importantly for our purposes, in the concepts and assumptions they may come to invoke regarding language, meaning, and reading. It is we, modern literates, who hold special beliefs about reading and interpretation that make other orientations to writing seem faulty or primitive. As we saw in Chapter 4, quipu are "read" in ways that preserve meaning rather than in a way that preserves particular wording and in that way are quite different from logographic or alphabetic scripts. Quipu remind the tellers of significant events whereas some other scripts specify the verbal form of the idea. Yet beliefs about writing may not change even if the script does. So, for example, in the Middle Ages no distinction was drawn between writing systems and mnemonic systems. Carruthers (1990) and Leclercq (1961) pointed out that reading and memorizing were taught as a single activity and that the primary use of writing was as a record against which to check one's memory. Modern readers, as we shall see, use texts in a quite different way.

Cultures without writing systems for preserving wording not only have physical devices for preserving factual information, they also employ poetic devices including symbolic devices such as homophony, metonymy and metaphor to make information memorable by preserving the verbal form. Vansina reports that in Rwanda a poet will refer to a king as a hunter of zebras. The listener is expected to translate "killer of zebras" as a lion, recognizing that as a homophone of the king's title, the lion of Rwanda. Finnegan (1988, pp. 48–49) describes some of the forms of word play appreciated by the Limba, forms of onomatopoeia (words analogous to our "kerplunk"), simple puns (imitating children's whines as the sound of a young goat), nonsense words, mimicry, exaggeration of tone and length, all of which "reveal an attitude of self-conscious awareness to language." Gaur (1984/1987, p. 21) tells us that the Yoruba of Nigeria use puns to convey messages. Young lovers may send one another strings of cowrie shells, six on a string to convey "I like you" because the word *efa* means both "six" and "attracted" and eight on a string to convey "I agree" because ejo means both "eight" and "agreed."

Havelock (1982), building on the work by Parry (1971) and Lord

(1960), developed a theory of how cultures without writing cope with the problem of preserving longer texts representing significant or sacred events. "Poetized speech" managed by memory specialists such as oral poets or wisemen, he argued, may serve as an oral encyclopedia, that is, a storehouse of important cultural information. In Havelock's view much of the "glory that was Greece" was the product of this oral rather than literate culture. Recent work has tempered Havelock's conclusions somewhat both because of a better understanding of writing systems and of the softening of the boundary between the "oral" and the "literate" (Lynn-George, 1988). Finnegan (1988, p. 72) reviewing her own and others' work in this field concluded that "the old idea of lengthy memorized transmission over centuries or even millennia may no longer be tenable, but over shorter time spans memorized transmission certainly takes place."

To summarize this point: memory for what is said, that is the actual words of an expression, poses little problem in cultures without writing so long as the text is short and the delay brief. Longer texts, if specially crafted, can be preserved over longer periods of time. Mnemonic devices, coupled with figures of speech and metrical, poetized speech, permit the storage and retrieval of the verbal form of culturally significant information. Yet, verbatim memorization seems a uniquely literate activity, assuming as it does, the availability of an original or fixed version against which memory may be checked. Without such a transcript there is greater latitude in what is accepted as exactly what was said. As a result direct and indirect quotation may not be as sharply distinguished in oral contexts and in oral societies more generally.

Memory for what the speaker or author intended by what was said poses different sorts of problems in oral and literate cultures. Even if one successfully remembers something close to the very words employed by a speaker – no small feat – how is one to pass on the manner in which the original was expressed? One means, widely exploited in at least some forms of written discourse, is to employ speech act and mental state terms such as "state," "deny," "imply," "concede," "allege" and the like. These verbs indicate the reporter's belief as to how the original speaker intended the expression to be taken.

How is this handled in oral discourse and in oral cultures? In fact, it need not be a problem. Just as the content of an utterance may be repeated, its manner of speaking may be imitated as well. A sneering intonation can be imitated just as easily as the linguistic form of the content.

But the primary means for reporting how the speaker intended his or her utterance to be taken – the illocutionary force of an utterance – is through verbal descriptions of the manner in which the utterance was expressed – eagerly, hesitatingly, sternly, forthrightly, meekly, and the like – and through speech act verbs – said, asked, told, insisted, claimed, and the like. Do the linguistic resources for characterizing the illocutionary force of an utterance differ between oral and literate cultures?

At least some lexical and syntactic resources are available in oral cultures for referring to the type and manner of reported speech. The study of speech acts in a variety of non-literate cultures has only begun and even then has not been done with a view to contrasting how speech acts are reported in speech as opposed to writing. Hence, it may be somewhat misleading to construct a "synthetic oral type" (Bloch, personal communication, March, 1990). Yet some evidence is available which may be generalized to indicate how speech acts are reported in non-literate cultures. Stross' (1974) account of Tzeltal metalinguistics is indicative. A full range of speech acts occur including descriptions, apologies, announcements, and promises. Linguistic means for referring to these speech acts takes the basic form of a term for speech, "k'op" plus a modifier to indicate the kind of talk: examples include such things as "truthful talk," "talk within the heart," "mistaken talk," "threatening talk" and the like.

Rajaonarison (personal communication, March, 1990) a native speaker of Malagasy, a traditional language of Madagascar, reports a variety of terms for referring to and quoting the speech of another person. The basic form is to employ a term for "talk" which can then be qualified by adding a second term to represent the kind of talk – question, denial, acceptance, with feeling, and qualified again to indicate manner – forcefully, repeatedly, directly and the like.

Feld and Schieffelin (1982) found a rich set of metalinguistic terms in the language of the Kaluli, a traditional society of Papua New Guinea including the basic "say," "ask," and "tell" as well as "speak," "hear" and "understand." Terms that provide some indication of how the original speaker intended an utterance to be taken were handled by adverbs of manner such as "speaking sadly," "speaking softly," and "speaking forcefully."

Distinctive genres and the lexical means for referring to them have also been discussed. Feldman (1991) provides an analysis of the specialized genre employed by two traditional cultures, the Wana of Indonesia and the Ilongot of the Philippines. Feldman points out that both have special genres for handling sensitive topics by means of indirect speech forms which call for and bring into prominence issues of interpretation. Feldman notes that the Ilongot have several genres including conversation conducted in "straight" language, as well as a form of discourse for magical spells and formal oratory (purung) conducted with a special code called "crooked" language for which issues of interpretation also arise. She concludes that while writing may extend the length or depth of such analyses, "the matter of establishing a text and reflecting on it cannot require writing" (p. 56).

Yet it is not clear that oral cultures make the same distinctions or elaborate them to the same degree as literate cultures do. Feldman's analysis suggests that the Ilongot acknowledged that crooked speech, essentially metaphorical discourse, called for interpretation but there is no indication that they also understood that straight speech is subject to misunderstanding and requires interpretation as well; the problem of interpretation, the need for a systematic search for an underlying intention, may be recognized only in a particular form of discourse. In fact, in her analysis of speech acts, Rosaldo (1982) noted that Western assumptions about the distinctive intentions of the speaker lying behind any statement or command seemed inappropriate for the Ilongot. She reported that assertives, that is simple statements of fact, are not systematically distinguished from declaratives, that is, claims and edicts which create a truth rather than report one. Consequently, what is true is what one can get another to accept, not an objective account of a pre-existing fact. Furthermore, Rosaldo found that commissive speech acts such as promises which express a personal intentional undertaking were absent as were expressive speech acts which represent underlying feelings such as gratitude and regret.

Duranti (1985) reporting on the interpretive strategies of the

Samoans noted the absence of means for distinguishing an utterance from its underlying intention. What an utterance means depends upon what others take it to mean. Consequently, a Samoan speaker will not "reclaim the meaning of his words by saying 'I didn't mean it'" (p. 49). It means what the listener takes it to mean; the meaning is not seen as inhering in the words.

McCormick (1989, 1993) in examining the influence of Spanish on Quechua, a Peruvian language, found that bilinguals borrow from Spanish for anything other than the basic notions of "say," "tell," "ask" and the like. When translating from Spanish to Quechua, speakers have no speech act terms such as "deny." It comes out as "say it is not true" or else the Spanish term is used.

Heeschen (1978) who studied this problem in perhaps the greatest detail, pointed out that Eipo speakers, traditional peoples of West New Guinea, have an abundance of ways for talking about what had been said, frequently adopting general verbs for a more specific linguistic purpose. However, there were, by his standards, limited lexical means for referring to language structure, to truth, and to speech acts. In all cases such reference was tied to content and linked to non-verbal behavior. Thus linguistic judgments referred to such infelicities as stuttering rather than ungrammaticality; judgments of truth-telling and lying were not based strictly on truth – irony, understatement and impoliteness were all considered examples of lying; and speech act types were marked non-lexically by "non-verbal behavior and paralinguistic features" (pp. 174–175). Nonetheless, speakers had little difficulty in expressing a full range of meanings and distinguishing among them even if they lacked specific terms for referring to them.

Thus, it is impossible to deny that any natural language, including the more recently studied sign language (Klima & Bellugi, 1979), has the syntactic and word-forming resources to cope with any set of ideas; in that sense there are no primitive languages. Second, not only can oral languages cope with the the requirements of communication in face-to-face contexts, they have the resources to allow for quoted, that is, remembered information both through preserving the ideas via mnemonic systems and in a more exact verbal form through sayings, recitation under ritual conditions and through poetized speech.

Finally, oral cultures possess metalinguistic concepts to discuss at least some aspects of what was said and how it was to be taken. Traditional cultures are said to do with memory what literate or bureaucratic societies do with writing. These similarities lead many anthropologists to conclude that there is no great divide separating pre-literate or oral cultures from literate ones (Feldman, 1991; Finnegan, 1988; Scribner & Cole, 1981).

But these similarities should not blind us to the important differences. First, writing introduced a new awareness of linguistic structure, especially the verbal form in contrast to the conveyed meaning, which added precision to the notion of what, precisely, was said. In the absence of writing, recounting what someone has said and their manner of saying it is likely to vary dramatically from one reporter to the next. Ong (1982, p. 65) has pointed out that even the most critical words of Jesus, "This is my body ... This is the cup of my blood" were reported differently by each of his disciples. And as mentioned, both Goody and Finnegan reported the latitude which oral poets revealed in their interpretation of what was meant by "the same words" – as long as it had the same meaning, they thought of it as being composed of the same words.

The literate's awareness of words and wording had some conceptual implications at least in the Western tradition. Havelock (1982) was the first to suggest that the oral Homer talked and thought about language in quite a different way from the literate Aristophanes:

Archaic terminology has described human language synthetically, as song, speech, utterance, saying, talk. (Neither *epos* nor *logos* originally signified the separated word.) In the Aristophanic critique one detects an increasing tendency to view language as though it were broken up into bits and pieces of separate passages, divided into lines, measures, feet, stanzas.

(pp. 289–290)

Palmer (1980) noted the evolution in classical Greece of technical prose suitable for the expression of what had been seen, inferred, conjectured and the like.

Vansina (1961/1965) pointed out how the literate historian can analyze the traditions preserved in the versions of the oral tradition in order to find out the truth. This ability to distinguish between the facts of the matter and the forms of the telling was not ordinarily visible to those who passed on the oral tradition. The reason is simple. The literate historian could collect up the versions, transcribe them to form documents, and then compare the documents, looking for tell-tale signs of interpolation as well as for invariants. Goody (1987) has provided an abundance of evidence for the importance of writing for making lists, tables, analogies, syllogisms, for explicitly representing forms of argument, and for preserving and comparing narrative accounts.

Secondly, the need to cast events into poetic or memorable form provided constraints on telling that necessarily made the poetized version differ from what would have been conveyed in a direct account. In fact, Havelock proposed that the elaborate panoply of gods and heroes of the Homeric epics were used, perhaps even invented, to make significant cultural information memorable. Consequently, memorized epics reported "a panorama of happenings rather than a program of principles" (1982, p. 226). While some more recent writers (Lynn-George, 1988) have called into question the validity of assigning Homer rigidly to the oral side of the oral-literate dimension, there seems less doubt that memorization introduces different constraints than freely invented and yet preserved discourse. Only when freed from the constraints of memorization, Havelock suggests, could texts be formulated and *preserved* which addressed such traditional issues as "What is justice?" or "What is the good?" or "What is magic?" or "What is mind?" philosophically, that is, as theoretical issues.

Third, just how successful such techniques are for the verbatim preservation of longer texts remains unclear. While Finnegan refers to "lengthy memorized transmissions" she also acknowledges that a basic feature of oral forms of discourse, including oral literature, is "their lack of fixity. There tends to be more linguistic elasticity, less idea of verbal accuracy" (p. 57). Goody (1987), too, noted that while memorization occurs, there is some latitude as to what is meant by a correct reproduction; "there is little evidence of exact copying, of verbatim reproduction" (p. 151). In fact, the concept 'verbatim' is a relatively modern word coined only in the fifteenth century.[2] Memorization,

---

[2] I am indebted to J. P. Small for pointing this out.

without writing, is only misleadingly called "verbatim." Hunter
(1985) has argued convincingly that verbatim memory of longer texts
does not occur unless there is a written text against which memory can
be checked. Without such a verbatim record dispute about particular
wordings are likely to be unresolved because recall of wording is
strongly influenced by the semantic or meaning properties of the text.

This point is important for what follows for if, in oral contexts,
there is dispute as to meaning, that dispute cannot be solved by more
precise attention to the wording of a text, or consequently, to its
precise meaning – for that precise wording will be lost. Complex
assumptions are involved in determining how carefully one attends to
the lexical and syntactic properties of a text (as we shall see in Chapter
6). But if the text is not fixed precisely, appeal to wording as a basis for
resolving disputes regarding meaning is likely to be replaced by appeal
elsewhere, namely, to the authority, whether wiseman or poet, or to
the muses. This point may be stated another way. With a written text,
interpretation can turn into a research enterprise with the preserved
wording serving as one kind of evidence in the formation of a
judgment. In an oral context, such judgments rely more heavily upon
authority or majority opinion.

A somewhat spectacular exception to that rule is the Vedic tradition, the memorization and study of the ancient scriptures of Hindu-
ism, which was conducted exclusively by oral means. While some have
argued that writing must have been involved at some stage (Goody,
1987), for present purposes it is not necessary to deny that such study
and analysis could be done orally but only to insist that whatever
system is employed, oral or written, will specify the categories and
relations in terms of which we think about speech and language.
Writing has offered up concepts for some properties while leaving us
blind to others.

And finally, and perhaps most importantly, the preservation of
speech acts takes a somewhat different form, I suggest, in oral
tradition than in a written one. In oral context, a poet, orator or
conversationalist tends to rely on direct quotation (see Vansina, 1961/
1965, pp. 58–59) of the words of the speaker, to some degree of
accuracy, using his own tone of voice to convey the speech act
involved. Chaytor (1945) says of oral narration: "the audience wanted

a story with plenty of action and movement, the story, as a rule, showed no great command of character drawing; this was left to the reciter for portrayal by change of voice and gesture" (p. 3). To report the speech of another, the oral story teller uses such verbs as "say," "tell," "ask" and "answer" to mark the fact that the speech is not the speaker's own freely invented discourse, and, secondly, uses "change of voice and gesture" to mark the type of speech act.

In reading a written text, a new burden falls on the reader to reconstruct the speaker's or writer's attitude to the text and a new burden falls on the writer to characterize that attitude through exclusively lexical means. As we have seen, in reporting another's speech an orator can report not only the words employed but also the speaker's attitude to those words, that is, the speech act; the orator does not need to say "He insisted that ..."; the orator can simply repeat the claim *using an insistent tone of voice*. To make writing serve the same functions that speech has served, new verbs and new concepts have to be invented, concepts such as "literal" and "metaphorical" as well as those expressed by the terms "stated," "insisted" or "implied," which when nominalized, could yield such novel entities as "conjectures," "statements" and "implications." These are the things out of which modern epistemology was constructed (Febvre, 1942/1982, p. 355).

In a similar vein, Janet Astington and I (Olson & Astington, 1990) noted the massive borrowing of vocabulary from Latin into English that occurred in the sixteenth and seventeenth centuries. A conspicuous part of this borrowing included the speech act and mental state verbs that have come to play such a large part in recent psychology and philosophy of mind. Speech act verbs are those that can take the place of the verb *say* while mental state terms are those that can take the place of the verb *think*. An indication of the borrowing of terms for referring to what people say, write and think, is given by the facts depicted in Table 5.1.

As an aside, it is interesting to note that in this sense drama is a simpler linguistic form to write than prose; in drama the actor is left the task of deciding how to "interpret" the lines to the audience. A prose writer, on the other hand, is ordinarily required to tell the reader how to interpret those lines. In a sense reading requires every reader to become an actor; the reader has to "interpret" the lines he or she

Table 5.1. *Date of first known use in English of some speech act and mental state verbs*

Germanic		Latinate	
believe	OE	assert	1604
know	OE	assume	1436
mean	OE	claim	ME
say	OE	concede	1632
tell	OE	conclude	ME
think	OE	confirm	ME
understand	early ME[b]	contradict	1570
		criticize	1649
		declare	ME
		define	ME
		deny	ME
		discover	ME
		doubt	ME
		explain	1513
		hypothesize	1596 (Greek)
		imply	ME
		infer	1526
		interpret	ME
		observe	late ME
		predict	1546
		prove	ME
		remember	ME
		suggest	1526

[a] OE = Old English (before 1150)
[b] ME = Middle English (1150–1350)
(late ME 1350–1450)
Source: The Oxford English Dictionary

reads just as an actor has to "interpret" the lines for an audience, by uttering the lines with the correct expression. However, the modern prose reader's task is much simpler than the actor's as the reader is aided in this task by the writer exploiting a new range of speech act and mental state terms that explicitly indicate how the writer intends the reader to take the content of the utterance. Text thus shaped up for reading rather than performing is what gives prose its distinctive character.

So it is in this way that writing comes into its own. Ironically, writing comes into its own because of the limitations of the writing system not, counter to our usual assumption, because of the limitations of speech. As writing systems evolved they came to be seen as representations of the lexical and syntactic properties of the language; speech act properties carried by stress and intonation are not captured by the script. Just as the history of writing systems can be seen as employing graphic means as representations of the phonological and morphological properties of speech, so the elaboration of speech act verbs such as "claim" and "insist" as well as punctuation marks including the period, exclamation mark, and quotation mark can be seen as lexical and graphic means for representing speech acts (Parkes, 1992). Distinctions marked informally in speech, such as rising intonation or raised eyebrows, have to be explicitly represented by graphic means in writing. The question mark, to cite a single case, is a duplication of the first letter of the Latin word *quaestio* which was reversed and written above the period at the end of the sentence (Halliday, 1985, p. 33). Thus the use of the question mark depended upon explicitly representing, that is, categorizing the utterance as a question.

The problems involved in explicitly representing the force of an utterance were as significant as those involved in the invention of the alphabet to represent the verbal form. In both cases, writing is largely a matter of inventing communicative devices which can be taken as explicit representations of aspects of language which were expressed non-lexically in speech and thereby bringing those aspects of linguistic structure and meaning into consciousness.

The view that writing provides a model for speaking permits us to reassess the issue of whether or not oral cultures have the same conceptual and linguistic resources as literate ones. Theories of literacy from Levy-Bruhl to McLuhan have implied that the absence of a particular linguistic or literary form in an oral culture indicated an absence of the corresponding conceptual structure. Anthropologists such as Finnegan, Sperber, Bloch, and Heeschen, looking more directly at social forms of discourse, claim that similar forms and distinctions are made in both oral and literate cultures. Both could be right. Writing adds less than it explicates.

What writing requires, and what the history of literacy achieves, is the evolution of graphic communicative devices which then serve as explicit models of phonology, morphology, and syntax, but also of speech act and discourse properties whether handled by grammar, by prosodic and paralinguistic cues such as tone, intonation and stress, or by non-verbal context. The history of literacy, in other words, is the struggle to recover what was lost in simple transcription. The solution is to turn non-lexical properties of speech such as stress and intonation into lexical ones; one announces that the proposition expressed is to be taken as an assumption or an inference and whether it is to be taken metaphorically or literally. But in making those structures explicit, that is representing them as concepts, and marking them in a public language, those structures themselves become objects of reflection. That is what makes possible what we may think of as literate thought and literate discourse.

To summarize: in cultures where writing is available, writing becomes a medium of choice in a number of domains because of its permanence (Clanchy, 1979; W. Harris, 1989). But what writing gains in permanence it loses in comprehensiveness. The literal "death of the author" entails that the author cannot be consulted as to how the text was to be taken. Writing readily preserves the lexical and syntactic properties of speech but loses the voice-qualities of the speaker including stress and intonation, the "silent language" revealed in bodily clues manifest in the eyes, hands, and stance as well as the cognitively shared context, all of which in oral contexts indicate how the utterance is to be taken. The problem for writing then becomes that of inventing devices, including lexical and syntactical ones, which can compensate for what is lost. And the problem in reading is in mastering those clues and the hermeneutical techniques which provide some indication of how the writer intended the text to be taken.

The problem became acute in Western culture in reading sacred texts in which the illocutionary force was often unspecified. Just how was one to take Jesus' statement "This is my body"? The attempt to recover the illocutionary force of such an utterance engaged many of the best minds for a millennium. The traditional arts of rhetoric, like the specialized genres employed in traditional societies, are attempts to manage illocutionary force. Appeals to the king took a particular form which marked the subservience of the appellant, sermons attempted to persuade the listeners to live a life of virtue, and poetry was to inform and entertain (Murphy, 1971). It was not enough to say the right words; they had to be said in such a way as to assure their appropriate uptake.

Even the remarkable illuminations framing medieval Bibles and Books of Hours can be seen as non-verbal devices for indicating how the accompanying texts were to be understood. Morrison (1990) has provided a fascinating account of the changing role that these illuminations played in the expression of meaning in the twelfth century. Earlier illuminations were a critical part of the text. The interpretive assumption was that the words together with the pictures presented modes or components of information which when pulled together by the reader provided an epiphany, a revelation, of the true meaning, which ultimately was God. Consequently, texts were written in a "nuclear" manner consisting of a series of points or parts which, while not related logically, led the viewer or reader to form a synthesis. In the eleventh and twelfth centuries illumination changed its character in that images became subordinated to the text which came, increasingly, to be seen as the primary conveyor of meaning. And with the emphasis on the text came, Morrison suggests, the greater concern with the logical form of a text, with single, clear lines of argument and universal unambiguous meanings of terms. This linearity was also reflected in the development of a single linear perspective in art. Thus advances in the visual arts reflected changes in ways of reading – a theme we examine in Chapter 8.

So the illuminations in the manuscripts of the Middle Ages like the rubricated versions of the Christian Bible in which the words of Jesus were printed in red ink are means for indicating illocutionary force of a text, that is, as supplements to the text rather than as part of the text itself. When texts begin to provide verbal indications of how any expression is to be taken, we have the beginnings of modern prose.

Why is illocutionary force not represented lexically or syntactically in language in the first place, for if it had been, literacy would require little more than learning the script? To some extent it is: questions are represented by subject–verb inversion, commands by subject deletion, and assertions by full subject predicate constructions. But other more subtle features are expressed by intonation, stress, presupposition and genre choice. Why are those features not represented lexically? My guess is that illocutionary force is the most primitive part of language, the part of language shared with other animals and readily detected by infants (Bruner, 1983). These features were preserved through evolution, new lexical and syntactic resources being added to these. Orders, for example, are expressed through grammatical means as well as through shrieks and howls. Grammar evolved to express propositional content; writing systems, to the extent that they model the grammar, preserved the grammatical and lexical aspects of an utterance. What remained to be invented were devices for representing the illocutionary force, devices which, so far as possible, indicated just how the speaker or writer intended his or her utterance to be taken. Some such devices exist in all languages for as Leech (1983) pointed out all languages possess some metalanguage for indicating how utterances are to be taken. However, the problem became acute not so much in writing as in interpreting sacred texts where it became a matter of dogma as to how particular utterances were to be taken. That was the domain in which a systematic articulation of intentionality was worked out. We shall examine this problem in Chapter 7 when we consider the history of reading.

The significance of writing for economic and bureaucratic activities is quite clear and relatively well established (Clanchy, 1979; Eisenstein, 1979; Goody, 1987). But the significance of writing for its role in *explicating* intentions – of turning attitudes towards what oneself or others say into concepts – is not. I believe it to be only a slight overstatement to claim that the use of writing for representing the ways the speaker intends his utterance to be taken and the subsequent attempts to shape up writing to represent adequately these ways of "taking" was to have a more dramatic impact on our representations of ourselves and our world than its more obvious recording functions. Texts written to circumvent the limits of simple transcription are, by definition, texts written to be read; such texts mark the beginning of written prose and ultimately of texts as representations.

Paradoxically, the understanding of literal meaning of an utterance was to await the development of an understanding of illocutionary force – how the author intends the text to be taken. In the next chapter we shall examine just what is involved in interpretation and review recent research on children's developing understanding of what texts mean and what speakers and writers mean by them and the role that literacy plays in this development.

6 THE PROBLEM OF INTERPRETATION: THE RECOVERY OF COMMUNICATIVE INTENTION

....

Reading precedes interpretation.

(Quintilian)

Not to interpret is impossible.

(Italo Calvino, *Mr. Palomar*)

The Christian Bible tells the story of an Ethiopian eunuch, the keeper of the queen's treasure, who was reading the prophet Isaiah when Philip, an evangelist, approached him and asked "Do you understand what you are reading?" to which the Ethiopian replied "How can I, unless some one guides me?" (Acts 8: 26–35). When interpretation becomes impossible, we require a theory, a set of concepts, to guide us. That held by the Ethiopian, it appears, is that the correct interpretation depends upon insider information, the expert.

Although the problem of interpretation is relatively conspicuous when one is dealing with written texts which have been carried from one context to another, it is implicit in all of language use. All understanding is interpretation, as Gadamer (1975) has pointed out. People do, after all, say things and mean things by them. They make requests, give advice and commands, they tease, joke and lie, they simply report on states of affairs, they exaggerate, understate, and imply, and they cooperate, ridicule, and patronize. As we saw in the last chapter, in face-to-face discourse a listener has access to both the verbal form of the utterance and to the speaker's style, stance and tone as well as context to determine what is meant. And if failure occurs the listener's simple "What?" or even a failure to respond calls for a revision.

But problems of interpretation become serious when one is faced with a transcription of what was said, the transcription capturing only the content of the utterance and not its tone. The speaker's attitude has to be inferred by the reader. That too is ordinarily done unreflectively, the resulting interpretation being ascribed to the text as "what was said." But now, with no author available to refute spurious interpretation, the result is a kind of interpretational anarchy, each interpretation being taken by some individual or group as "what was said." If the authority of the church or state intervenes, a series of bureaucratic rules and procedures by means of which to establish the "true" meaning may evolve. These rules and procedures, accompanied by a set of beliefs and assumptions, constitute a theory of interpretation which can be more or less conventionalized or shared by the community of interpreters. Consequently, as mentioned in the last chapter the theory of interpretation, hermeneutics, is the theory of interpreting texts which are written. Hermeneutical theory evolved for the analysis of sacred texts for which the correct interpretation was taken to be a matter of life and death (Gadamer, 1975; Nicholson, 1984). The term hermeneutics is derived from the name Hermes, the Greek god who voices and interprets messages (Padel, 1992, p. 7).

To interpret, then, and to have a concept of interpretation are quite different things. The concept or theory of interpretation is what makes the process of interpretation conscious and subject to rational considerations. Whereas interpretation may be a universal feature of any symbol user, the concepts of interpretation are cultural artifacts subject to revision, to developmental and historical change.

The traditional meaning of interpretation going back to the classical period was "to reveal" or "render clear and explicit" the meaning of a passage or text; the more modern meaning, on the other hand, is more subjective, namely, "to construe" or see in a particular light. Only in the modern sense could interpretation be characterized as "merely" an interpretation. The older meaning of the verb *interpret*, to reveal the meaning, is close to the verb *understand*. *To understand* is a factive verb (Kiparsky & Kiparsky, 1970; Vendler, 1970) which is to say that, like the verb *know*, it entails the truth of the complement. To know that Suzy is lazy implies the truth of the grammatical complement, "Suzy is lazy." Conversely, one could not know that Suzy was lazy if she was not. One may "believe" it but one could not "know" it if it were false. Similarly, to understand a text is to *know* what it means. To interpret a text, however, entails not that one *knows* what it means but rather that one *thinks* that it means such and such. It is sufficient that one arrive at a meaning, not necessarily *the* meaning. Consequently one may indeed interpret a text but have no concept of an interpretation. Furthermore, when one acquires a concept of interpretation it may be either that of revealing what the text says or that of construing a text in a certain way. If the former, a meaning once arrived at is taken to be *the* meaning. This was true for people in pre-modern times, and, as we shall see, is true for young children growing up in western cultures. Roughly speaking, the seventeenth century view which many writers refer to as "Modernism" was the invention of a new solution to the problem of interpreting texts; what these same writers refer to as "Post-modernism" is recognition that there is no ultimate solution.

The availability of a concept of interpretation is what allows interpretation to be recognized as interpretation; it is what makes interpretation conscious or as Nicholson (1984) suggests, brings interpretation from the background where it is more or less automatic to the foreground where it is subject to deliberate, reflective analysis. Once foregrounded an elementary concept of interpretation would allow for such distinctions as that between what was said and what was meant, that is, for an understanding of what lies behind, beyond or within what was said. The so-called Post-modern concept of interpretation would allow for the element of subjectivity, for inference to the best explanation. It was this notion of interpretation that allowed Mr. Palomar to think of all experience as interpretation.

The syntactics, semantics and pragmatics of interpretation

What are these interpretive processes that one may become conscious of? Interpretation involves the management of the three aspects of linguistic structure which are conventionally referred to as syntactics, semantics and pragmatics (Morris, 1938). Basically, the syntax allows the expression of relations between a subject and a predicate. Both spoken and written language exploit the same grammar but they do so in systematically different ways. Chafe (1985, 1991) argues that the basic unit of speech is an "idea unit" – it consists of a clause which is composed of a verb and one or more noun phrases, it has a single intonational contour, it is composed of about seven words and it lasts about two seconds; it seems to correspond to the amount of information a speaker can focus on in consciousness at a point of time.

Written language respects these idea units but subordinates them to the grammatical structure of the sentence. A sentence is composed of one main clause to which may be appended one or more subordinate clauses linked to the main clause by conjunctions or relative pronouns.

Chafe has suggested that the increased processing time available to the writer, coupled with the possibility of editing, allows the formation of well-rounded sentences. "Sentences in spoken language are often difficult to identify, and their function is problematic. They are probably not units of cognitive processing and memory" (Chafe, 1985, p. 111). Idea units play that more immediate cognitive function. That is not to say that people cannot learn to speak like a book as apparently many of the medieval scholars did (Carruthers, 1990). To revert briefly to the argument of the last chapter, people introspect the grammar of their speech in terms of their writing system and, hence, may judge casual speech to be "loose and unruly" or "ungrammatical" and learn to shape their speech to the norms of the written mode.

Halliday (1985, 1990) too, has shown that on average spoken clauses are shorter than those which are written, and that the grammar of spoken language is more "intricate" than that written. He suggests that a primary device for both making the clause structure more orderly and for increasing the length of clauses in writing is what he calls "grammatical metaphor," the most common type of which is nominalization (see also Macaulay, 1990). It is the device by means of which "applaud" becomes "applause" and "infer" becomes "inference." Written texts are peculiar in the way they turn such actions into entities. Moreover, the device permits the formation of complex, technical discourse. An expression such as "decreased crack growth rate" may seem incomprehensible until it is seen as the accumulation of simpler facts: Glass cracks; cracks can grow; crack growth proceeds at a rate; crack growth rate can be decreased. Notice how the verbs "crack" and "grow" become nouns and are added to the noun phrase thereby creating a complex entity "crack growth rate" and at the same time sum up the argument within a grammatically ordered sentence. Halliday traces this grammatical style to seventeenth-century scientific writing. The product, Halliday suggests, "is the construction of an 'objectivized' world through the grammar of the written language" (1990, p. 16).

The semantics of language specifies the relation between the subject and referent – between the word and the object referred to – , and between the predicate and the property ascribed to the object, relations that determine issues of truth and falsity of the expression. These relations are easily calculated when the expression refers to something immediate or obvious, such as "The cat is limping" when "the cat" refers to the cat in front of me and "is limping" assigns a property to the cat, the property being either truly or falsely assigned to the object.

But the matter is far from simple, as for example in our Ethiopian story mentioned above in which the text being read stated: "As a sheep led to the slaughter or a lamb before its shearer is dumb, so he opens not his mouth." Who, the Ethiopian wants to know, does this "he" refer to, the Prophet or someone else? Different answers to that question, as we know, separated Christian from Jew. Differences in interpetation, then as now, were often attributed not to the ambiguity of the text but to the intransigence or credulity of the other.

Or to cite another example. When the American Declaration of Independence declared that "All men are created equal," to whom did the subject "all men" refer? The American Civil War was fought, in part, over whether or not the expression referred to slaves. Other battles had to be fought to establish whether it also referred to women. Issues of semantics become more complex when non-literal forms of expression are employed, forms such as metaphor and irony in which the question becomes not what does an expression refer to but how does it refer and leads inevitably into issues of pragmatics.

The pragmatics of language is concerned with audience-directed intention – how the speaker or writer intends the utterance to be taken. Simple pragmatic function is specified by grammatical mood: Declarative mood represents statements offered as true, Imperative mood represents commands to be complied with, Interrogative mood represents questions to be answered. Pragmatic theory in the form of Speech Act Theory represented in the work of the later Wittgenstein (1958), J. L. Austin (1962), Searle (1969) and Grice (1989) first showed that grammatical mood is not a reliable indication of the pragmatic type of an utterance. Different grammatical moods such as questions and commands both require a response from the listener, and are, therefore, seen as members of a single class of Directives. On the other hand, a single grammatical mood, the Declarative, is used to express both Assertives such as "It will rain" and Commissives such as the promise "I will come."

Furthermore, Austin (1962) distinguished the locutionary act, what was said, strictly speaking, from the illocutionary force of the utterance, the audience-directed communicative intention. Force could, on occasion be explicitly named – "I state ..." – although normally it is not. Searle (1969) distinguished five different types of illocutionary force: Assertives (I state ...), commissives (I promise ...), directives (I command ...), declaratives (I christen ...), and expressives (I congratulate ...). These categories are themselves somewhat "pragmatic" and may or may not exhaustively represent possibilities of how speakers or writers intend expressions to be taken. But they mark a significant advance over the grammatical mood theory as an analysis of how speakers or writers intend their expressions to be taken.

A speech act, then, is an intentional act to express some propositional content with some illocutionary force. Such acts assume a set of conditions which must be met if the speech act is to serve as an adequate representation of a speaker's communicative intention. Conversely, knowledge of these conditions may be exploited by speakers to produce indirect speech acts, what Grice (1989) called "conversational implicatures." Grice stated these conditions as a set of maxims which exploit the assumption that utterances not only express propositions but fit into a cooperative, goal-oriented, social activity. Because speakers honor these maxims – to be informative, truthful, and relevant, and to be clear how their contribution advances the co-operative project – speakers can convey more than they actually say. To mention one of Grice's widely quoted examples: if a music critic reports of a soprano "Miss X produced a series of sounds that corresponded closely with the score of 'Home Sweet Home,'" the speaker implicates, by the maxim of manner, that the performance lacked the musical qualities expected of a soprano. The reviewer did not say so in "so many words" but the listener or reader knows that that is what he or she intended to convey (Grice, 1989, p. 37).

Grice's analysis was offered primarily as an account of conversational implicatures, not the pragmatics of writing. But it highlights in a systematic way, the central problem of interpretation. How is one to recover the illocutionary force of an utterance when it is not lexically specified or even mis-specified as in Swift's *A modest proposal*? In writing, both the relationships between ideas and the writer's attitude toward them must be lexicalized as the stress and intonation that marked them in oral discourse is lost. If it is not lexicalized the attempt to recover the speaker's audience-directed intention may call for a systematic hermeneutical theory. What does "All men are created equal" really mean? What does "Corn is deer" really mean? Different interpretive assumptions yield different answers to those questions.

When the author's attitude to what is said is maintained over longer stretches of discourse than a single sentence, the resulting form of text is referred to as a rhetorical form or "genre." To understand a joke one must know what a joke is, that is, one must have the appropriate concept. Young children tell faulty riddles, for example, and laugh uproariously before they actually understand what a riddle is. The same appears to be true for concepts of story, poem, song, parable, prayer and the like. Rhetorical forms differ from culture to culture, between oral and literate cultures as well as within them and the evolution of genres and of systematic means for distinguishing and interpreting those different forms is an important aspect of literacy. Writing has permitted the evolution of one particular genre of broad applicability, written prose, which has come to play a dominant role in modern scientific, bureaucratic cultures. We have already mentioned some of the ways that writing contributed to the development of such a genre.

We have discussed three aspects of linguistic structure that must be coped with in any interpretation. In oral discourse these structures can generally be left in the background with the listener or speaker focusing on the content of the discourse. Interpreting written texts and writing such texts requires that aspects of interpretation which were handled by contextual, prosodic and paralinguistic means be handled purely lexically and grammatically. Representing them explicitly in the language brings these structures into consciousness and turns them into objects of reflection and systematic management. The particular problems that we have mentioned are those having to do with the management of complex syntax which creates complex entities and allows the explicit management of cohesion of a text, those having to do with the semantic issue of assigning reference to expressions, and those having to do with the pragmatic issue of managing how the listener or reader takes the expression.

We may get a clearer picture of what is involved by examining how children cope with the problems of interpretation that arise in dealing with expressions.

Children's understanding of what is said and what is meant

First, a word about the use of both developmental and cultural–historical data in evaluating a theory of literacy and cognition. Since Levy-Bruhl, psychologists and anthropologists have been cautious of equating children with members of traditional societies. Levy-Bruhl, as we mentioned earlier, abandoned the concept of "primitive" thinking because it tended to equate the minds of aboriginal people with those of children. No such equation is implied herein. Rather, the argument is that while different cultures in different historical periods specialize their discourse in different ways and to different degrees, these new more specialized structures of knowledge are built upon earlier more fundamental concepts. Thus the cultural evolution of conceptual systems may run parallel to the child's acquisition or construction of his or her own conceptual system. Ferreiro (1991) has recently made the same point in her discussion of the parallels between the history of writing and children's acquisition of literacy. In both cases the order is due to the fact that some constructions are prior to others because they are constitutive of those that will follow. In a simple case the concept of a syllable may precede the concept of a letter both historically and developmentally because the concept of a letter requires that it be seen as a constituent of a syllable. The same, I suggest, holds for concepts like thinking, meaning, and interpretation. The concept of interpretation is built out of the concepts of thinking and meaning: to interpret is to think it means. Thus the claim is that conceptual development is orderly whether that development proceeds historically or ontogenetically. Unlike theories of "primitive" mentalities, however, it does not assume that these concepts are necessarily more true or more valid than the ones they developed from; concepts are acquired because they are useful either directly or indirectly for some purpose.

To return to our theme. Children's grammatical competence is well developed by the time they enter school. Indeed, grammatical development is so rapid and completed so early that many writers believe grammatical competence to be largely innate (Chomsky, 1980; Pinker, 1989). Written language, however, presents a new set of demands on that competence. Aside from the fact that children have to learn the conventions of the standard language, much of their earlier implicit syntactic knowledge must be made conscious and deliberate. Specifically, lexical and grammatical markers must be substituted for information which was earlier carried by prosodic and paralinguistic cues. The explicit notion of a sentence, that grammatical unit which is to be followed by a full stop, is one that troubles many young writers for many years. Although some say that is not a problem (sic)!

One such development has been nicely described in the work of Michaels and Collins (1984). Children were asked to retell a narrative in which two men played a part. The problem for the children was that any use of the expression "the man" would be ambiguous. Two strategies were employed by children for dealing with the problem. Some children used gesture and intonation to distinguish the two men, for example, stress fell on the word "man" when it referred to the character who had been referred to earlier. The second strategy was to use adjectives and relative clauses to distinguish them, for example, "the man who was picking the pears ..." Although these strategies may be equivalent in oral context, only the latter is directly applicable to reporting the narrative in writing. Indeed, Michaels and Collins refer to the latter strategy as literate-based suggesting that such competence improves with schooling.

Children's understanding of the semantic issues involved in interpreting an expression constitutes a vast literature only a part of which bears on literate interpretation. The one aspect of semantic development of relevance is children's competence with decontextualized language in which meaning is to be gleaned exclusively from the linguistic form rather than from contextual and non-verbal clues. A good example is Inhelder and Piaget's (1959/1964) finding that if pre-school children are shown a group of five animals composed of three ducks and two rabbits and are asked: "Are there more ducks or more animals?" they tend to reply "More ducks 'cause there's only two rabbits." When asked to repeat the question they sometimes reply, "You said 'Are there more ducks or rabbits?'" That, of course, is not what was asked. Donaldson (1978), too, found that pre-school children when shown five toy cars, four of which are put into corresponding garages, one remaining free, and asked "Do all of the garages have cars in them?", tended to interpret the question as "Are all of the cars in the garages?" and so answer "No." Donaldson concluded that to overcome their difficulties children would have to learn to pay "scrupulous attention to the wording" of the question. Attention to the meaning of words and expressions shorn of their contextual and intonational features is a normal feature of written but not of ordinary conversational discourse. Consequently, it makes up an important part of both the oral and the written discourse of the school (Watson & Olson, 1987).

Children's understanding of the speaker or writer's audience-directed intentions has been examined in cases in which what a speaker says is not a full or a literal representation of what was meant or intended. Such conditions occur when a child hears an ambiguous utterance, when the child encounters an indirect speech act, and when the child encounters some form of metaphorical or ironic discourse.

Robinson, Goelman, and Olson (1983) showed that pre-school children have grave difficulties in distinguishing what a speaker says from what he or she means by it. Like Lucy in the famous Charlie Brown cartoon, children, and perhaps many adults, insist on their identity (see Figure 6.1).

In a typical experimental task, a five-year-old child, separated from another child and a group of pictures by a small barrier, and wanting a particular picture with a small blue flower on it, requests of the second child that she pick up the picture of the "blue flower." The listener picks up and offers the wrong picture, one with a *large* blue flower. Not only will the child tend to blame the listener for picking up the wrong blue flower, the speaker will go on to claim that she had actually asked for the *small* blue flower. That, indeed, was what the speaker wanted but, by our standards, not what the speaker had said. By the

Figure 6.1   PEANUTS

time they are seven or eight children distinguish what the speaker said from what the speaker "should have said," "meant," or "wanted" (Torrance & Olson, 1985).

Children not only come to understand possible discrepancies between speakers' intentions and their expressions at this period but also to understand that a listener's interpretations may be discrepant from their own interpretations of an utterance. Ruffman, Olson and Torrance (1990) report a study in which children overhear a speaker tell a listener that a particular toy is in "the red drawer" when, in fact there are two such red drawers. The child, who has been shown which of the two red drawers the toy is in, is then asked if the listener will know which drawer the toy is in. Children under four years of age say that he will know, those over four say he will not. Thus, it appears that in the late pre-school and early school years children come to understand some of the relations between an utterance and the intentions of speakers and the interpretations of listeners. In both cases they distinguish what the sentence means or refers to from what the speaker means or the listener understands.

These children also understand that someone could misunderstand, that is, that someone given an ambiguous message, could come to hold a false belief. A simple example of this comes from a study by Ash, MacLaren, Torrance, and Olson (1991). Children were shown three small wooden blocks, two of which were white. The child was shown that a gold star was affixed to the bottom of one of the white blocks. A second child (or a puppet) was then introduced and told that "The star is under a white block." The child was then asked, "Could the listener think the star is under this one (while pointing to the white block the subjects know to be incorrect)?" Children five years or older correctly say that he could think that; those younger that he could not.

Hedelin and Hjelmquist (1988) provide a recent example of the youngest children's tendency to identify what was said with what was meant. Children were shown a collection of animals including a black dog and a white dog all of which were fed in turn except for the white dog which remained standing outside the barn. Children were told to pass on to the newly arriving zoo keeper the message that "The dog is hungry." The zoo keeper, after listening to the child's reported message asked "Did you say the white one was hungry?" Interestingly, the majority of three year olds answered "Yes," thereby identifying what was said with what was meant. Most of the five year olds answered "No." Thus, by age five, most of these Swedish children made this distinction at least in the simplest, clearest possible cases.

Torrance, Lee, and Olson (1992) carried out a similar study to see if children could distinguish a statement from a paraphrase. They asked children, the youngest of which were three years of age and the oldest, ten, to make judgments as to whether or not "Teddy Bear" should be awarded a sticker on the basis of how Teddy responded to various requests. On one series of trials Teddy's task was to say exactly what a story character, Big Bird, had said when he came into the kitchen. These were the verbatim trials. On a second series of trials, Teddy's task was to say what the person wanted; he did not have to "use the same words." These were the paraphrase trials. Test trials were preceded by practice trials in which children were helped in judging whether Teddy had "listened right or wrong." The order of the two types of trials was counterbalanced. As predicted, children under four were unable to judge correctly when Teddy should get a sticker both for the verbatim items and the paraphrase items. Three-quarters of the four and five year olds got the paraphrase items correct while failing the verbatim items. Only when they were six years of age and older were children able to get both types of items correct. What they found most difficult was to withhold a sticker from Teddy when Teddy was to say the same words "Big Bird is hungry" but had said, rather, a true paraphrase "Big Bird wants food." Thus, although they can repeat an utterance verbatim as Hedelin and Hjelmquist showed, only when they are six years of age or older are they capable of distinguishing systematically between a verbatim repetition and a paraphrase. It is a conflation of what was said with what was meant.

Children become somewhat more sensitive to what was said, that is, to "the same words" when confronted with a written text (Keenan, Olson, & Torrance, 1990). Three- and five-year-old children were shown drawings of simple objects beneath which were simple captions. One drawing, for example, showed Charlie Brown, the celebrated cartoon character, below which was printed the caption "Charlie." Children were informed that this was a picture of Charlie Brown and that the caption said "Charlie." Following this the children were asked a series of questions one of which was "Is this a picture of a little boy?" to which all three year olds said "Yes." They acknowledged that a picture could be "read" in more than one way. But when asked the analogous question about the caption "Does this say 'a little boy'?," they replied "No," indicating an early understanding of the fact that texts preserve a verbal form not a set of meanings. Thus, while children are quite happy to say that a speaker "said" something when that something is only the intended meaning, they are less willing to do that with a written text. Bonitatibus (1988) was the first to report such findings.

Children's discovery of the distinction between what is said and what is meant builds upon the rather pervasive set of distinctions that children acquire when they begin to understand intentional mental states at about four or five years of age and which, following Perner (1991), we may refer to as "first-order" metarepresentations. They begin to understand the very possibility that someone could believe something false. They begin to ascribe thoughts to themselves and others, they begin to understand tricks and surprises and they begin to distinguish accidental from intentional actions (see Astington, Harris & Olson, 1988; Perner, 1991; Wellman, 1990). At about the same time that they grasp the idea that a belief could be false, they also grasp the parallel idea that an utterance could be false and they thus begin to understand such notions as lies and secrets. There is, it appears, a close relation between the concepts expressed by the speech act verb "say" and the mental verb "think." These basic concepts are acquired very early by Western children and it would be surprising indeed if they were not universal although research is only beginning on this topic.

Understanding intentionality, however, does not imply an understanding of communicative intention, of what one means by what one says. What one means by what one says or writes is a matter of what one *wants* a listener to *think*, or *thinks* a listener *thinks*, a second-order relation. For that reason concepts of meaning are acquired somewhat later in Western children and may or may not be universally acquired.

To cope with this problem of communicative intention children must acquire some notion of subjectivity, that is, how beliefs appear to the holder of those beliefs. Whereas at four or five years of age children could, from their own point of view, say that someone thinks (falsely) or knows (truly), only when they are six or seven years of age do they begin to acknowledge that the holder of a false belief "thinks that he knows" a "second order" metarepresentation (Perner, 1991). While four- and five-year-old children can acknowledge that John falsely believes such and such is the case, they have difficulty stating John's own attitude to his belief. When asked: "If we ask John, 'John, do you know where the chocolates are?' what will he say?" these children reply, incorrectly, "No" (Perner & Howes, 1992.) And while they understand that Charlie is, inadvertently, bringing Lucy the wrong shoes, when asked: "Does Charlie think he is bringing the shoes that Lucy wants?" these children reply, incorrectly, "No" (Olson, Howes, & Torrance, in preparation). Thus, while these children have little difficulty in ascribing beliefs they may have difficulty understanding another's attitude to their beliefs or in granting an appropriately subjective status to their own. This is what is involved in understanding communicative intention, that is, what a speaker or writer thinks a listener or reader thinks.

To advert to an earlier distinction, we could say that what children
have achieved at the "first order" level is an understanding of understanding; what they acquire at the "second order" is an understanding
of interpretation. At the first level they characterize the beliefs and
intentions of speakers and listeners exclusively from their own point of
view. Children understand that someone may misunderstand as long
as the judgment is made from their own perspective. And they
themselves may grant that they had misunderstood once they discover
the truth of the matter. What they have yet to come to terms with is
how that knowledge is viewed by its holder. They have yet to come to
understand the possibility of another's beliefs about understanding
and misunderstanding. When they make a statement they may know
what they want a listener to think but yet not know or be able to
anticipate what a listener will *think* that they *mean*. Failure to do so is
to identify as the meaning of an expression their own interpretation of
it.

The tendency to identify their interpretation with what the text or
the author of the text said continues to be a problem through the
school years. If children are asked to distinguish what was said from
the inferences they have drawn in the course of interpreting what was
said, even eight- to ten-year-old children frequently fail. Beal (1990)
read stories which had an implicit inference in them and children were
asked to indicate if the story actually "said" the implied fact. One story
read:

Cindy's family went to the beach. Cindy made a sand castle. The waves were
big that day. Her sand castle got smashed. Her father helped her make
another one.

The children were then asked if the story "said" the waves smashed
the sand castle or if they had "figured it out." Only nine- and
ten-year-old children correctly answered that they had figured it out.
Beal concluded: "Once the child has interpreted the text, its words
literally appear to represent his or her interpretation. The child cannot
then clearly identify the inferences and assumptions that were made in
order to understand it" (p. 1022). Similar results have been reported
by others (Ackerman, Szymanski, & Silver, 1990; Bell & Torrance,
1986; Newman, 1982). Thus when readers or listeners make an

inference in the process of interpretation even older children and some adults fail to recognize that any interpretation has taken place; they project the interpretation back into the text, claiming that the texts actually mentioned the inferred fact. Presumably they will have to be even more sophisticated to recognize that the text implied the fact; it was not simply an inference by the reader.

Astington and Olson (1990) presented university undergraduates with the following multiple-choice item:

It's Adam's birthday tomorrow. Barbara is just sneaking out of the house to buy a present for him when he sees her and asks her where she is going. Barbara says, "We're out of milk. I'm going to the store."
A   Barbara means that she is going to buy milk.
B   Barbara concedes that she is going to buy milk.
C   Barbara asserts that she is going to buy milk.
D   Barbara implies that she is going to buy milk.

Only about half of the undergraduates chose the correct verb "implies"; the majority chose "asserts." Perhaps only those "strictly brought up" as J. L. Austin once put it, would notice the difference. Nonetheless it indicates the difficulty readers have in deciding what is asserted and what is merely implied, that is, between what is said and what is meant.

The say–mean distinction is fundamental to all interpretation in that it allows the independent specification of the meaning in the language – what was said – and of the communicative intention of the speaker – what was meant. It is not simply a matter of learning more about language but simultaneously of learning something about intentional states. This is the basis for the claim that literacy, with its focus on precisely what was said, is related to an increased understanding of subjectivity, of precisely what was meant. This is the subject of the penultimate chapter of the book.

The concepts for referring to what a person *says* and *means* and what a text *says* and *means* are fundamental to the more elaborate speech act and mental state concepts that are commonplace in adult literate discourse, concepts such as assume, infer and interpret. For example, the concept of *interpret* may be composed of the coordination of two first level metarepresentations, in this case, "*think* it *means*"; *under-*

stand, on the other hand, may be the product of coordinating the simpler concepts "*know* it *means*" (Olson & Astington, 1990). Astington (1988) found that only in the middle school years did children successfully distinguish the concepts of *assertion*, *prediction* and *promise*. Younger children thought you could promise things you had no control over and that a promise was not a promise unless it was kept! As mentioned, while it is quite likely that the first order metarepresentational concepts are universal, it is possible, indeed likely, that second order ones are not.

Once children grasp the distinction between what is said and what is meant they are in a position to sort out the more complex relations that hold between the two including indirect speech acts and figurative uses of language.

Interpreting indirect speech acts

Indirect speech acts are interpreted quite appropriately by even very young children by virtue of their appropriateness to particular contexts and particular social relations. Teachers have been observed to say to their classes: "I hear talking," or "I see chewing gum" which are intended to lead to the end of the talk or of the gum. Assertions by teachers are used and interpreted by children as disguised commands (Sinclair & Coulthard, 1975).

Even when the illocutionary force of an utterance is expressed verbally, that expression may be ignored if it is at variance with the informal, non-verbal cues. In one of our studies, pre-school children were told to repeat certain utterances, such as "Say 'chickens have feathers'" to which they duly replied "Chickens have feathers." But when told "Say 'Sit down'," they promptly sat down. When told "Tell me if you can put the penny in the cup," they put the penny into the cup. In such contexts children tended to take a request for information as a command for action (Mitchell-Kernan & Kernan, 1977; Olson, 1980).

A listener, then, judges illocutionary force of indirect speech acts partly by non-verbal clues, clues inaccessible to readers. As writing represents only the grammatical form of an utterance, alternative means must be devised for signalling how the utterance is to be taken.

Figure 6.2   SALLY FORTH

These means are primarily lexical either through characterizing the manner: "literally speaking" or "with alarm" or naming the speech act as in: "I promise that . . ." If no indication is given as to how the text is to be taken, more complex interpretive strategies may be required.

Interpreting figures of speech

Irony, sarcasm, understatement and hyperbole are all cases in which what is meant by the speaker differs from the meaning the utterance conventionally expresses. Unlike ambiguity in which one fails to provide all the information necessary, these figures of speech are "literally" false. If one has just been swindled by an associate and reports this by saying "He's a fine friend," the incongruity between the conventional meaning of "fine friend" and the situation in which it is used, especially when accompanied by an ironic tone (Capelli, Nakagawa, & Madden, 1990; but see also Winner & Leekam, 1991), is sufficient to allow the listener to detect the intended meaning, namely, "He's no friend at all." Children presented with ironic statements such as the one above tend to treat them as true (He really is a fine friend after all), as lies (The speaker is lying), or as mistakes (The speaker meant to say terrible friend) until they are eight or nine years of age (Winner, 1988; Winner et al., 1987). This point is nicely illustrated in the Sally Forth cartoon shown in Figure 6.2.

Situational irony implicit in such cases as that of the psychologist who suffers a nervous breakdown or the shoemaker whose children go barefoot (Lucariello, 1989) also tend to elude younger children. Autistic subjects, whose difficulty is usually attributed to a lack of understanding of the mental states of others (and themselves), have been shown to be able to treat utterances as if they were coded messages but fail to treat them as expressions of the intentions of others. Consequently, they generally fail to grasp irony, joking and metaphorical expressions (Frith, 1989; Happé, 1993) for which what is meant is discrepant in some way from what is said.

Puns present an analogous difficulty in that they play on the independence of a word from its contextual meanings. Consider the following example of a six-year-old child's response to a riddle based on a pun. The transcription of the conversation was as follows:

Adult What has four wheels and flies?
CHILD No response.
Adult It's a garbage truck, see, it has flies flying around it.
CHILD Garbage trucks can't fly.
Adult No, but flies can.
CHILD But they haven't got wheels.
Adult That's true. So that one wasn't too funny was it.
CHILD No.

(Laboratory notes, September, 1988)

The child fails to see that the word "flies" may be interpreted in two ways. The solution to such comprehension problems depends, then, upon an understanding of the fact that words and sentences can have a meaning independently of the intentions of the speaker. Such an understanding calls for the addition of new concepts to the child's inventory, namely, the concept of word and its meaning in contra-distinction to the concept of the thought or intention expressed by that word.

The argument to this point is that while interpretation is required for all language, concepts of interpretation may, and in fact do, develop in children well into the school years. This is equally true for the understanding of genre or forms of discourse.

Understanding genre

We earlier noted in the American Declaration of Independence the difficulties in interpreting the noun phrase "All men." Is the author

speaking "roundly" or "precisely"? Is this a factual claim or a theoretical ideal? None of this is specified in the text so determining how the
author(s) intended it to be taken can only be addressed by making
some interpretive assumptions. Children acquire knowledge of these
genres and the interpretive assumptions appropriate to each well into
the high school years if they acquire them at all.

How an utterance is to be taken depends on its rhetorical form or
genre – pleas, sermons, stories, poems, parables, narrative and expository prose and the like. Our question is how does writing alter genre
and more importantly does it allow the formation of distinctive genre
such as logical prose? And how do children come to acquire these
distinctions?

Bruner (1986) has proposed that there are two classes of literary
genre which specify two distinct modes of thought and which he refers
to as narrative and paradigmatic modes. Narrative is more fundamental in that we invent stories and continuously revise them in the
attempt to make events, including our lives, comprehensible to ourselves and others. Paradigmatic modes are metarepresentational
means of turning the "and then" structures of narrative into the causal
relations expressed in coherent, logical prose. Although both modes
have their oral and written counterparts, the latter is particularly
important to the literate formation of an "archival research tradition."
Stories can be told and retold, changed and revised but the product is
not a text. It is the story which is updated not the text. This is in sharp
contrast with a literate archival tradition in which it is not only the
story which is the object of analysis and revision but the text itself
(Eisenstein, 1979). Such accumulative, synoptic texts, like maps, are
the products of many minds and many hands; they are not merely
compiled but coordinated, criticized and reorganized into structures
of great explanatory power. Such texts are one of the main legacies of a
literate tradition.

Non-narrative texts take a variety of forms which have evolved
historically. Murphy (1971) has recently translated and edited three
medieval rhetorical texts, one dealing with letter writing, one with
poetry and one with preaching. A letter was to be divided into five
parts: salutation, securing of good will, narration, petition and conclusion. A poem, according to *The new poetics* of Geoffrey of Vinsauf

(c. 1210 AD), was to have the following form (which I quote verbatim as the text exemplifies what it describes):

Let the beginning of your poem, as if it were a courteous servant, welcome in the subject matter. Let the middle, as if it were a conscientious host, graciously provide it hospitality. Let the ending, as if it were a herald announcing the conclusion of a race, dismiss it with due respect. In each section, let everything in its own way do honor to the poem; neither let anything in any section sink or in any way suffer eclipse.

(Murphy, 1971, p. 35)

Sermons, too, were to have a proper form consisting of introduction, division, proof, amplification, unification and conclusion. In addition one could also appeal to any of thirty-five figures of diction, nineteen figures of thought, or ten tropes for ornamentation.

Rhetorical form is the product of designing extended texts so as to manage, so far as possible, how they are taken by an audience. As such they are devices for handling illocutionary force. And as interpretation requires that one detect audience directed intention, it requires an awareness of rhetorical form.

While medieval rhetoric focused on means for achieving a particular effect in the listener or reader, modern hermeneutical theory focuses on means for achieving shared understandings. Hence, the kind of competence which students are expected to achieve now-a-days is not merely to grasp the rhetorical form but to understand something of the mind of the writer and of the writer's assumptions about the mind of the reader.

What progress do children make in this direction? While even quite young children are adept at recognizing jokes, riddles, stories and poems, older students and literate adults have difficulty in recognizing rhetorical cues by which an author indicates how a written text is to be taken or for that matter recognizing that a text could be taken in some other way than that which immediately comes to mind.

The central achievement in reading texts critically is a new consciousness of what a text *could have meant* or *could mean* to a putative reader. Readers frequently fail to consider how texts could be understood or misunderstood by readers other than themselves. Children decide what a poem means rather than "deciding what to believe

[a] poem means" (Norris & Phillips, 1987). Only the latter brings the decision process into focus. Haas and Flower (1988), too, pointed out how undergraduates, while expert at paraphrasing and summarizing, were limited in their ability to analyze and criticize. Wineburg (1991) noted how even knowledgeable students directed their attention to what a text meant, its referential meaning, whereas professional historians reading the same texts were much more concerned with authorial intention and rhetorical form. Professional historians distinguished what the author was attempting to get some reader to believe from what they themselves were, in fact, willing to believe. Students failed to ask themselves why is the author saying this? what assumptions is the author making about the audience? what does the author want the reader to think? do I really think that? and so on. To read a text rhetorically is to set the text not only in its context but also in terms of its putative writer and its putative audience. The difficulty, it may be argued, is that both readers and the psychological theories advanced to explain them focus on the recovery of content as if the writer was irrelevant and as if they, the current reader, was the intended reader.

Wineburg (1991) has recently developed this view, crediting Gibson (1950) with the insight that a skilled interpreter is conscious of two readers, him or herself as actual reader and a "mock" reader. The mock reader is a model of what a hypothetical reader would think upon hearing or reading a text; the actual reader is a model of what the reader actually thinks. With some texts no gap may exist between these two modelled readers; but on other occasions the actual reader may note the gap between what the speaker or author intends the putative reader to believe and what the actual reader is willing to believe. When great enough the gap may lead to criticism or rejection of the text.

Some of the difficulties children have in learning to write expository prose may be explained the same way. Children may remember certain facts and theories but they are less able to keep in mind how statements of those facts and theories may be interpreted by any reader other than themselves or of what it may take to convince an unsympathetic reader. Consequently, children adopt a "knowledge-telling strategy" in which they simply report all they recall on a topic (Scardamalia & Bereiter, 1985). Only later do they begin to accommodate to the rhetorical demands of a piece of writing and to coordinate the available knowledge with their rhetorical goals. Facts and beliefs have to be reconceptualized as playing certain roles in a discourse structure, roles such as claim or evidence for a claim, which a putative reader would recognize. Put simply, beginning writers are often capable of making statements on a topic; they have difficulty in indicating just how the reader is expected to take those statements. It is a problem of managing the force of an utterance more so than its content.

We have discussed children's increasing competence in interpreting utterances and texts and their corresponding metaknowledge of what goes into formulating and justifying an interpretation. Learning to deal with written texts is significant in that it presents children with texts in which the propositional content is well represented but for which the cues to illocutionary force are largely lost. Readers must learn an important set of concepts and they must learn to use often subtle clues to infer how the writer intended the text to be taken. Even college students asked to comment on the differences between a popular and a scientific article frequently fail to identify their different sources (J. W. Astington, personal communication). When children become conscious of these clues and share them within an interpretive community, they will have acquired a hermeneutics, a science of interpretation.

Oral hermeneutics

Although hermeneutics originated as a science of interpretation of written texts it is useful to compare, however briefly, the question of how problems of interpretation are managed in an oral tradition. The hermeneutics of a literate tradition tends to focus upon the precise wording and grammar of the text as well as the author's bias and intention with a view to developing explicit rules and procedures for getting from a text to an interpretation. Let us then compare these procedures with those of the oral traditions we examined in the last chapter.

Feldman (1991) and McKellin (1990) have provided elegant examples of the differing modes of interpretation present in traditional oral societies. Feldman examined the interpretive activities involved in dealing with specialized "oral" genres. These forms of discourse are examples of the "marked" forms earlier described by Bloch (1975) in that they involve a particular form of language, delivered in a special way, and employed in specialized contexts for a particular purpose. Feldman chooses these genres for analysis because they are clear cases of language use in which what is said is metaphorical or ambiguous and hence becomes the object of interpretation by others. Such "texts" are characterized by oblique reference, ambiguity and hedges of various sorts and they are designed to raise issues of dispute without seriously offending the listener. The phrasing and repetition assures that the critical expressions are stored in memory and these phrases then become the objects of further discussion and provide the basis for a consensually agreed upon interpretation which may go beyond what was actually said. The method is admirably suited to resolving disagreements that could otherwise turn into serious personal and social problems. Interestingly, the province of Ontario has recently acknowledged the importance of this procedure for resolving social problems by legalizing "native justice" as an alternative to the more formal court procedure.

McKellin (1990) has provided a parallel account of how potentially dangerous social issues are dealt with by the Mangalese of Papua New Guinea. Again the genre involves the use of allegorical discourse with hermeneutical procedures for arriving at a mutually agreed upon interpretation. The Mangalese avoid open displays or discussions of intentions and consequently advance their own understandings of the behavior of others through metaphors and allegorical oratory, symbolic tokens and dream interpretation. Allegories, "Ha'a," are a form of veiled speech in which talk about, say, betelnut, may actually refer to a marriage arrangement or the exchange of a pig. A token, such as a betelnut with a carved design, may represent the same message. When such a token is presented, the recipients are free to take it any way they want for the allegory is little more than a hint or allusion to its "intended" meaning. Much talk may proceed as to the "meaning" of the allegory and the offerer may deny it means anything if the message threatens to provoke confrontation. Yet meanings are successfully shared thereby.

To cite an example of McKellin's: sprouting coconuts, somewhat inedible, were offered as a gift at a feast. The recipient suspected this may imply that the giver of the sprouting coconuts was unhappy with the poor gift he had received on an earlier occasion. When this interpretation was offered, the giver of the poor coconuts denied it, saying merely that the coconuts just happened to be handy – they conveyed no meaning. A year and a second poor gift later, the recipient of the coconuts was berated and reminded of the earlier sprouting coconuts which were now claimed to have been given as a warning the previous year.

Such episodes exemplify the use of indirect speech forms which are the object of interpretation and which are referred to as being a particular type – "wrapped speech," as the Wana refer to their poetry – which recruits a different mode of interpretation than that for "straight speech." Similarly, they illustrate a kind of indirect discourse in which the direct and the indirect meanings come apart in analysis with, for example, the coconuts as the "real" meaning and "complaint" the indirect meaning.

Our question now is how these distinctions relate to those we have examined from literate cultures. To oversimplify somewhat, there seem to be few interpretive problems that cannot be handled in oral, face-to-face contexts although there may be some categories of linguistic events which are less differentiated in oral than in literate cultures. Recall the findings of Heeschen (1978), reported in the last chapter, that among the Eipo figures of speech such as irony and overstatement were not distinguished from lies. And recall Duranti's (1985) finding that traditional Samoans seemed reluctant to think of meaning intention apart from what was actually said. Furthermore, as we noted in Chapter 2 (p. 45), the notion of literal meaning may be unique to traditions deriving from Aristotle. Interpretive problems arise primarily in interpreting written texts because, as we noted in the last chapter, writing provides little indication of how the texts are to be taken. It is for dealing with written texts that an elaborate, explicit hermeneutics is required. Once acquired, of course, this elaborate interpretive machinery may be redeployed for the analysis of one's own and other's speech. In this way concepts of wording, meaning, and intention, of distinctions between saying and meaning, between literal and figurative, come into the discourse of the school and into literate family life.

Nor are genres universal. Recognizing genre is one example of recognizing illocutionary force. As we noted, what is said is easily represented in writing and is relatively easily translated into other languages; how it is to be taken, because it is expressed non-verbally, is both difficult to represent in writing and difficult to translate. An illustration of the difficulty of recognizing the force of an utterance comes from the studies of logical reasoning conducted by Luria (1976) which we discussed in Chapter 2. Luria, it will be recalled, embedded inferential tasks, syllogistic in form, into simple narratives:

In the Far North, where there is snow, all bears are white. Novaya Zemlya is in the Far North and there is always snow there. What colour are the bears there?

Non-literate, rural peasants tended to resist the logical inference that the bears *must* be white. Indeed, they typically responded by saying "I don't know; there are different sorts of bears." Luria's inference from such studies, as we noted, was that non-literate subjects tended not to reason logically. Yet the subject in question, had later replied: "Each locality has its own animals: if it's white, they will be white," a correct logically derived inference from a premise! Critics have suggested that the task is not valid because it is relevant only in an artificial school context. In my view the problem is a very general one in interpreting a written text (even if in this case the written text was read to the subject). The general problem is one of assigning an appropriate illocutionary force to an utterance when that force is not explicitly labeled. The puzzled subject in the experiment does not know whether to take the expression as the assertion of a factual truth, a wild conjecture, a commonly held view, or a personal suggestion. The author intended that it be taken as a premise; the listener took it as an implausible conjecture. Experimenter and subject alike failed to recognize the problem as a problem of genre.

That is not to say, however, that Luria's problem is identical for literate and non-literate subjects. As we noted, non-literate subjects are able to solve such problems if they are presented as pretense (Scribner & Cole, 1981). Pretending something is true, however, is not the same as assuming it to be true. The latter is required for the syllogism in which the assumption becomes a premise. Premises and assumptions are abstract metalinguistic notions of particular relevance to a special written genre of discourse. All cultures presumably have conditional expressions such as "What if . . ." which are in some ways conceptually equivalent to premises. What appears to be specialized in literate discourse is the extent to which these practices are turned into concepts, made orderly and systematically applied. All cultures use indirect expressions but only some systematically distinguish the literal from the metaphorical and set out rules for their appropriate use.

Oral and literate hermeneutics are equally suited to their tasks; both are specialized uses of language and both require complex interpretive strategies. But, as we noted, they differ in important ways. In the oral societies we have discussed, interpretation belongs only to particular, marked genre of discourse such as oratory and poetic discourse and ceremonial occasions all of which are characterized by the use of indirect, metaphorical speech and other symbols. In a literate context, metaphor does not belong to a specialized genre but may be used, if marked as metaphor, in any kind of context or any form of discourse. Similarly, special interpretive procedures appear to be reserved for this special kind of oral discourse – only indirectness calls for inter-pretation. In modern literate culture on the other hand a usual assumption is that the meaning of every utterance, literal or meta-phorical, while open to interpretation, is knowable. And finally, there is some indication that in oral cultures greater weight is given to the importance of consensus in assigning an interpretation – the meaning is what the group will accept as its meaning. Literate culture is more conducive to diversity in interpretation, the divergences arising from somewhat idiosyncratic readings of particular texts with more atten-tion to particular wordings and correspondingly less attention to context and other non-verbal indications of illocutionary force, that is, indications of how the original utterance was intended to be taken.

In literate culture, special procedures have evolved for dealing with the information which is lost in the act of transcription, namely, with illocutionary force, the putative audience-directed intentions of the author; interpretation becomes bureaucratized. Aspects of oral discourse that were carried by stance, voice and tone are now either ignored or reconstructed, often laboriously, from other clues within the text, or explicated through a new set of concepts and a new genre of discourse. Once in possession of explicit concepts for interpreting texts we may, like Mr. Palomar, see them as useful for interpreting everything else. But, as we shall see in the next chapter, these interpretive assumptions have also changed historically. Their changes constitute pivotal points in the history of reading and the history of thinking.

7 A HISTORY OF READING: FROM THE SPIRIT OF THE TEXT TO THE INTENTIONS OF THE AUTHOR

....

[Twelfth-century] readers would peruse texts with a kind of redactive criticism, editing them and seeking epiphanies between the lines.

(K. F. Morrison, 1990, p. 68)

The conceptual changes that ushered in modernity, that is those changes that occurred between the Middle Ages and the Renaissance, may be seen as a matter of learning to read in a new way. It was a matter of moving away from reading between the lines to reading what was on the lines – giving increased importance to the information explicitly represented in the text. New ways of reading gave rise to new ways of writing texts and both gave rise to new ways of thinking about the world and about the mind. These are the proposals we shall examine in this and the next two chapters.

Quite different practices can and do go on in the name of reading. One of the important contributions of historians has been to show that ways of reading have changed historically. These changes arise both from the structure of the texts themselves and the assumptions about the meaning of a text. In line with the theory developed in the preceding chapter, these historical changes may be traced to revised procedures for determining how texts are to be taken – the management of illocutionary force.

The late Middle Ages, roughly the twelfth to the fifteenth centuries, are often thought of as a dormant period with intellectual life reviving in the Renaissance. Medieval historians have done much to show that the conceptual developments associated with the Renaissance were in fact worked out in the twelfth and thirteenth century, long before they served as the intellectual basis of the Renaissance and the popular movements associated with the Reformation.

Attitude to texts – issues of interpretation – were central to these developments. At the beginning of this period, texts were seen as a

boundless resource from which one could take an inexhaustible supply
of meanings; at the end of the period, the meaning of a text is austerely
anchored in the textual evidence. This definitive notion of meaning of
a text thus permitted a firm distinction between what a text means and
what is seen in a text by the overzealous as well as a new understanding of the relation between the objectively given and the subjectively
construed – that which was mis-taken from the text.

The matter is not simple for the meaning of a text could not be
resolved by a careful scrutiny of the words alone, although that was a
critical part of the process, it was a matter of recovering or imputing
intentionality to the writer. This, of course, fits our theme. Writing
systems readily capture (represent) syntactic structure but not the
pragmatic structure; a written transcription may allow us to know
what was said but not how the speaker intended it to be taken.
Recovery requires a conscious analysis, a theory, of interpretation.
Thus at the end of the Middle Ages, Aquinas announced the solution
to the interpretive problem of the Middle Ages by saying that the
"literal meaning" of a text is that meaning intended by the writer. The
understanding of reading changed from that of "epiphanies" or revela-
tions of meanings to the methodical recognition of authorial intentions. Let us examine this development in some detail.

Fixing a text

The transition from remembering what someone said to the fixing of
an original or standard text with a definitive meaning in writing may
seem simple. The text, we would think, is simply a memory or a
transcription of what was said and the meaning is simply what he or it
meant. This apparent transparency of written texts is, in fact, the
source of a serious interpretive problem. The attempt to develop a
standard version, the original, required the evolution of a particular
concept of a text and correspondingly a particular concept of what was
involved in reading or interpreting a text. It was a task that took up the
better part of a millennium, absorbed the best talents of an empire,
and laid the stage for modern science and philosophy.

The problem arises from the fact that utterances rarely say what
they mean. They imply, hint, insinuate, and indicate as well as state,

assert and define. Just as Blake aspired "To see a world in a grain of sand" so one may see the reflections of meaning in an utterance or a text. It is a modern anthropological insight that cultures may be seen as a kind of "text" which may be endlessly characterized or interpreted by means of "thick descriptions" (Geertz, 1973).

The scholars of Charlemagne's day read religious texts in just this way. For them too, the actual words or forms are merely the tip of the conceptual iceberg, the real meanings lying far beneath the surface and detectable only by internalization and meditation. In fact, reading in Charlemagne's day is somewhat similar to reading the post-modern, or reader-response way – what a text means is what a reader takes it to mean. But that assumption when made about traditional written texts proved to be a major obstacle to the birth of modern ways of reading texts and thinking about nature.

As we saw in Chapter 5, texts in principle are never complete representations of what is said orally. Writing lacks devices for representing the illocutionary force of an utterance, that is, indications of the speaker's attitude to what is said which the reader may use to determine how the author intended the text to be taken. The history of reading is largely the history of attempting to cope with what writing does not represent. Lacking a theory of illocutionary force, readers and writers alike attempted to cope with the problem of intentionality by the traditional means we discussed in Chapter 6 including the theory and practical arts of rhetoric.

Both the theory and practice of reading altered significantly from the time of Augustine (d. 430) to the time of Thomas Aquinas (d. 1274). During this time the very issue of "fixing a text" and of "establishing what a text means" came to the fore and a series of proposals were advanced in the attempt to solve the problem. The main properties of this development were set out in Beryl Smalley's remarkable work *The study of the Bible in the Middle Ages* (1941). A large body of work on this topic by such writers as Febvre (1942/ 1982), Febvre and Martin (1958/1976) as well as more recent work by Stock (1983), Nicholson (1984) and Morrison (1988, 1990) has greatly extended our understanding of these developments.

The history of reading in the West is largely the history of reading the Christian Bible even if, as we shall see, that tradition was deeply influenced by classical Greek, Arabic and Jewish traditions. The early Christian tradition, largely as a reaction against the Jewish concern with the "letter of the law" and strict ritual observance, countered that "the letter killeth but the spirit giveth life" (II Cor. 3: 5). The purpose of interpretation was to recover that "spirit."

Moreover, the ways of reading were greatly influenced by practices of translation of sacred texts. As any translator knows translation has to be dominated by the sense not the very words of a text. Thus St. Jerome who translated the Christian bible into Latin wrote that there was no loss of meaning if a word or two were added to a text (Morrison, 1990). Reading, based on a consciousness built up through translation according to the sense, placed little emphasis on the very words of a text.

The problem may be stated this way. In the Middle Ages the letter was seen as the verbal form of the text and the spirit as its meaning or significance – one version of what it says versus what it means. But until the late Medieval period and the early Renaissance there were neither clear procedures for working out precisely what the text actually said nor for determining what it literally meant. The earlier method was to think of the word and its meaning as analogous to the body and its soul. The purpose of reading or listening to a text was to see through the text to the spirit: "Blessed are the eyes which see divine spirit through the letter's veil" as Claudius of Turin put it (Smalley, 1941, p. 1), or what Morrison, cited in the epigraph to this chapter, described as "seeking epiphanies between the lines" (1990, p. 68). Thus the spiritual exposition generally consisted "of pious meditations or religious teaching for which the text is used merely as a convenient starting point" (Smalley, 1941, p. 2). St. Paul's contrast between the letter and the spirit "inspired luxuriant methods of exegesis intended to disclose what was unsaid in what was uttered" (Morrison, 1990, p. 247).

Although it was only in the thirteenth century that humanists began systematically to develop notions of a more literal understanding, an understanding which made it increasingly difficult to read "between the lines" some earlier writers had taken tentative steps in that direction.

Disturbed by the attention to the spiritual interpretation at the expense of the literal, Augustine (d. 430) argued that every text has a literal meaning thereby giving "the 'letter' a concrete chronological reality which it had never had before" (Smalley, p. 10). Although the spiritual sense was considered to be much more important than the literal sense, Augustine defended the notion that the spiritual sense was always based on the literal and that every text had a literal meaning.

The theory for determining spiritual meaning was elaborate indeed. As mentioned the letter was thought of as body and one gained access to the spirit by looking "through" the text; one glimpsed the spiritual meaning as if reflected in a mirror. Of Origen, an early church father, Smalley says:

Scripture for him was a mirror, which reflected the divinity now darkly, now brightly; it had body, soul, and spirit, a literal, moral, and allegorical sense, the first two for 'simple believers' who were 'unable to understand profounder meanings', the third for the initiates, the gnostics, who were able to investigate *the wisdom in a mystery, the hidden wisdom of God.*

> (Smalley, p. 5, emphasis mine)

Disputes about the meaning of a text arose, nonetheless, in the course of formulating commentaries on the text. Unlike the Jewish tradition which allowed some latitude for interpretation – it was the correct oral reproduction of the verbal form that mattered most – the dogmatic nature of the Christian Church required that "correct" interpretations be distinguished from "incorrect" ones. The theory of interpretation that developed, borrowed in large part from Jewish and Arabic sources, and which was employed in much of the Middle Ages, articulated the four-fold meanings of sacred texts. The four levels were made memorable in the Jewish tradition by the acronym "PRDS," pronounced "Pardes" which stood for the four forms of meaning: P for plain sense, R for oblique meaning, D for homiletic, and S for mystical meaning. Dante's (d. 1321) exposition of the Christian view is exemplary:

In order to make this manner of treatment clear, it can be applied to the following verses: "When Israel went out of Egypt, the house of Jacob from a barbarous people, Judea was made his sanctuary, Israel his dominion." Now if we look at the letter alone, what is signified is the departure of the sons of

Israel from Egypt during the time of Moses; if at the allegory, what is signified to us is our redemption through Christ; if at the moral sense, what is signified to us is the conversion of the soul from the sorrow and misery of sin to the state of grace; if at the anagogical, what is signified to us is the departure of the sanctified soul from bondage to the corruption of this world into the freedom of eternal glory.

(Dante Alighieri, 1317, 1973, p. 99)

But it was also agreed that the significance of a religious text is endless; the search for the spiritual meaning led one to interpret in a way that they thought of as mystical: "Understanding came not through such indirect means as words and images, but directly through the effects [of those words and images] and the inward feeling of enlightened love" (Morrison, 1990, p. 52). We moderns would think of such epiphanies as unbridled subjectivity.

Augustine's contribution to the solution was to see the letter as possessing a meaning, a literal meaning. But how was one to determine that literal meaning? "The patristic tradition had no agreement as to the meaning of 'literal' and 'historical'" (Smalley, p. 27). Even Augustine taught that opinions about the literal sense of a text could be taken as true "provided that they were not unedifying" (Smalley, p. 101). Moreover, literal meaning was scarcely worth seeking since as far as Christians were concerned, it was the spiritual sense that mattered. All religious texts were thought of as needing a key to their understanding; that key was given primarily by its role in the doctrine and worship of the Church and secondarily through the personal experiences of those who lived the doctrine, especially the lives of the Saints. The texts themselves were not seen as providing the key.

It was the church fathers working in the twelfth century at the Abbey of St. Victor in Paris, in particular Hugh of St. Victor (d. 1141) and his student Andrew of St. Victor (d. 1175) who recognized the significance of the literal meaning of scripture and who developed a scholarly, systematic approach to interpretation by "substituting research for revelation" (Smalley, p. 104). Hugh, for example, chided some of his teachers for taking "'the letter killeth' [as] an excuse for preferring [their] own ideas to the divine authors" (Smalley, p. 69). As we shall see this was to become a central theme in the writings of Francis Bacon some three centuries later when he defended careful observation in science by declaiming "God forbid that we should take a dream of the imagination for a pattern in the world" (Bacon, 1620/1965, p. 323).

Hugh also provided a definition of literal meaning in terms of what the author wished to say. That meaning in turn was to be settled not by prayer and meditation resulting in epiphany but rather by appeal to new sources of evidence based on textual, historical and geographical research. To aid literal interpretation Hugh prepared two chronicles and a map of the world as well as precise drawings of Noah's ark. In a rhapsodic summary that suitably allegorizes the theme of this book, Smalley writes of Hugh:

He is making the letter a proper subject for study . . . He wants to understand the literal meaning of Scripture exactly, so as to visualize the scene. He had that curiosity which set explorers in quest of Eldorado and led to the discovery of a continent.

(1941, p. 72)

Yet, while Hugh made the study of the literal meaning of a text into a naturalistic enterprise, he never questioned the traditional view of the subservience of the literal to the spiritual meaning of scripture; that was a turn that we identify only with the Reformation. But before that final step could be taken a clearer notion of literal meaning was required.

The contribution of Andrew of St. Victor to this enterprise was to advance the understanding of the historical meaning of a text. Andrew, who "wrote for himself" (Smalley, p. 95) advanced his and his contemporaries understanding of the historical meaning of scripture by borrowing both knowledge and technique from his Jewish colleagues.

The "Jewish way" of reading the Old Testament, as Andrew of St. Victor referred to it, was to render according to the actual words of the text thereby providing new insights into its meaning. Andrew admired this Jewish way even if in the eyes of Andrew and his twelfth century contemporaries, Rabbinical scholars employed "serpentine wile" to evade the "manifest witness to Christ" which they found in the Scriptures (Smalley, pp. 139–142).

While Andrew had learned from St. Augustine that each biblical text had a literal meaning, his discussions with the Jewish scholars led him to identify the literal meaning of a text with what the Jews say about it; "if you want to know the literal sense, go to the Jews" (Smalley, p. 142).

The Jews in question were those of the school of Rashi (1040–1105) who like their Christian contemporaries were concerned with the problem of reading sacred texts. Before Rashi, two forms of biblical interpretation were prominent, the *halachic* and the *aggadic*, the former was reading the text so as to adduce rules for living, a form of exegesis that became frozen with the closing of the Talmud about 500 AD. The latter was the midrashic method of interpretation which regarded biblical texts as "a peg upon which to hang moral doctrine and edifying tales" (Smalley, p. 122). The midrashic method is the Jewish equivalent of "spiritual" interpretation in the Christian tradition.

Rashi, equipped with a newly produced grammar and a dictionary, developed a third method of interpretation, the literal or rational. He attempted to write a literal exposition of the whole Old Testament, emphasizing the chronology and geography of the period, examining the cultural context in which the text was written and explaining supernatural events in terms of natural causes. Thus, God's appearing in a vision to Joseph is interpreted as Joseph dreaming of future greatness because of what he thought about during the day. This "discovery" of the literal led to an antagonism for the more imaginative interpretations of the midrash:

... whosoever is ignorant of the literal meaning of the Scripture and inclines after the Midrash of the verse is like a drowning man who clutches at a straw to save himself. Were he to set his mind to the word of the Lord, he would search out the true meaning of the verse and its literal purpose.

(Quoted by Smalley, p. 122)

The Christian attempt to provide a definitive literal meaning, then, took an important step in identifying the literal meaning of a text with that meaning held by the Jews. By combining evidence from chronologies and geographies with the cultural and historic knowledge of the Jews and by resolutely avoiding appeals to the miraculous, Andrew was able to advance both knowledge and technique for determining

the literal sense of scripture: "No western commentator before
[Andrew] had set out to give a purely literal interpretation of the Old
Testament, though many had attempted a purely spiritual one"
(Smalley, p. 140). But just what the content of the "letter" was
remained a matter of judgment. During the Middle Ages "there were
no rules for defining [the literal meaning], just as there were no rules
for establishing one's text" (Smalley, p. 140). Andrew's strict attention to the literal at the expense of the spiritual, the natural at the
expense of the miraculous, marked an important step in developing
such rules.

The text that Andrew took as worthy of analysis was the surface
meaning not its deep meaning. He undertook to expound *iuxta super-
ficiem littere*, that is, according to the surface of the letter. He sought
the "simple surface meaning," the literal sense of scripture rather than
its spiritual mysteries. Recovery of that surface meaning required the
examination of a number of sources of evidence, both contextual –
historical and cultural – and textual – grammatical and lexical. Its
recovery could be seen as the product of research rather than as a gift
of the spirit.

It was this concern for the literal meaning that turned the attention
back to the very words, the verbal form of a text. Literal interpretation
unlike spiritual interpretation depended critically upon just what
words were used. Consequently, there was a new concern with and
respect for the original wording of a text. The careful fixing of the
verbal form of a text, including making corrections in existing texts in
the attempt to recover the "original," became the primary concern of
Renaissance humanists. The Vulgate, St. Jerome's Latin translation
of the Bible, for example, had referred to a person "Mehusim." On
textual basis, and by comparing various readings of passages, one
writer showed that the text should have read "of Husim," thereby
cleaning up the text and "abolishing a purely illusory personage called
Mehusim" (Smalley, 1941, pp. 170–179). This was simply a small step
in the right direction. As long as the written text was treated merely as
the retrieval cue for the spiritual meaning or as an object against which
to check one's memory, producing a standard text with fixed wording,
grammar, uniform punctuation, consistent chapter and verse indicators had a low priority. Systematic textual design was achieved only

beginning in the thirteenth century. As mentioned earlier, Carruthers (1990) celebrates the importance of memory in the Middle Ages and at the same time plays down the role and significance of writing. But in so doing she greatly underestimates the role of writing in the evolution of a modern concept of literal meaning and in the desire to purify and restore texts to their original form, a major legacy of the Middle Ages to the modern era.

A clear conception of literal meaning appeared only in Maimonides' *Guide for the perplexed* (1190/1963) and Thomas Aquinas' *Summa Theologica* (1267–1273/1964–81) both master works of the thirteenth century. Maimonides provided new naturalistic explanations for what Christians had thought of as "mysteries," by showing that the form of the text was a product of the mind of the author and the author's audience-directed intentions. Biblical writers talked of the hand of God because those were terms that simple folk would understand; the authors chose the words they did because that was how events had struck them:

> The reader of the description believes that it contains superfluous matter, or useless repetition [one of the things that readers thought must indicate some deeper, mystical meaning], but if he had witnessed the event of which he reads, he would see the necessity of every part of the description.
>
> (1190/1963, pp. 381–382)

Thus, for Maimonides, reading required that one have an understanding of the audience-directed intentions of the writer. Only if one studied the text in its context would the reader understand why the writers had spoken or written as they did.

Aquinas begins his *Summa* with the somewhat traditional conception of the literal and the spiritual senses. He takes God to be the author of Scripture. But he proceeds to develop the distinction in a new way pointing out that human writers express their meaning by words. What the human authors intend constitutes the literal sense; the literal sense was the legitimate object of scientific study and research. The spiritual sense is what the divine "author" expressed by the *events* described by the human author; the spiritual sense was the object of theology. Only scripture had both senses. Aquinas thereby granted a complete autonomy to the text and its literal meaning.

Interpretation was thereby naturalized and yet God could be revealed through the events recounted. I find Aquinas' solution absolutely dazzling; a brilliant solution to a problem that had plagued scholarship for a millennium. Yet it must be remembered that he remained medieval in his belief that the deeper meanings and the higher truths were available only as a gift from God. Although a naturalistic literal meaning now stood shoulder to shoulder with spiritual meaning, it by no means threatened to displace it. The view persisted that although scripture had a literal meaning it was also a divine encyclopedia, a written cipher from which all real truths could be derived. Such readers thus continued to live in what we moderns think of as an "enchanted" world (Ozment, 1980).

Luther's theory of reading, the theory we associate with the Reformation, was a rather direct outgrowth of Aquinas' view of literal meaning. Luther took as the real true meaning of scripture the historical or literal meaning, the meaning that was available for all to see if they read carefully. The meaning of scripture relied not on the dogmas of the church but on a "deeper reading of the text" (Gadamer, 1975; Ozment, 1980). Readings or interpretations were to be grounded openly in the text and were not to be dependent upon Church dogma, cabbalistic traditions, or private inspiration. The search changed from one for revelation to one for meaning. One was to seek the meanings *on* the lines rather than the epiphanies between them.

In his assumption that texts had a single, historical meaning and that that meaning was lodged in the words, visible for all to see, and not dependent upon any private or privileged insight, Luther was a model of the new way of reading. Luther's categories for thinking about interpretation were in great flux from 1509 until 1521. By the end of that period he had adopted a simple biblicism, essentially identifying the intended meaning with the textual meaning. But this was not a simple fundamentalism. Luther never thought that the texts could be interpreted casually. Like other late medieval scholars he read the texts in their original languages, was knowledgeable in philology and in the relevant cultural anthropology, and interpreted texts in their textual context. Consequently, textual interpretation was seen as dependent upon linguistic knowledge as well as on knowledge about the putative intentions of the writers. Readers had learned, we may say, how to manage the illocutionary force of textual statements. Such recovery required serious and systematic study and the judicious use of evidence, for only in this way could literal meaning be identified with intended meaning.

This conception of the literal meaning of scripture was sufficiently robust to allow Luther to claim that the levels of meaning which previous writers had seen as "in the text" were fantasies, dreams, extrapolations, and interpolations, constructed to sustain the "dogmas of the church." Thus was the stage set for Protestantism.

Luther, like his Protestant contemporaries, was positivist in regard to interpretation, however. He believed that the intended meaning of a text could be determined with certainty and, consequently, that a text could only be read correctly one way. Cranmer, Archbishop of Canterbury, and author of the *Book of common prayer*, too, "took for granted that *a text* had *a meaning* that would be equally apparent to all who read it" (Tyson & Wagonheim, 1986, p. 13) and that such a prayer book would therefore draw together all the people of England into one common belief.

The significance of Luther's move was to treat written texts as autonomous representations of meaning. It was the belief that texts could speak for themselves; they did not require authority or dogma to get from the text to the interpretation. Luther's emphasis on the importance of literacy was based on the assumption that everyone who could read could consult the text for themselves and thereby use the text as evidence to judge the validity of an interpretation. Interpretation, we could say, was both naturalized and democratized.

We now think Luther was wrong; texts, especially texts created in one culture and read in another, never wear their intended meanings on their sleeves. Scripts fail to provide a model for communicative intention which has, therefore, to be inferred from textual and contextual clues. There is always the possibility of seeing undiscovered meanings in texts – witness Freud's reading of the Oedipus myth. But the importance of the revolution in reading should not be minimized. By interpreting texts strictly in terms of their properties, both textual and contextual, as if meaning depended upon nothing other than what was said, it was possible to shed the enormous weight of significance and meaning that the medieval readers had read into a text. This new way of reading provided the conceptual basis for the Reformation. Equally important, it suggested a new way of reading the Book of Nature as we shall see presently.

A history of the notion of literal meaning is an important part of the history of reading. For readers in the early Middle Ages, the literal meaning of a text was a mere stepping stone to the real or spiritual meaning. What Hugh and Andrew and later Aquinas did was to distinguish and justify an attention to the literal meaning, which they considered to be the intended, historical or referential meaning. What Luther did was to exclude all meanings other than that literal, historical, intended meaning. What has changed since Luther's time is that we no longer assume that earlier writers thought of their texts as we think of our own. Luther's mistake, if I may be so bold, was to assume that ancient writers thought and spoke and meant in much the same way that he himself did. He spoke, wrote and read "literally" and assumed ancient writers had done the same. We no longer assume that the ancient writers used categories like our own, especially, categories like meaning and intention. Interpretation, we grant, requires that we recover how earlier writers and speakers intended that their utterances be taken in their own cultural context. Thus Frye (1982, pp. 61–62) has argued that the Bible's literal meaning is its poetic or metaphorical meaning for that arguably is how it was spoken and taken by its producers. Only in the seventeenth century did the literal meaning shift to what Frye calls "the descriptive phase of language."

It is worth quoting Frye (1982, p. 23) more fully for his Vicoean view of stages of language use are close to those advanced here as stages of reading:

[In the first phase] Homer's language is metaphorical to us, if not necessarily to him. In his poetry the distinction between figured and literal language hardly exists ... With the second phase, metaphor becomes one of the recognized figures of speech; but it is not until the coming of a different conception of language that a tension arises between figurative and what is called "literal" meaning, and poetry begins to become a conscious and deliberate use of figures. In the third phase ... a descriptive writer will tend to avoid as many figures of speech as he can, on the ground that they are "merely verbal" and interfere with the transparency of description.

Only in this third phase did texts become representational and suitable instruments for science, philosophy and history. What Luther apparently failed to recognize was that the Bible's literal meaning is the poetic or metaphorical meaning and not the descriptive, referential meaning characteristic of the modern prose he and his contemporaries were creating.

That the evolution of a defensible concept of literal meaning should be long and difficult runs counter to both our commonsensical assumptions and our current cognitive theories. In both cases, the literal meaning is deemed to be unproblematic, the harder work of comprehension occurring in "making" meaning, constructing meaning, drawing inferences, making glosses, capturing gist, understanding metaphor and the like. The history of reading and interpretation which we have just examined suggests just the opposite. Medieval readers never have had difficulty in reading between the lines, in taking a hint, listening for allusion and nuance – in seeing a world in a grain of sand. What they had difficulty doing was just what Andrew of St. Victor was teaching his contemporaries to do, namely, capturing the meaning which is warranted by the text and "confining interpretation to the text" (Olson, 1977) and in so doing recognizing and rejecting the meanings that were read into a text.

So what, precisely, is this literal meaning that the medievals were so intent on capturing? Grasping the literal sense does not come simply from staring at the words – as we saw in the last chapter it depends on syntax, semantics and pragmatics, the latter dependent upon historical and cultural knowledge. But above all it depends on understanding how texts were to be taken, that is, how they were used by speakers or writers to produce certain effects in listeners and readers. Thus, critical to grasping the "literal" meaning is an understanding of audience-directed intentions – what the author wants the putative audience to do or think. To capture the literal meaning requires that the reader have a model of both the speaker and writer and the reader or listener. But now this reader being modeled is not simply the reader him or her self, but a model of some historical or hypothetical reader, what in the last chapter we called the putative reader. The activity of modeling that audience-directed intention required careful analysis of the text and its context. The fixed text could serve as the evidence against which possible interpretations were adjudicated.

That this was the goal becomes clear if we look at Andrew's style of interpretation. An important strategy for determining the historical meaning of a text was to ask not just "What does this text mean?" but also "Why does the author say this?" "Who is the author addressing?" "What does the author want the listener or reader to do or to think?" Thus Andrew asks "Why is it said to Jeremias?" (Smalley, 1941, p. 113) and he refers to the human author of the text (rather than to God as author) thus: "He [Moses] has just recapitulated what he said above . . . he explains . . ., he dwells on the things which concern the common man, and which the untaught, less gifted mind can understand . . . He told us that God said . . ." (Smalley, 1941, p. 107); and again, "The prophet teaches his readers that . . ." (p. 115) and so on. This indicates, I suggest, that Andrew, perhaps for the first time, interprets the text in terms of audience-directed intentions – as a text produced by a historically real person and addressed not to himself as a Christian, but to a particular historical audience. He reads the text, we may say, objectively, that is, as an object of study rather than as an object of reverence. The same is true, as we have noted, in the interpretive strategy of Maimonides, Aquinas and Luther.

The central achievement in reading texts this way is a new consciousness of what a text *could have meant* or *could mean* to a putative reader. As we saw in the last chapter, readers frequently fail to consider how texts may be understood or misunderstood by readers other than themselves. Critical readers attend not simply to what a text says or means but in addition attend to the authorial intention and rhetorical form distinguishing what the author was attempting to get some reader to believe from what they themselves were, in fact, willing to believe. To read a text literally, then, is to set the text not only in its context but also in terms of its putative writer and its putative audience.

Once one clearly distinguishes what the speaker or writer was attempting to get some particular reader or audience to think or believe from what the current reader him or herself actually believes, the interpreter will have taken an important step in understanding interpretation. If a reader fails to distinguish these two readers, himself and the intended, texts will be interpreted in the medieval way; if he distinguishes the two, as did Andrew of St. Victor, he will read in the early modern way. Not every sentence in a sacred text was directed to the reader and not every expression was to be taken in the same way. What was involved was a new understanding of and a new ability to analyze the meaning of an expression so that that meaning could be used as evidence for determining how the author intended his listener or reader to take that expression.

It is easy to imagine why earlier readers may have found it difficult to distinguish these two components, content and force, or what was said and how it was to be taken. As long as reading was primarily oral reading, the tone of voice was a critical part of reading even if it had to be added (without access to a score) by the reader. Saenger (1982, 1991) has importantly contributed to the idea that reading, and not just writing, has a history by providing clear evidence that silent reading became a useful skill only after the development of word-segmented texts which became routine in the twelfth century AD. Writing a text to be read silently required the explicit markings, either lexical or via punctuation, to indicate how texts were to be taken. Such a requirement may have made the absence of indication of illo-cutionary force of earlier texts more obvious and the search for more precise means for marking illocutionary force lexically, more pressing.

As we shall see in the next chapter, once conscious of the unma-nageably diverse ways of taking a written text, seventeenth century writers attempted to bring interpretation under control first by favor-ing expressions of direct, verifiable observation and second by explicitly marking how each utterance was to be taken. Certainly, the post-modern emphasis on what the reader makes of a text and the abandonment of the search for "the one historical meaning" would strike our early modern authors not merely as wrong but as perverse. They had seen far too much of that in what passed for the "spiritual" interpretation of scripture.

Readers hoping to find a hand-wringing apology for my earlier (1977) oversimplification of the concept of "literal meaning" will come closest to gaining satisfaction at this point. To my earlier claim that for seventeenth century readers "texts simply meant what they said" I would now admit that texts always mean more than they say. What a text means depends upon not only the sense of the expression as specified by the grammar and lexis, but also on the illocutionary force of the expression, which when explicitly marked indicates the author's intention as to how that expression is to be taken by a real or putative audience. On the other hand, I would insist that the force of an utterance is not "made up" or "read into" a text by the reader but is, at least in part, recoverable on textual and contextual grounds. The central problem of interpretation is to recognize the force of an utterance. Interpretive problems are particularly pressing in dealing with written texts for which indications of illocutionary force are absent or indirect and readers must make use of subtle textual and contextual cues to decide how an expression is to be taken. It was the attempt to make those interpretive decisions routine, that is, to make texts which both say what they mean and explicitly indicate how they are intended to be taken, which led to the revolution in the ways of reading texts, and eventually to the invention of new ways of writing them.

8 READING THE BOOK OF NATURE: THE CONCEPTUAL ORIGINS OF EARLY MODERN SCIENCE

· ·

There are two Books from which I collect my Divinity, one of God [Scripture], another of His servant Nature.

(Thomas Browne, 1643).

At the death of William Harvey in 1657 his friend Abraham Cowley composed an "Ode upon Dr. Harvey" to celebrate his achievements in medicine and, more importantly for our purposes, in epistemology. Harvey had not only discovered the circulation of the blood, he had done so by means of a new way, a Protestant way we may say, of reading the Book of Nature. Cowley wrote:

Thus Harvey sought for truth in truths own Book
The creatures, which by God himself was writ;
And wisely thought 'twas fit,
Not to read Comments only upon it,
But on th' original it self to look.

(Cited by Frank, 1980, p. 103)

Cowley attributes Harvey's success to his willingness to consult the Book of God's own creatures – the Book of Nature – for himself rather than relying upon the ancient authorities who Cowley demotes to the role of commentors. The attitude contrasts sharply with that of the biblical story of the Ethiopian eunuch with which I introduced Chapter 6. For the Ethiopian the meaning of a text was to be found by consulting an authority; for Harvey, it was to be found in reading the text, in this case the Book of Nature, for oneself.

But as we saw in the preceding chapter, the new route from text to interpretation was not a naive one. It involved a new understanding of how to use textual clues to make up for what was lost in simple transcription; textual clues could indicate not only what was said but also how the text was to be taken. "Correct" reading required both. Whereas for the Medieval rhetorician the "ways of taking" a text was the expansive art of the preacher, for the Reformers it was the austere art of reading. Harvey, Cowley said, was reading the Book of Nature this new way.

Harvey, then as now, was seen as a symbol of a new age in the life of the mind. So much so that an enormous secondary literature has grown up around Harvey and the other major figures associated with what Alfred North Whitehead called "the first century of modern science." The seventeenth century was marked by the work of Gilbert on the lodestone (the magnet), Galileo on the laws of motion, Harvey on the circulation of the blood, Boyle on the laws of gases, Hooke on microscopy. It was also the century of the great mental philosophers Descartes, Locke, Hume and Berkeley. It was the century of the descriptive art of the Dutch masters and the century that at least set the stage for the realist narrative fiction of Defoe and Fielding.

Any period has an impressive list of achievements each of which, whether in science, theology, art or literature, has its own history and it would be perverse to account for them with a too general formula, a zeitgeist. And indeed specialist disciplines have been built around each of these movements. But even if we consider a single domain, science, we still have one recalcitrant fact to face, namely, that the developments in seventeenth century science were made in extremely diverse fields of study, ranging from planetary motion to the circulation of the blood, to observation on the lodestone, to microscopic studies of the teeth of snails. Thus something more than simple domain-specific knowledge would seem to be involved. Indeed it may be argued that science, literature, art and religion shared a new attitude to language and even employed a common form of discourse. My purpose in this chapter is to examine how the ways of reading and interpreting texts which had evolved during the Renaissance could have contributed to those new ways of thinking about nature, mind and language that burst upon the scene in the seventeenth century.

In order to see how the seventeenth century scientists "read" the Book of Nature it is useful to review how they thought about reading and writing generally. For as we shall see their attitude to language, words, and texts is duplicated in their attitudes to the perceptible properties of the natural world. To that end we shall first discuss the emerging notions of how texts are to be written and read, and then turn to the main topic of this chapter, how the Book of Nature was to be "read."

Medieval and Modern discourse

It is by now well established that seventeenth-century writers were in full possession of a new awareness of language, of signs, of ideas, and of discourse which permitted them to see earlier uses of signs and forms of discourse as flawed. Their new awareness, as we saw in the last chapter, was built upon those advances in ways of reading that first developed in the monastic religious culture of the thirteenth and fourteenth centuries. In the seventeenth century this new understanding is manifest in the development of a new factual, prosaic form of discourse (Reiss, 1982), a new understanding of signs – specifically a clear distinction between the meaning of a sign and the idea it represented – (Aarsleff, 1982), and a new understanding of representation generally (Foucault, 1970; Hacking, 1975b). Let us consider these developments in turn.

Reiss (1982) has contrasted Medieval discourse, which he calls a discourse of patterning with Early Modern, that is, seventeenth century, discourse, which he calls "analytico-referential" discourse. Discourse of patterning was that form of writing suited to the form of reading we discussed in the last chapter in which readers were expected to form their own synthesis and to detect meanings hidden in events (Morrison, 1990, p. 121). The medieval rhetorical arts set out the multiple ways of taking or interpreting texts for their multiple levels of significance.

An example, admittedly extreme, of the discourse of patterning, is that of the erudite physician and astrologer Paracelsus (1493–1541) best known for his invention of sympathetic medicine – treating like with like: "[Nature] made liverwort and kidneywort with leaves in the shape of the parts she can cure … Do not the leaves of the thistle prickle like needles? Thanks to this sign the art of magic discovered that there is no better herb against internal prickling" (1922–23/1958, XIII, pp. 376–377; cited by Hacking 1975b, p. 42). Paracelsus, we may say, read the Book of Nature in the same way that many, indeed most, of his contemporaries read the Book of Scripture.

The key to his reading was the detection of signs, a generous God having provided signs for everything needed by man. Paracelsus consulted both the classical works of Galen and the great book of the firmament, the patterns in the stars. He wrote:

The second book of medicine is the firmament ... for it is possible to write down all medicine in the letters of one book ... and the firmament is such a book containing all virtues and all propositions ... the stars in heaven must be taken together in order that we may read the sentence in the firmament. It is like a letter that has been sent to us from a hundred miles off, and which the writer's mind speaks to us.

(XI, 171–176; cited by Hacking, 1975b, p. 41)

Both the writings of Galen and the writings in the firmament had to be read correctly to make a correct diagnosis and to suggest a cure. Just as the points of a stag's horns indicate its age, so the position of the stars could indicate the correct remedy for an illness. For Paracelsus, signs were everywhere. Such signs were to be interpreted by resemblance, reasoning was by analogy, and a universal vitalism ordained that there was a sympathy among all things (Reiss, 1982, p. 49). Every surface sign implied a deeper, hidden meaning which could be "divined" by the specialist.

Early Modern writers disparaged such reading as "rhetorical" or "poetic" and as unsuitable for serious discourse (Hamilton, 1963; Kittay & Godzich, 1987) because the texts and signs on which such reading was based were hopelessly polysemous and ambiguous, they alluded to deep, occult or mystical meanings and they were open to, indeed invited, reading between the lines. Serious discourse, they claimed, required a kind of writing which was analytical or representational in which words stood for things, the kind of discourse we think of today as written prose. Such writing required reading on, not between, the lines.

An eloquent spokesman for the new discourse was Francis Bacon, lawyer and statesman and Lord Chancellor of England before his political disgrace in 1621, who wrote extensively on the foundations of empirical science. His views best represent the intellectual and social revolutions of the seventeenth century (Webster, 1975; Reiss, 1982). In a series of works, chief among them *The advancement of learning* (AL, 1605), *Redargutio philosophiarum* (RP, c. 1608), *The New Organon*

(NO, 1620) and *The Great Instauration* (1620) Bacon offered an account of how to make language transparent to the world it was to represent. He offered a discourse of things to replace the old, and as he thought barren, discourse of words. Old knowledge, even logical proof, he claimed, was merely verbal and may not correspond to ideas or to things:

A syllogism consists of propositions, a proposition of words, and words are the counters or symbols of notions or mental concepts. If then the notions themselves, which are the life of words, are vague, ignorant, ill-defined (and this is true of the vast majority of notions concerning nature) down the whole edifice tumbles.

(*Works*, VII.125: Cogitata et Visa [CV])

Aphorisms were particularly untrustworthy for they operate "much as the mysteries of the faith do" (*Works*, IV.52: *NO*). Rather than set forth ideas plainly they "leave the wit of man more free to turn and toss" (*Works*, XIV.182: Maxims of the law).

In fact, Bacon discussed the new kind of discourse that he advocated as a kind of writing, what he called "literate experience" (*Works*, VIII.133: *NO*). Ordinary reasoning from raw experience is flawed, he thought, leading to anticipations and to imaginations and thus to allegory – relations based on resemblance and similarity. Literate or methodological experience, on the other hand, involves "the art or plan for an honest interpretation of nature, a true path from sense to intellect" (*Works*, VII.78: *RP*). In the past invention was done by [allegorical] thinking rather than by writing, but "Now no course of invention can be satisfactory unless it be carried on in writing" (VIII. 136: *NO*, I.ci).

Bacon's talk of this kind of discourse as "writing" is itself a kind of metaphor. As Reiss (1982) points out, Bacon advanced an elaborate analogy between texts and nature. Knowledge, for Bacon, is produced when the mind meets things in this special kind of language Bacon referred to as "writing." Writing involves setting the order of expressions with the order of things. The minimal parts of the world correspond in a way to the minimal parts of written language. Bacon, in fact, elaborated this metaphor by talking about the alphabet of the world – the language of creation – which one could learn to read by careful observation and analysis. This language was not the language of Adam (Aarsleff, 1982), the right *names* for things, but rather the language in which the natural world was written by the creator. That language was composed of a sort of alphabet, a table of elements, the correct reading of which was the correct perception of things. Once that language of the world was read it could be turned into knowledge by setting the spoken or written language into correspondence with it. Reiss (1982, p. 205) writes: "For him, writing is not a mere record. It is the very foundation of knowledge, whose recording it will then make possible as well: writing precedes and follows knowledge." Bacon, like Harvey – at least if Cowley's eulogy is to be trusted – saw scientific discovery as a matter of the correct reading of the Book of Nature.

Not only did the discourse change from one of patterning or analogy to one of reference and representation, the conception of signs changed correspondingly. Arguments about signs go back to antiquity (Long & Sedley, 1987). But they took on a new urgency in the early modern period. Hacking (1975b) points out that Paracelsus, like other writers of the "low" sciences of astrology, healing, and alchemy failed to draw distinctions between types of signs; the motions of the planets could be "read" no less validly than books could. Hacking comments: "In our conceptual scheme the names of the stars are arbitrary and the points of the antlers are not. For Paracelsus both are signs. [For us] the resemblances between words and stones, herbs and comets, are now lost" (1975b, p. 40). Indeed, we find it startling that anyone ever did see such resemblances.

Even such distinguished readers and writers of the Middle Ages as Augustine and Anselm, thought of signs as a two-term relation between the sign and the thing signified. Medieval scholastics such as Abelard and others who had been influenced by Aristotle, insisted on a clear distinction between signs, ideas and reality, a three-term relation (Stock, 1983, p. 378).

The distinction was fully exploited by seventeenth-century writers. "Galileo himself always recognized that signs (whether mathematical or linguistic) fall in between what is taken as the conceptualizing mind and the world of objects" and that consequently, "knowledge is a sign-manipulating activity" (Reiss, 1982, p. 33). Words and other signs could be manipulated independently of the things they represented in the attempt to make them correspond to the ideas in the mind.

With the clear distinction between words, ideas and reality, words came to be seen increasingly as potentially mischievous and misleading. Galileo, distrusting words, preferred mathematics for his physics. Locke (1690/1961) referred to words as a "perfect cheat"; Many writers urged the "study of things to the Rabble of Words" (Eisenstein, 1979, p. 700). And the Royal Society took for its motto: "*Nullius in verba*; in the words of no one." Representation and misrepresentation became central concerns. Francis Bacon, our spokesman for the new science, wrote:

Although we think we govern our words ... certain it is that words, as a Tartar's bow, do shoot back upon the understanding of the wisest, and mightily entangle and pervert the judgment. So that it is almost necessary, in all controversies and disputations, to imitate the wisdom of the mathematicians, in setting down in the very beginning the definitions of our words and terms, that others may know how we accept and understand them, and whether they concur with us or no. For it cometh to pass, for want of this, that we are sure to end there where we ought to have begun, which is in questions and differences about words.

(The advancement of learning)

Aarsleff (1982) has argued that the remarkable achievements of the Early Modern Period are attributable, in part, to the distinction they drew between ideas and signs. Words were seen as "cheats" but ideas could be entertained independently of signs and could be based on non-verbal sources such as observations. Observation, therefore, provided a new route to knowledge; one could read the book of Nature, God's book of creatures, directly. Signs, expressing these ideas, could then be judged as true or false of the world they represented.

Correspondingly, the autonomy of ideas from words, provided the basis for the mental philosophy of Descartes, Hobbes, Locke, Hume and Berkeley. Hacking (1975a) refers to this period as "the heyday of ideas" because of the certainty those philosophers had in the two fixed points, namely, things and ideas, with words taking up the shaky middle ground. Descartes, for example, had written, "So long as I confine my thoughts to my own ideas, divested of words, I do not see how I can easily be mistaken" (*Principles*, Sec. 22, 1637–44/1968) especially if we examine our ideas "isolating them from each other and scrutinizing them separately with steadfast mental gaze" (*Rules*, Rule XII). Both a new understanding of signs and a new understanding of ideas as subjective, mental entities, were made possible by clearly distinguishing them. We shall return to the topic of ideas and minds in Chapter 11.

What, then, is a representation? This problem is at the root of a host of philosophical problems but perhaps we can make some progress with this question if we recall that in the Middle Ages words, like images, were seen as having a natural connection to things – words had a true name given by Adam at creation, and images were identified with the objects they stood for – both were seen as intrinsic parts of the object – the relation is one of metonymy. Images could be sacred and therefore worshipped and to deface the word is to deface the object. Blasphemy was a punishable crime under the Inquisition and even today "Propane [sic] language is prohibited" as the sign in the skating rink I played in as a child read. Scribner and Cole (1981) reported an interview with a group of unschooled Vai informants about the arbitrariness of signs. The experimenters had asked if the sun could be called the moon and vice versa. The consensus of the group was that it could not but, interestingly, one of the group offered the Adamic theory of signs, saying "Anything that God created, His talking, the names He gave to things, cannot be changed" (p. 141).

Signs are seen as arbitrary only in the Early Modern period when words are seen as having a meaning by reference to ideas rather than directly by reference to things. Then the word loses its direct tie to the thing, it is no longer the correct name for the thing but merely represents or stands for the thing. The temptation to believe in word magic is further lessened; to deface the word is neither here nor there, it is a mere convention. But by distinguishing sign from idea the route is opened to the problem of the correctness, truth and appropriateness of representation.

The notion of "representation" has been most thoroughly examined in the writings of Foucault (1970) who points out that only in the seventeenth century did language and other sign systems come to be seen as representations. Signs are no longer seen as natural to their object but as conventions; not copies or mimesis (Morrison, 1982) but as representations in a medium (Gombrich, 1960). Gilson (1957) expressed this point brilliantly by saying that prior to Giotto a painting was a thing; from Giotto to Cezanne a painting was a representation of a thing. The graven image gave way to the picture. As we shall see in reference to the work of Alpers (1983) the idea of correct representation eclipsed the notion of symbolization in the art of the seventeenth century Dutch masters.

How are we to explain this development? The accounts we have reviewed focus upon the new understanding of the world, of language, and of ideas. I would reverse the emphasis and suggest that the new attitude to signs, to ideas, and to reality were produced by a new way of reading – the reading of signs in terms of their surface properties, their literal meanings. This too, requires some explanation.

In the preceding chapter I argued that one of the achievements of the late Middle Ages, particularly in the hands of the Aristotelian Scholastics, was to read scripture in terms of its "literal meaning." We noted the new concern with the exact correct text, separate from commentary, with due attention to word meaning, etymology, syntax, context and intention of the writer and the writer's view of the reader. Even if the interpretation required a high degree of study and scholarship, that reading was to be strictly tied to the properties of the text, or as the Reformation writers were to put it, to the meaning "grounded openly" in the text. The signs were not seen as concealing deep, mystical truths but rather as openly revealing their meanings, for all to see. A text required careful reading not the gift of personal illumination, revelation or epiphany.

This kind of reading, according to the sense, in spite of its complexity, was seen by seventeenth-century readers and writers as more or less "algorithmic," as more or less mechanical and as available to everyone if they followed correct procedures. Calculating square roots is an example of an algorithmic process; although the process is complex, if the simple rules are obeyed the correct solution will be found. Recall, too, that this was a set of beliefs about the correct method of reading; practice obviously diverged considerably from the belief. Twentieth-century readers would probably agree that reading is never algorithmic; all reading requires something like inference to the best explanation. But the assumption that such algorithmic reading was possible allowed a new and distinctive way of reading nonetheless and it allowed, for the first time, notions like figurative language, interpretation and commentary to take on a pejorative sense. To cite one case, Hobbes (1651/1958, p. 38) insisted that serious discourse avoid metaphor for "metaphors are like will-o-the-wisps."

To read algorithmically implied that all readers relying on these methods obtain the same reading or interpretation and that they obtain it on every re-reading. The correct interpretation was seen as obtainable because it was grounded openly in the text, apprehensible by the senses. It allowed a clear distinction between what was in a text and what someone may read into a text. It came to be, as we saw, the Protestant way of reading scripture.

But once this method of reading scripture was developed it was a rather simple step to assume that nature could be read in the same way. Hence, Bacon's assumption about the "alphabet" of nature. Both scripture and nature could be read by careful examination of the surface properties of the "texts" in question. Neither relied on deep meanings, hidden secrets, mystical interpretations, or a gift of the spirit; the meaning of either was written openly for all to see if one knew how to read "according to the senses."

Reading the Book of Nature

Bacon's discussion of reading the Book of Nature according to the alphabet of the world becomes more comprehensible when we recognize that Bacon was working from the "root" metaphor we encountered in the eulogy to Harvey. Bacon, like Harvey and his contemporaries, worked on the assumption that science consisted of correct reading of the Book of Nature. It was that which allowed him to think of the world as a kind of an alphabet.

It was a commonplace of the Middle Ages to speak of nature as God's book. The metaphor was carried into the early modern period. Thus Bacon (1620/1965) spoke of "the book of God's word and the book of God's work." Again, Bacon comments that true knowledge can be found only in "the volume of creation" (*Works*, IX. 371).

Galileo (Galilei, 1623/1957), too, used the metaphor of the Book of

Nature. In his *Letter to the Grand Duchess Christina* (Galilei, 1615/ 1957) he quotes approvingly from Tertullian: "We conclude that God is known first through Nature, and then again, more particularly, by doctrine; by Nature in His works, and by doctrine in His revealed word." Again, in his *Saggiatore* (Galilei, 1623/1957) he suggested that it was written in the language of mathematics. The advantage of mathematics, as I have mentioned, was that it was less prone to ambiguity and, hence, to "interpretation."

Robert Boyle, a friend of Harvey who went on to become a founding member and curator of the Royal Society held as a personal creed: "There are two chief ways to arrive at the knowledge of God's attributes; the contemplation of his works, and the study of his word" (Pilkington, 1959, p. 14). "There are two sources from which I collect my divinity," wrote Thomas Browne, a seventeenth-century cleric who was also a member of the Royal Society, talking of two Books, that of Scripture and that of Nature (Eisenstein, 1979, p. 455), as we saw in the epigram to this chapter. While the metaphor of the Book of Nature was preserved, the ways of reading that book changed with the development of new ways of reading Scripture.

In practice as well as in theory there was a clear connection between scientific methodology and Protestant theology, a connection we have discussed as involving a common way of reading. Robert Boyle who is widely known as the father of Chemistry, in addition to his role in the Royal Society also wrote such books as *Some motives and incentives to the love of God* (*Works*, 1772). Boyle, as mentioned, was a friend and follower of Harvey who took anatomy in general and circulation of the blood in particular as evidence for the existence of the divine being. Boyle celebrated the enlightenment that could arise from "dead and stinking Carkases [for in] those forsaken Mansions, [one could see] the inimitable Workmanship of the Omniscient Architect." Boyle wrote that when:

I study the Book of Nature, and consult the Glosses of Aristotle, Epicurus, Paracelsus, Harvey, Helmont, and other learn'd Expositors of that instructive Volume; I find my self oftentimes reduc'd to exclaim with the Psalmist, *How manifold are thy works, O Lord? in wisdom hast thou made them all.* Psalm 104: 24.

(Cited by Frank, 1980, p. 121)

The route to knowledge was the correct reading of the Book of Nature; humans, at best, wrote glosses.

While the metaphor was old, the "correct" way of reading, the methodical or mechanical or "algorithmic" way of reading according to the textual properties themselves, was new. For when that method of reading was applied to Nature, it turned the writings of the ancients into mere commentaries on the real text, the Book of Nature. As such they may be either criticized or set aside completely while one reads the Book of Nature for oneself. This is what Cowley said Harvey had done. Or course, we know otherwise. Harvey had carefully studied Galen and Vesalius; he just never regarded their work as an alternative to careful observation and thought (Bylebyl, 1979).

This new way of reading, whether of Nature or Scripture, was on the basis of the evidence available to the senses – what was grounded openly for everyone to see in the text or to see in Nature. Texts not so grounded, metaphorical texts for example, were to be read "largely" if at all. The product was not only a new understanding of scripture but also a new, "objective" understanding of nature. For objectivity is just reading the Book of Nature according to the evidence available to the senses.

The very notion of objectivity in science presents a difficulty for twentieth-century readers. Since the time of Kant, we have contrasted the *noumenal* world, the world of things in themselves, with the *phenomenal* world, our subjective, personal or private experience of those things. That distinction, in turn, rests on a more fundamental distinction between the knower and the known, a distinction which Havelock (1963) argued may have its root in writing. Ong adds:

By separating the knower from the known ... writing makes possible increasingly articulate introspectivity, opening the psyche as never before not only to the external object world quite distinct from itself but also to the interior self against whom the objective world is set.

(Ong, 1982, p. 105)

The distinction between the knower and the known continues to be fundamental. But in current epistemological thought, the known has become subjective, composed of bodies of beliefs, rather than of objective truths. Kant despaired of ever knowing the noumenal world and proposed instead that we add such basic psychological concepts as space, time and causality to our ontology. Pure objectivity was abandoned as unachievable (Cassirer, 1957). In recent times, this subjectivity has been described in terms of the "theory-ladenness" of observation (Hanson, 1958). In this vein, philosophers of science such as Kuhn (1962) have argued, convincingly I believe, that all scientific knowledge presupposes a perspectival framework or "paradigm" which makes even scientific knowledge fundamentally psychological in nature. At the same time some historians of science such as Polanyi (1958, p. 16) have argued that knowledge in science is personal, committing one "passionately and far beyond our comprehension, to a vision of reality." If so, the development of objectivity in the Early Modern Period would seem to be a Pyrrhic victory – small gains at enormous expense – or else just an error, a step in the wrong direction.

Although seventeenth century writers were optimistic that the application of the appropriate methods, what they thought of as the correct reading of the Book, whether Scripture or Nature, would provide access to religious truth and allow the discovery of the ultimate structure of reality, we in the twentieth century recognize the dogmatism of their religious views and the unattainability of their scientific goals. Our generation aspires to the more modest goal of formulating theories, hypotheses and claims, and criticizing them in the light of the best evidence. In the place of objective truths we are happy to have warranted assertions and justified beliefs.

All is not lost. If we adopt what I think of as a discourse-based epistemology which appeals to such discourse categories as *claim* versus *evidence* we can find a rather direct mapping to the older and bolder epistemology of the seventeenth century which distinguished the *given* from the *interpreted*, the *facts* from the *theory*, and the *observations* from the *inferences*. Even if we are unwilling, these days, to defend a hard and fast distinction between the given and the interpreted, we can still see the contribution of the seventeenth century's concern with objectivity to the development of present scientific thought if we note the rather straightforward translation of *theory* to *claim* and *fact* to *evidence for a claim*. True, the concepts have shifted in the translation but any achievements of the former can be preserved through the translation. That is, if we take "their" observations as "our" evidence, we may preserve their achievements even as we relativize them. Today's fact which provides evidence for some more general theory or claim may be tomorrow's theory or claim for which new evidence is required. And so on. Thus twentieth-century epistemology relativizes rather than abandons seventeenth-century epistemology.

How to read the Book of Nature

The metaphor of the Book of Nature cut two ways. First, it allowed the set of concepts devised for "reading" Scripture to be applied to nature. Epistemology, the correct method for studying nature, was applied hermeneutics, the correct method for studying Scripture. The key, we may recall, was to read according to "sense," the surface or literal meaning open for all to see. The meaning of scripture was to be "grounded openly" in the text. Spiritual meanings and allegorical meanings in general came to be seen as the inventions and imaginings of the readers rather than grounded in the intentions of the author or the meanings in the text. Just as one had to distinguish the literal meaning of the text from its putative allegorical meanings, so too, in reading the Book of Nature one had to distinguish the "patterns in the world" from the "dreams of the imagination" as Bacon (1620/1965, p. 323) was to put it.

Just how this was to be done was set out by Robert Boyle in his accounts of his experiments with the vacuum pump carried out in the 1660s and which have been recently examined in detail by Shapin (1984) and Shapin and Schaffer (1985). Boyle (1772) believed that everyone who witnessed his experiments with the vacuum jar would see just what he had seen. He described his experiments in such detail that it was as if the reader was present with him in his laboratory. What he and anyone else present in the laboratory would have seen constituted a "fact," the true concern of the new science. Hypotheses, conjectures and the like were "clearly man-made and could, therefore, be contested" (Shapin, 1984, p. 502).

Consequently, Boyle left a "conspicuous interval" between the descriptions of his experimental findings and his occasional "discourses" upon their interpretation (Boyle, 1772, Vol. 1, notes 1, 2;

see Shapin, 1984). He marked the texts falling on one side of that interval by such modals as *probably, might be, and perhaps*, while those on the factual side, he asserted boldly.

Robert Hooke, a student of Boyle, and also a member of the Royal Society of London, expressed the same concern. In the Preface to his major work *Micrographia* (1665/1961), he sets out his goal as describing nature "as it is" contrasting observation with mere guesses, conjectures and conclusions:

> Wherever [the reader] finds that I have ventur'd at any small Conjectures, at the causes of the things I have observed, I beseech him to look upon them only as doubtful Problems, and uncertain ghesses, and not as unquestionable Conclusions ...
>
> (The Preface, p. 5)

> ... I indeavoured (as far as I was able) first to discover the true appearance, and next to make a plain representation of it.
>
> (The Preface, p. 24)

Reading nature and writing about it, then, was based on the distinction between what was in the mind as opposed to what was in the world. It was an attempt to honor Bacon's injunction not to mistake a "dream of the imagination" for the "pattern in the world." The injunction applied equally to reading the Book of Scripture and the Book of Nature.

If properly read, there would be no conflict between the two books. Galileo, for example, held that "the true senses of scriptural texts" will concord with "physical conclusions [based on] manifest sense and necessary demonstrations" as long as one clearly distinguishes "the meaning of the Bible ... from his own *interpretation*; ... not what is in the Bible, but what he has found in himself and imagines to be there" (Galilei, 1615/1957, p. 186). The distinction between what was in the text or world and what was seen to be in there, was sufficient to divide not only "true" from "false" religions but also the pseudo-sciences from the genuine sciences: astronomy from astrology, chemistry from alchemy, mathematics from numerology, predicting from foretelling and the like (Toulmin, 1972; Hacking, 1975b).

As an example of the semantic shift involved consider the concept of *foretelling* and its more modern equivalent *predicting*. Both mean saying something about the future. However, foretelling implies the ability to tell the future by means of signs, analogies, and allegories, the invention of which depends on the possession of special powers. Prediction also depends upon signs, but now on signs which can be read mechanically, by anyone without the possession of special powers. The first is part of the "enchanted" world in which dreams of the imagination are not clearly distinguished from the patterns in the world. Predictions were to be based on objective, that is observable, facts.

Locke (cited by Aarsleff, 1982, p. 57) too, associated the correct way of using language with the correct way of investigating nature. He claimed that words are useful only if they are based on attention to "obvious appearances" and "sensible qualities" and anyone who thinks otherwise "will never become a chemist but remain an alchemist."

And this was the distinction that was honored in the new attempt to represent the world, to put, as we may say, the world on paper. How to take a text, what to treat as given and what as a product of the imagination is, of course, the issue of the consciousness and management of the illocutionary force of a proposition. When the means were developed for determining how texts were to be correctly taken, the one true historical meaning free from fantasy and imagination, the same means could be applied to the observation of nature. Stars could be seen as stars rather than as divine messengers (although the latter was, and is difficult to shed completely). Understanding how to take texts and how to "take" nature will provide the basis for a theory of how literacy contributed to modern thought.

Cassirer (1951) in his account of the philosophy of the Enlightenment provides a cogent summary of this new attitude to discourse:

... truth is revealed not in God's words but in his work; it is not based on the testimony of Scripture or tradition but is visible to us at all times. But it is understandable only to those who know nature's handwriting and can decipher her text. The truth of nature cannot be expressed in mere words ... [but] in mathematical constructions, figures and numbers. And in these symbols nature presents itself in perfect form and clarity. Revelation by means of the sacred word can never achieve ... such precision, for words are always ... ambiguous. Their meaning must always be given them by man ... In nature ... the whole plan of the universe lies before us.

(p. 43)

But right reading of either Scripture or Nature depends not only upon the method, according to the surface features, whether senses of texts or appearances of nature, but also upon the issue of final authority. Who is to decide what a text means or what the Book of Nature truly says? What or who is the final arbiter? Recall Cowley's and Boyle's dethronement of the ancients by referring to them as mere commentators on a text; the real text, they said, was written by God and observable by man.

A new way of reading, then, depended not only on new means for reading and writing but also, at least if it was to supplant more traditional ways, required the establishment of some court to rule on the validity of readings or interpretations. Church and Crown had traditionally provided authority to decide on correct reading of scripture and correct interpretation of the law. This point is well known in regard to law; law without courts is pointless. Anderson (1989, p. 84) points out that "unless the right of interpretation is 'democratized', the mere existence of written laws changes little." So too, careful writing exploiting literal meanings would carry little weight unless there was some means of establishing agreement as to the correct reading of the Book of Nature. The court to establish the correct reading was none other than the idea of the "testimony of the senses," what anyone could see "with a faithful eye" as Hooke put it. William Harvey wrote: "trust nothing I say; I appeal to none but thine eyes." Robert Boyle wrote his experimental reports in such a way as to turn readers into "virtual witnesses," describing only things that readers would have seen with their own eyes if they had been present (Shapin, 1984, p. 500).

But the "testimony of the senses" available to everyone is again not a cause but an implication of the new epistemology. Recall that the drive to isolate the literal, historical, intended meaning resulted in procedures, a hermeneutics, for deciding complex cases. Interpretation was to be "grounded openly" in the text, but yet it also involved lexical, syntactic and historical scholarship to decide many cases. Historical grounds for an interpretation may seem to be hardly "openly grounded" in the text. But in a sense they were. We should think of "grounded openly" as based on strict, specifiable method, a mechanical or methodical way of examining and weighing evidence.

The algorithm need not be simple, nor need it be infallible. But it must be seen to be mechanical and not dependent upon the whim or inclination or fantasy of the interpreter. Neither tea leaves or chicken guts, nor allegory or aphorism can be read algorithmically. Scripture, the Protestants thought (falsely, many would say) and nature, the early modern scientists thought (falsely, many would say) could be so read because they were clearly written by the unswerving hand of God.

Reading God's other book, the Book of Nature, then was a rather straightforward application of the principles of reading that had developed for reading scripture towards the end of the Middle Ages. That method was one of reading "according to the sense," the literal, or surface meaning of the text. Such close or strict reading allowed for the first time interpretation and commentary to be thought of pejoratively. Interpretation and commentary were ancient practices and concepts of interpretation were equally ancient. What was new was the sense that they were debased coin relative to the true understanding that could be derived from careful reading and strict observation. What was required to turn the method into an institution was both a set of texts – scripture and nature, a set of interpretive practices – according to the sense, and a court of appeal for determining the correct reading. That court was democratized by the assumption that judgment was to be based on the evidence plain for all to see. In fact, even with a method and a court, what is "plain for all to see" never arrives at unanimity. Protestant sects, like the heretics before them, continue to find new "readings" and scientific schools continue to find new models. But that is not the point. The point is that the method for reading Scripture turned out to be useable for reading everything else; Protestantism and Modern Science were the products.

This, of course, is not the end of the story. Protestantism failed, some would say spectacularly, to arrive at the true, ultimate meaning of scripture and the empiricism of early modern science failed, ultimately, to yield the true knowledge of the book of Nature. The relative success of the method in the two domains is informative. The algorithmic method of reading "according to the sense" was largely inappropriate for reading scriptural texts in the first place. Scripture, whether Bible, Koran, Veda or Talmud is a product of an oral tradition in which the literal–metaphorical distinction is not readily honored; indeed culturally significant texts say, mean, imply, allude and allegorize often all at once. We may return to Frye (1982, p. 61), a scholar who has devoted his life to interpreting these texts, who says: "The primary and literal meaning of the Bible, then, ... is the metaphorical meaning." Utterances such as "The kingdom of heaven is within you" or that "God in three persons" do not fall easily into the analytical categories of literal as opposed to metaphorical meaning. They literally meant what we now think of as merely metaphorical.

Yet there is no way of going back to the mystical readings of the later Middle Ages, either of scripture nor of nature. One who, these days, reads :

Sermons in stones,
Books in babbling brooks
And good in everything.

(Shakespeare, *As you like it*, II, i, 17–20)

is either mad, in love or a deconstructionist!

The new way of reading was sufficient to underwrite a new "writing" of the world, the attempt to represent the newly discovered world on paper. That is the subject of the next chapter.

A HISTORY OF WRITTEN DISCOURSE: FROM MNEMONICS TO REPRESENTATIONS

Emperor Lothar III's great deeds were inscribed on lead tablets and buried in his tomb so they would never be forgotten.

(K. F. Morrison, 1990, p. 215)

Beginning in the thirteenth century texts began their transformation from dramas into documents.

(K. F. Morrison, 1990, pp. 247ff)

As we saw in Chapter 5, if one is to rely upon writing as a means of preserving significant information, some attempt must be made to make up for what is lost in simple transcription. Scripts readily capture, record or represent verbal form – lexis and syntax. The attitude of the speaker to that verbal form, varying from enthusiastic endorsement to cynical disdain, is not captured by an alphabet. The elaboration of lexical and graphic means to represent speaker's attitude and thereby bring it both into awareness and under control, represents a major achievement, comparable in significance, I suggested, to the invention of a script. Indeed, it could be suggested that the elaboration of these graphic means for representing the force of an expression is what turns scripts into writing systems.

In this chapter we turn to the problem of how these new resources for specifying intended meanings in writing developed and how that development made possible the notion that a text can stand as a representation of a writer's intention rather than merely as a mnemonic for remembering that intention. It was a development, as we shall see, that was built upon new ways of reading and writing texts. In the chapter following this we shall examine how these new resources were exploited in building representations of the world, in putting the world on paper.

Creating texts which represent rather than merely remind involved three correlated achievements. First, means had to be developed for

creating texts with determinative, monological meaning – the traditional problems of literal and textual meaning; second, texts had to be
created which could be seen as adequately representing and therefore
standing in the place of the putative intentions of the writer; and third,
texts had to be seen as adequately indicating how they are to be taken,
whether as factual or speculative and whether literal or metaphorical.
Let us consider them in turn.

(1) Texts as reminders versus texts as representations

As long as texts, like speech, are seen as carrying multiple levels of
meaning – of hinting, alluding, insinuating, allegorizing as well as
stating, with significant aspects of meaning to be indicated by context
and intonation – it is impossible to say exactly or definitively what a
sentence or text means. Further, as long as texts serve primarily as
transcriptions of the lexical and syntactic properties of speech they
could at best assist one in remembering what was said but could not
fully represent how it was to be taken. In face-to-face contexts, the
solution is relatively simple. The way to decide the intended meaning
of an oral utterance is to keep talking until some understanding and
agreement is reached. The actual language utilized in the process
cannot be taken *as* the definitive agreement; the agreement is the
mutual understanding.

Even when writing enters the picture the relation between
reminders and representations may not change. As long as written
texts are seen as imprecise expressions of intentions and consequently
potentially polysemous, written texts could not constitute the agreement; the agreement would remain the meeting of minds. Any written
record would serve merely as equivalent to an authenticating signature. The text would again not constitute the agreement; it could only
remind readers of the agreement just as a mark or a seal would do.

There is historical evidence for just such a development. Pindar and
Aeschylus, the first who commented on the subject, thought of writing
as a reminder of spoken utterances (Havelock, 1982, p. 201; Thomas,
1989, p. 21). The view persisted through the Middle Ages (Camille,
1992, p. 18). Written records were thought of and treated as reminders
rather than as representations. Clanchy (1979) has shown how auth-

ority devolved to a written document in the eleventh and twelfth centuries in England. Prior to the reliance on documents, ownership of a piece of property would be transferred by a witnessed ceremony and the transfer of some symbolic object. Even when written deeds came to be used it was common to attach to the piece of paper some less symbolic item, such as a clod of earth, to authenticate the agreement. By the thirteenth century the *Magna Carta*, a carefully negotiated, signed and sealed written document could stand as the agreement. Having signed such a document there was no possibility of a signatory evading the specified conditions by saying that that was not what he had intended; the document represented the intention. Illich (1991) provides a colourful description of how oral oaths came to be replaced by documents:

In an oral society, a man has to stand by his word. He confirms his word by taking an oath, which is a conditional curse called upon himself in the event that he should become unfaithful. While swearing, he grasps at his beard or his balls, pledging his flesh as a troth ... Under the literate regime, the oath pales before the manuscript: it is no more the recall but the record that counts.

(pp. 39–40)

Not only were early documents treated as reminders rather than representations, the general belief about writing supported this use. Carruthers (1990) provided overwhelming evidence that the medieval writers thought of writing on paper as essentially equivalent to writing on the mind: "reading and memorizing were taught as they were in antiquity, as one single activity" (p. 101). Indeed, written texts were used in the Middle Ages primarily for checking one's memory rather than as objects of representation in their own right. Thus monks in training were urged to provide themselves with tablets on which the Psalms were written, not so they could consult them, but rather "so that when they stopped they could sharpen their memory with the help of their companion" (p. 88). Knowledge was in the mind; writing was mnemonic, a reminder. Carruthers cites Isidore of Seville's definition of the purpose of letters as allowing one to "hold things in memory" and "enable us to hear again and retain in memory the voices/words of those who are not actually present" (p. 106). Perhaps in this context the irony of writing down the great deeds of Lothar and then burying the text "so they would never be forgotten" becomes comprehensible (Morrison, 1990, p. 215). Perhaps not.

If writing is simply mnemonic, written signs cannot be taken as adequate representations of the beliefs and intentions of the writer and hence capable of standing in the place of those beliefs and intentions; the sign simply reminds one of the intended meaning. Indeed, as long as writing preserves only the lexis and syntax, then non-lexical aspects of audience-directed intention, that is, the speaker's attitude to what is said, is lost and must be recovered from other sources such as memory of the histrionic sound of the original speaker's voice or the context in which it was spoken. Under such conditions there is no possibility of closing the gap between what a word or sentence means and what one means by it (Grice, 1989). Signs are just reminders; the signs themselves cannot be taken as adequately representing meanings intended by the speaker or writer.

The view that writing is merely mnemonic has a second implication. As we saw in the last chapter, the evolution of modern thought depended upon the distinction between signs and the ideas they represented. But that distinction could not be made as long as meanings were thought of as in the heart rather than in the sign. Thus the view of writing as mnemonic is congruent with the medieval view of signs.

So how did written texts come to be seen as having a definitive meaning which adequately represented a writer's intention and which could, therefore, stand as a representation of that intention? The answer lay in the invention of graphic and lexical devices for indicating not only what was said but also how it was to be taken. Relations between propositions could be marked explicitly through grammatical and lexical means – we discussed relative pronouns and subordinating conjunctions as well as nominalizations in Chapter 5 – and attitudes to propositions could be expressed through the use of indirect discourse which gives free reign to the lexicalization of speech act and mental states. The effect was that both what was said and how it was to be taken could be indicated in the text and recovered without the need to consult either the author or a specialist in interpretation. The consequence was that the text came to be seen as autonomous, as an adequate representation of what the writer intended. It was no longer merely a reminder of what was meant; it represented that meaning. The route is open to the deliberate attempt to create texts as archival representations of the facts of the world (see Bäuml, 1980, p. 249).

(2) Texts without voice

A popular refrain of post-modernism is "the death of the author." The author is replaced by "the birth of the reader" (Barthes, 1977). The story of literacy is somewhat different. The death of the author is replaced by the development of texts which, in a sense, speak for themselves. They lose the "voice" of the speaker or writer to become what has been called "autonomous" or "authorless text" (Harris, 1989; Olson, 1977). Gellner (1988; pp. 70–71) states: "The most significant thing about writing is that it makes possible the detachment of affirmation from the speaker. Semantic content acquires a life of its own." How can this come about?

Rousseau (1754–91/1966) pointed out how the substitution of marks for voice loses track not only of the personal voice or "signature" of the author but also loses all indications of intonation and emphasis. He was speaking as a modern, silent reader. McLuhan reminds us of James Joyce's character Mrs. Equitone who spoke like a book in a measured, scripted manner. But how did text come to be thought of as voiceless and, hence, to be read silently?

Early writing was seen as capturing voice; writing spoke to those who could read. Havelock (1982) points out that Greek writing had to adjust speech in order to produce a new form of written discourse. Earlier writing tried to emulate speech. The content of what was written was thought of as "something that is being said aloud rather than silently stated or recorded. It has the quality of an oral announcement addressed to a particular occasion or to a particular person." Thus many early inscriptions "spoke" to the reader. The caption on a physical object may read: "I am Nestor's cup" or "Mantiklos dedicated me" or "Whoso steals me will go blind" (pp. 190–191).

Levy-Bruhl (1923; 1910/1926) provided many accounts of how written texts were seen by those unfamiliar with writing as "saying" things, that is as speaking and hence as instruments of divination. Harbsmeier (1988) cites an eighteenth-century account given by a freed slave named Equiano, of how people unfamiliar with writing responded to books:

A Bechuana one day asked what's that on the table there? When he was told that it was books, and that these books told news, he put one of the books to his ear, but being unable to hear any sound, he said: this book doesn't tell me anything, and put it back on the table saying: "Might it be asleep?"

(p. 254)

Jaynes (1976) has made interesting use of this attitude to written inscriptions in his theory of the evolution of consciousness, arguing that prior to the invention of writing, remembered events were sometimes experienced as spoken in the mind by a god or a spirit rather than as the product of one's own memory and imagination. He provides ample evidence of this attitude in both the Homeric epics and in the biblical prophets who hear the voice of the gods or of God speaking to them. The argument against this view is that although some people in heightened "spiritual" states may indeed experience their ideas as a visitation, normal cognition for most of the people most of the time was then for them, much as it is now for us. Nonetheless, it remains entirely possible that the dividing line between what is seen as originating in the mind and what in the world was in fact redrawn with the beginning of writing and again in the Early Modern period.

Just as writing can be seen as the attempt to give marks "voice," so the process of reading may be seen as giving voice to written texts; the written text merely provided clues to producing the real oral form. The vast literature on "oral interpretation" is devoted to the process of restoring particular properties of voice – intonation, phrasing, pausing and the like – in the process of reading a text aloud. The attempt is to read in such a way as allows the audience to hear the voice of the writer of the text rather than just the voice of the reader. Even when reading for ourselves such famous orations as Churchill's "We will fight" or Martin Luther King's "I have a dream" we may mentally reconstruct their voices as well as their words. What the written text does is to preserve the words, not the voice. Reading in the Middle Ages was primarily oral reading: the restoration of the voice was critical to capturing the intended meaning. Dom Leclercq (1961) wrote:

... in the Middle Ages, as in antiquity, they read usually, not as today, principally with the eyes, but with the lips, pronouncing what they saw, and with the ears, listening to the words pronounced, hearing what is called the "voices of the pages."

(pp. 18–19)

Clanchy (1979) points out that the same was true of Medieval writing. Eadmer of Canterbury, an eleventh-century cleric thought of composing in writing as "dictating to himself" (p. 218). We moderns acknowledge that the recovery of "voice" is important to poetry and to oral reading, particularly the oral reading of dialogue, but deny that it is important to the silent reading of prose; we allow lexicon, syntax and genre to determine the meaning. We read "He insisted that the book was his" without mentally "hearing" the insistent tone. Lexis comes to bear more and more of the tone.

It is relatively obvious how written records could contribute to the loss of the speaker's voice; transcription represents the words of Churchill, Martin Luther King, men and women, boys and girls, kings and subjects, with exactly the same letters, the same script. Voice along with stress and intonation and other markers of illocutionary force are lost when utterances are transcribed but can be reinvented by the reader in some circumstances. Listener-directed intentions, what the speaker or writer wants the listener or reader to believe he or she means, may be represented in the utterance to the extent that they can be lexicalized in the utterance or its linguistic context. Crafting discourse so as to specify how the author wants his utterance to be taken is what allows that text to stand in for the intentions of the speaker or writer. But once that is achieved, or even assumed to be achieved, the text can be treated as meaning what it says – one need have no further concern as to the putative further meanings lying behind the text or between the lines. Interpretation becomes recovery rather than invention.

Detachment of a text from a speaker thus requires the development of alternative devices for representing what, in speech, is carried by voice. Some features are irretrievably lost – the stringy voice of T. S. Eliot and the sonorous voice of Dylan Thomas – cannot be captured in a writing system. But those aspects of meaning carried by voice such as the relation between clauses, the problem of cohesion (Tannen,

1985) and the attitude of the speaker to what is said can be managed to some extent through lexical and grammatical means. Those not managed can be disparaged or ignored. Only when both what was said and how it is to be taken are indicated in the text can the text be seen as autonomous. Texts will have moved from mnemonics to representations.

Let us contrast this attitude with that of oral texts and oral tradition. Some degree of detachment from the original speaker's voice occurs in the oral contexts when texts are memorized and cited or recited by another person. In ritual speech such as the circumcision rituals of Madagascar (Bloch, 1975) or for that matter our own recitation of the national anthem or the Lord's Prayer, whether in English or in Latin, the current speaker is not the author but a spokesperson. In such cases the relation between the "author" and the spokesperson is obscured. Biblical prophets such as Jeremiah tended to think they were not speaking for themselves at all but for God perhaps because they were quoting words earlier attributed to God. In quoting speech who is to decide what the true intention expressed by the utterance is? Who is to decide if an utterance is to be offered as a hint, a rhetorical question, a conjecture or a bold assertion? A performer in an oral context may have heard how an utterance was originally presented; the how is as poignant as the what. But as we noted earlier, in many cases the burden fell on performer as interpreter whose choice depends upon the needs of himself or his audience:

the audience wanted a story with plenty of action and movement, the story, as a rule, showed no great command of character drawing; this was left to the reciter for portrayal by change of voice and gesture.

(Chaytor, 1945, p. 3)

A reader is faced with the analogous problem. The words of the utterance are fixed in writing but the illocutionary force of the utterance may be left to the judgment of the reader. It is the reader who must provide "the voice." For some texts the reader will have great latitude. For others that "voice" may be fixed lexically by the writer. If the text is not seen as an adequate representation of what was meant, of meaning only what it says, the gap must be filled by the reader, whether oneself or priest or prophet – anyone who has the authority and is willing to take on that responsibility. Under such conditions the text cannot serve as a fixed or invariant representation of meaning or intention and cannot serve as the basis of an archival research tradition.

To summarize, in an oral context, a poet, orator or conversationalist tends to rely on direct quotation of the words of the speaker, to some degree of accuracy, using their tone of voice to convey the speech act involved. If this preserved discourse is to stand in for the original intentions of the speaker, both lexical means for representing the speaker's listener-directed intentions, essentially speech act verbs, and a set of concepts including that of literal meaning must be invented and employed consistently. When both the appropriate concepts and the lexical resources were available writers and speakers could set out to create texts which could serve as autonomous representations of meaning. It is no longer seen as necessary to consult the author as to what the text means; the text may be taken as adequately representing a specific intended meaning. Texts have begun the important journey from dramas to documents (Morrison, 1990, p. 247).

(3) Texts as literal or as metaphorical representations

The history of literacy is in part learning to construct documents which could serve as embodiments of and arbiters of meaning. Texts can serve such a function only if there is some clear indication of whether they are to be taken as "strictly speaking," "loosely speaking," and as literal or as metaphorical. Stated otherwise, they require some explicit management of illocutionary force.

Legal documents illustrate the formation of documentary texts which are to be interpreted strictly. Pollock and Maitland (1898), in their classical account of the development of English law, describe the origin and uses of Common Law "writs." These explicit written statements setting out a complaint which had to be answered were among the first types of documents submitted to "inform the jury" (Vol. 2, p. 628). Clanchy (1985) pointed out how these writs contributed to standardization not only of the forms of complaint but the complainants themselves. As every writ, being preserved, served as a precedent, the number of types of writs was restricted and their manner of interpretation routinized. Nuance of meaning was sacrificed to the gain in bureaucratic convenience; on the other hand, an enormously increased number of cases could be dealt with because of their standard forms and routine interpretation. Secondly, anyone could file such a writ, thereby leveling to some extent the social differences that had dominated considerations of justice since feudal times.

It may be worth noting how such "writs" could come to be seen as autonomous representations of a complaint. Interpretation was routinized not only by formalizing "legalese," but also by fixing illocutionary force. The writ was a "claim." The convention determined the nature of the speech act involved. Legal writs are distinctive, then, not only in the use of standard language but in controlling formally the illocutionary force of the text to form a distinctive genre of discourse.

The use of writs and written evidence are early examples of treating written records as adequate representations of meaning – they are not employed simply as reminders of the personal beliefs and desires of their authors; their formulaic form allowed control both of the literal meaning and the speech act involved, both of which reduced openness to variable interpretation. If the complainant's original intention was lost sight of in interpreting the meaning of the document, so much the worse for that original intention. The document stands supreme. What becomes a matter of dispute is not in the intention of the claimant but the interpretation of the document. Such texts have become representations. It is worth noting that such speech act terms as "state," "claim," "evidence," "witness" came into systematic use in the formulation of such writs, terms which themselves help to determine how utterances are to be taken. So successful was the procedure that Robert Hooke (1665/1961) adopted the written, archival tradition of English Common Law as a suitable model for the writing and recording and accumulation of advances in science. Texts written to a formula which guaranteed, so far as possible, that they could be interpreted in only one way marked an important advance in the development of written prose.[1]

---

[1] The concept of evidence which played an important role in classical Greek science and philosophy was derived from law (Lloyd, personal communication, 1993).

The fact that it was so difficult to evolve a tradition in which writing could serve as an unambiguous representation of a speaker's intention should not be taken as implying that speech lacks the resources to make one's intentions clear. That is far from the case. Speakers can generally make their meanings embarrassingly clear; the trick is to make them sufficiently clear in writing so that one is willing to allow the text *itself* to stand as a representation of one's meanings – so that we can allow our text to stand as our emissary, so to speak. Plato, we may recall, was unwilling to grant writing such authority. To make the effort practicable required that the many strands of meaning which are frequently bound together in speech be distinguished and explicitly managed in writing.

The speech practices and the basic distinctions which were so difficult to capture in writing are present both in everyday speech and in oral cultures. The totemic beliefs that so puzzled Levy-Bruhl (1910/1926, pp. 118–122) such as the Australian Aboriginal belief that "A gum-tree is a frog," or the Huichol Indians of Mexico's belief that "Corn is deer," the Nuer belief that "Twins are birds" (Evans-Pritchard, 1956) or the Dorze belief that "the leopard is a Christian animal who observes the fasts of the Ethiopian Orthodox Church" (Sperber, 1975, cited by Lloyd, 1990, p. 19) are clear cases of what we would see as metaphorical discourse. Furthermore, as we saw in Chapter 5 many oral cultures distinguish "straight" from "crooked" speech, the latter referring to metaphorical and allegorical discourse. Such metalinguistic concepts are close to those exploited in dealing with written texts.

Yet the problem is not that simple, for metaphorical statements such as "Corn is deer" are taken as literally true by their makers. Anthropologists were unable to convince their informants that they did not literally mean what they said, that "Corn was *like* deer" for example (Sperber, 1975, p. 93.) Furthermore, interpretive practices show a relatively low degree of conventionalization – there is little theory of interpretation. McKellin (1990) and Duranti (1985) point out that what an utterance means depends upon how it is taken by the audience. Duranti, commenting on the interpretive strategies of the Samoans says, "A certain meaning is possible because others accept it within a particular context" (p. 47). The utterance, it appears, is not seen as a direct expression or adequate representation of the speaker's intention.

Thus what appears to be missing is not the ability to use language in a variety of ways including metaphor but the formation of a general concept of metaphor as distinguished from the literal meaning of the utterance. The distinction, it seems, is not explicitly contrastively represented in either the language or the thought of the Aboriginals, the Huichol, the Nuer or the Dorze.

Lloyd (1990) makes a case for the distinctively western origins of a clear conceptual distinction between the literal and the metaphorical and traces the origins of these concepts to the classical Greeks. Although Plato had a number of concepts which are almost synonyms for metaphor terms like "model" and "likenesses," it was only with Aristotle that an explicit contrast was drawn between the strict or proper meaning of a word or statement and the extended or metaphorical meaning. Lloyd points out that Plato in *Sophist* refers to "likenesses" as "a most slippery tribe," thereby using a metaphor to criticize a metaphor. Aristotle was much more systematic on this point condemning "metaphora" in his logic and his natural philosophy; clarity required the use of univocal terms and the exclusion of metaphorical expressions. In commenting on Empedocles' statement that salt sea was the sweat of the earth, Aristotle had written:

Perhaps to say that is to speak adequately for poetic purposes – for metaphor is poetic – but it is not adequate for understanding the nature [of a thing].

(Meteorology 357a24ff; cited by Lloyd, 1990, p. 21)

Stock (1983) discusses in detail the form that this debate took in the Middle Ages over the Eucharist. When readers encountered the biblical statement that Jesus took bread saying "This is my body" how were they to take that text? In the Middle Ages such texts were unproblematic; they meant literally, allegorically, morally, mystically and perhaps other ways as well. But such texts were increasingly problematic for Medieval scholars after the thirteenth century who were familiar with the Aristotelean distinctions as expressed in Latin and Arabic treatises. Was the text meant literally – as required by the doctrine of the Mass – or was it meant metaphorically? – the view that was largely adopted in the Reformation. Morrison (1982, pp. 235–236) points out that important Christian texts such as "This is my body; this is the cup of my blood" and "The Church is the body of Christ" were taken as figurative by both Luther and Calvin.

Stock adds that this interpretive tradition which distinguished the literal and the metaphorical was related to naturalistic, scientific thought:

Twelfth-century naturalistic thought could in theory have ... progressed without intersecting the rise of other interpretive traditions. But in practice it did not. ... The growth of a more literate society did for naturalism what it had done for the eucharist: it placed the whole matter on an intellectualist plane and dismissed as rustic, popular, and irrational all that did not accord with a *ratio* synonymous with the inner logic of texts.

(p. 318)

That inner logic was exploited in reading texts and nature, and in the new way of using writing as an explicit representation which itself could be treated as an object of thought.

It is tempting to assume that even if metaphor presented a problem, literal meaning is simple and universally exploited and understood. We all recall Molière's "Bourgeois Gentilhomme" who discovered that he had been speaking prose all his life. Of course, he had not; it takes years of specialized training to write prose or to come to speak it, as the unfortunate Mrs. Equitone, James Joyce's character who spoke like a book, and some others, do. The same is true of speaking literally.

Modern prose is a specialized form of language; it is specialized, I suggest, in that it is the form of language in which the textual/sentence meaning may be *taken* as the intended meaning. What the sentence means is seen as being sufficiently articulated that it can be taken as an adequate representation of what the speaker means. Since a speaker's intention is ordinarily somewhat richer than the expression, the adequate representation of that intention will require both a more elaborate, appropriately qualified, expression but also, and more importantly, an explicit representation of how the speaker intends the listener to take the utterance. Markers of illocutionary force, including grammar, lexicalization and punctuation, which indicate how the speaker intends the reader or listener to take the propositional content, whether, for example as a suggestion, a statement or a demand, must move inside the sentence structure. The result is modern prose. Boas suggested that the form of modern prose was shaped by the fact that it is "written to be read, not spoken" (Kittay & Godzich, 1987, p. 194).

To return to the theme of the last chapter, part of the problem arises from the fact that a script preserves only the verbal, that is the lexical and syntactic properties of the utterance; other aspects of meaning, such as the tentativeness or assertiveness of the utterance, marked by stress and intonation, will be lost in the transcription. Writing requires that these properties be represented graphically through punctuation or lexically by means of such verbs as "assume," "infer," "suggest" or the like, if expressions are not to be open to interpretation. Creating representations requires not only an understanding of these differences but conceptual and lexical control of them through marking how they are to be taken – providing explicit indications of whether it is intended as a threat or a promise, as metaphorical or literal, as fact or as conjecture and so on. While most if not all forms of discourse occur and are distinguished in oral speech and in oral societies, these distinctions tend not to be lexicalized. Speaker's attitude to a proposition is not explicitly stated. Consequently, it is difficult to control systematically. Secondly, the meanings of terms within the propositional content have to be well defined and systematically employed if literal meaning is to be preserved.

Once precise notions were worked out as to how written texts could explicitly represent speakers' audience-directed intentions, it became a relatively simple matter to recognize when readers or interpreters were reading things into texts or for that matter into nature. As we noted earlier, Francis Bacon (1620/1965, p. 323) could defend careful observation in science by declaiming "God forbid that we should take a dream of the imagination for a pattern in the world."

Once a new way of reading texts and nature was developed, a written form could be developed to match those habits of reading. Specifically, once the notion of a text with a single definitive meaning had been invented it was a relatively straightforward matter to begin to write texts which fit that model. The technical means involved creating dictionaries and elaborating punctuation but also inventing genre which exploited only a limited class of speech events and then labelling propositions as statements of fact, as conjectures, as probable causes and the like. Standard elementary textbooks, for example, consist of an unremitting flow of assertions, that is, statements offered as true.

What texts as representations required was not only a clear understanding of literal meaning – and which thereby saw metaphor as unreliable – but an understanding of how to control how texts were to be taken. Hence, the canonical way of taking texts was as statements which literally expressed what their readers would have seen with their own eyes had they been present. These are not statements without intended meanings but rather statements which are intended to be taken literally, as true to the facts they represent. When this goal is achieved even approximately, the text can stand in for the intentions of the writer; statements are no longer simply mnemonics for those intentions (cf. Bäuml, 1980, p. 265; Morrison, 1990, p. 215; Stock, 1990, p. 126).

Speaking or writing literally by design, that is writing modern prose, then, is nothing more than the attempt to control how the reader takes the text. Of course, this goal is never achievable; texts written to be read (or taken) one way may be taken quite another way. Bishop Usher in the seventeenth century took the book of Genesis to be written as a historical document and concluded that the world was created in 4002 BC. Such readings are sometimes enormously productive. The German anthropologist Heinrich Schliemann (1979) read the Homeric poems as geographic manuals and thereby succeeded in discovering ancient Troy. Helge Ingstad was able to discover the earliest settlement by the Norwegian Vikings at L'Anse aux Meadows on the northern tip of Newfoundland on the basis of a careful reading of the Norse Sagas (*Macleans*, August 5, 1991, p. 41). And Freud offered a "post-modern" reading of the Oedipus myth claiming that all boys love their mothers and unconsciously desire to kill their fathers. While such "misreadings" are never inappropriate, it is important not to confuse them with correct readings. The problem was framed in the seventeenth century as one of distinguishing what was "in" the text as opposed to what could be "read into" a text. Theories of interpretation attempted to formulate rules for succeeding with that enterprise.

In the twentieth century we are less inclined to state once-and-for-all what is in a text. We prefer to say that what is in a text depends upon what a reader can bring to a text. But what if the writer brings too much? The important point is that once it is recognized that texts may be read or interpreted in more than one way, the writer has at his or her disposal a variety of lexical and syntactic devices to specify, so far as is deemed necessary, how the text is to be taken. This is the only way to assure that the reader when bringing the meaning, brings only enough.

We may recall Foucault's (1970) discussion of the revolution in the understanding and use of signs. Signs in the Middle Ages had been thought of as an intrinsic part of things, their names, whereas in the seventeenth century signs became "modes of representation." Representations came to be distinguished categorically from the things represented. To represent truthfully, language must be brought as close as possible to the observing gaze, "and the things observed as close as possible to words." Scientific language becomes a "nomination of the visible" (pp. 129–132) and texts and images were created which narrowed or eliminated the interpretive gap between reading or viewing and the thing represented. The discourse involved is a neutral form of descriptive, reporting language, a kind of prose transparent to its object.

We can see the products of this new approach to the language and meaning of written texts most clearly in the Reformation and in the rise of Early Modern Science. Concepts and procedures developed for reading scripture and reading the Book of Nature as exemplified in the writings of Francis Bacon and his contemporaries, take a concrete form in the attempts to create representations of the world, to put the world on paper. That is the subject of the next chapter.

10 REPRESENTING THE WORLD IN MAPS, DIAGRAMS, FORMULAS, PICTURES AND TEXTS

••

Mapless leagues from nowhere.

(William Faulkner, *Big Woods*)

In her monumental work on the printing press as an agent of change, Eisenstein (1979) claimed that the Alexandrian achievements which came to an end with the collapse of the Roman Empire in the fourth century AD, were not surpassed until the invention of printing which allowed one to put "'the world on paper' for all armchair travellers to see" (p. 503).

The world on paper is an apt metaphor for analyzing the implications of literacy for by creating texts which serve as representations one came to deal not with the world but with the world as depicted or described. The notion of a paper world was used by Krul in 1644 for a collection of writings and drawings (Alpers, 1983, p. 193). More recently, a study of the cartographical publications from seventeenth-century Amsterdam was published under the title *The world on paper* (Amsterdams Historisch Museum, 1977). The same title *A world on paper* is used in a book on philosophy of science by Bellone (1980) which examined the significance of notational changes in the evolution of scientific concepts.

The notion of a paper world was not accepted enthusiastically even by those who most directly contributed to its creation. A common refrain amongst Renaissance writers, Galileo included, was the importance of turning away from books to study the things in themselves. Eisenstein reverses the claim suggesting that it was the accumulation of information *in* books, maps and diagrams that made possible the rapid growth of knowledge that we associate with Early Modern, that is seventeenth-century, science. This accumulation is what Popper (1972) has called World Three, the world of "objective knowledge," namely, the theories, models and other artifacts we use to think with.

Eisenstein is undoubtedly correct regarding the important role that printing played in the establishment of an accumulative archival tradition. That accumulative archival tradition, storing knowledge produced by many minds in a common representational format, as we saw in the last chapter, was preceded by a new understanding of texts and a new way of reading and writing them, namely, of seeing texts as representations. To review, as long as knowledge was thought of as in the mind, the usefulness of writing was limited; writing could only be seen as reminder not representation. To create representations is not merely to record speeches or to construct mnemonics; it is to construct visible artifacts with a degree of autonomy from their author and with special properties for controlling how they will be interpreted.

The new texts were developed on the basis of a new attitude to signs. Recall Gilson's epigram that until Giotto, paintings were things; after Giotto and until Cezanne they were representations of things. Science became a sign-manipulating activity.

The new attitude to signs which we examined in the last two chapters produced not only a new way of reading – according to the literal meanings – but also a new way of writing, writing as the creation of "representations." This new way of reading old texts was responsible for the development of a way of writing new texts, a new variety of literary form or genre. In this new way of writing, expressions were intended to be taken literally as meaning neither more nor less than what they said. The result was a 'neutral' and 'objective' scientific form of discourse with a "mathematical plainness of style" as the Royal Society of London (Sprat, 1667/1966) was to phrase it. Unlike Medieval discourse in which "a speaker said one thing so that another would be understood" (Morrison, 1990, p. 54) texts were written to honor the new principles of reading, namely, the management of voice, the management of intention, the management of linguistic meaning, and the establishment of a new court of appeal to judge correct interpretation, namely, the common reader.

In Chapter 8 we considered the possibility that reading scripture according to a formula or an algorithm which delivered its one, true, historical meaning, allowed one to read nature according to the same formula, in both cases on the basis of visible properties open for all to see. Reading a text according to its literal meaning, the meaning "grounded openly in the text," was sufficiently radical that reading the book of scripture yielded new heresies, one species of which succeeded as the Reformation, and that reading the Book of Nature according to the same principles produced Early Modern science. In Chapter 9 we considered the possibility that reading according to a formula, allows one to develop a new genre of writing which exploits the same formula. Writing a text according to this formula produces texts with just those properties that strike modern theorists as exemplifying an analytical form of discourse, and the new understanding of signs as *representations*.

We must set aside temporarily our twentieth-century or "Postmodern" suspicion that their goal was unachievable. What they invented, it turned out, was not a royal road to the ultimate truth of things but a new mode of discourse. What we now know which they did not was that even a simple description of the observed facts is not merely a true representation but an assertion made by a speaker, an insight I discussed earlier by reference to the recent work of J. L. Austin. The speaker and the speaker's attitude were not eliminated from the discourse but merely hidden or "occulted" as Reiss (1982) puts it. As we now know there is no representation without intention and interpretation.

We can see just how well seventeenth-century artists and writers succeeded in their attempt to put the world on paper by examining the evolution of representations in five domains: representational paintings of Dutch art, the representation of the world in maps, representation of physical motion in mathematical notations, the representation of botanical species in herbals, and the representation of imaginative events in fiction. The cases illustrate the dramatic impact upon the structure of knowledge and consequently the ways of thinking as one began to examine the world by means of explicit attention to the ways of representing it.

Representing the world in pictures: Dutch art of the seventeenth century

In her fascinating book *The art of describing* (1983) Svetlana Alpers attempts to show the common intellectual basis of Dutch art, geo-

graphical maps and microscopic anatomical drawings that co-occurred
in the seventeenth century. Her attempt is not merely to show that the
activities are correlated but rather to find out why they are related; she
attempts to identify the *episteme*, as Foucault called it, of the period.
The common ground, she suggests was the art of "description."
Description is usually thought of as a verbal art, a branch of rhetoric,
the power of words to evoke people, places, and events but for
seventeenth-century Dutch artists, the notion of describing referred
to the ways in which images could parallel the use of words in giving a
true account, of providing an accurate pictorial description. Medieval
icons did not simply or truly describe; they were objects of veneration.
For Dutch artists of the seventeenth century the descriptive function
of images was to be distinguished from the rhetorical one (p. 136).
Hence, the title of her book. Description shorn of its rhetorical,
dialectical form is what I have called *representation*.

Alpers provides convincing evidence that Northern, primarily
Dutch, art of the seventeenth century can be understood as a sustained
attack on the interpretive tradition in art, the tradition that sees
significance or meaning in all that is depicted. She contrasts the Dutch
"descriptive" tradition with the more general Renaissance tradition
which treats art as narration, as having a meaning or telling a story.
For the Dutch, "Attention to the surface of the world described is
achieved at the expense of the representation of narrative action"
(p. xxi).

Historians of art have long been concerned with the evolution of
new modes of representation – from the monumental to the aesthetic
images in classical times and from the iconic art of the Middle Ages to
the realistic images of the Renaissance. In Renaissance art, in addition
to its life-like realism, aesthetic norms required the subordination of
mimetic or imitative goals to narrative ones – a fine painting depicted
not only an object or event but also told a story: The dead Jesus in the
arms of his mother as in Michelangelo's (1475–1564) *Pieta* or the birth
of perfection as in Botticelli's (1446–1510) *The birth of Venus*. Gombrich describes the latter thus:

Venus has emerged from the sea on a shell which is driven to the shore by
flying wind-gods amidst a shower of roses. As she is about to step on to the
land, one of the Hours or Nymphs receives her with a purple cloak ...
Botticelli's Venus is so beautiful that we do not notice the unnatural length of

her neck, the steep fall of her shoulders and the queer way her left arm is hinged to the body. Or, rather, we should say that these liberties which Botticelli took with nature in order to achieve a graceful outline add to the beauty and harmony of the design because they enhance the impression of an infinitely tender and delicate being, wafted to our shores as a gift from Heaven.

(1950, p. 199)

Gombrich's analysis captures not only the aesthetics and the meaning of the Botticelli, it exemplifies how Italian artists of the period used visual images as mnemonics to retrieve well known themes; knowledge of those themes is what made the pictures meaningful. In fact Gombrich's book is essential reading for anyone who is interested in understanding what artists of the period were doing.

But the notion that art should tell a story, have a meaning, or hold a significance by means of retrieving a well-known classical or biblical theme, made it difficult for viewers, critics and artists alike to see any point to Dutch art of the seventeenth century. Dutch art is noteworthy for its peculiar devotion to the life-like portrayal of objects such as radishes, dead swans, and herring as well as simple domestic scenes such as a cook pouring milk into a pot or map-like landscapes, uninhabited by people. Alpers (1983) points out that applying the principles for interpreting Italian art to these Dutch paintings misleads some critics to read "meanings" into these paintings. Thus, Vermeer's painting of a woman by the window reading a letter (Alpers, p. 204), was sometimes interpreted, perhaps because of the fullness of her gown, as a woman pregnant by one who has left her and so on. Alpers argument is this interpretive stance is inappropriate for Dutch art of this period.

Indeed, contemporary viewers looking for "meaning" were puzzled by such art. Alpers cites Fromentin, a nineteenth-century commentator as asking "What motive had a Dutch painter in painting a picture?" And then providing the appropriate answer to that question: "None." (p. xviii). And Joshua Reynolds, the first president of the British Royal Academy after his trip to examine Dutch art said "The account which has now been given of the Dutch pictures is, I confess, more barren of entertainment, than I expected ... their merit often consists in the truth of representation alone" (Alpers, p. xviii).

The Dutch art of the seventeenth century, Alpers suggests,

exchanged narrative depth for surface description. The pictures were constructed not as mnemonics for remembered classical themes but as representations of things visible in the world. This is not to deny that aesthetic decisions reveal something about the artists themselves as Schama (1987) has argued, but rather that their intention is the literal, factual portrayal of concrete events. Alpers develops her theme both through the comments of the critics at the time and through an examination of the art itself. Typical of the commentators of the day was Samuel van Hoogstraten who in 1678 claimed that drawing is "imitating things after life even as they appear" (Alpers, p. 38). The importance of such careful visual inspection was not merely to see the world better but to disentangle what was there to be seen, from the interpretations read into it. Hoogstraten criticized the Italian Renaissance tradition of which Michelangelo and Raphael were leading exponents, of emphasizing beauty over truth in art, and "chides those who read *meanings* into the clouds of the sky" (Alpers, p. 77). Hoogstraten urged painters to use their eyes to see clouds as clouds and not as symbols of the heavens!

Hoogstraten's advice has been disregarded, perhaps for good reason, by some recent critics who insist that Dutch art is replete with allegorical and emblematic meanings (Schama, 1987).[1] Even so, the drive towards factual description in the art of this period marks a dramatic shift from the art of the Italian Renaissance.

Alpers traces the Dutch descriptive tradition to their contacts with British empirical or scientific tradition as represented by Bacon, Hooke and Boyle. They exemplified in their art what these scientists had urged in their science. Just as Bacon had claimed that

all depends upon keeping the eye steadily fixed upon the facts of nature and so receiving their images simply as they are. For God forbid that we should give out a dream of our own imagination for a pattern of the world.

(1620/1965, p. 323)

[1] Andrew Graham-Dixon quotes Schama as saying "The brush stood as a heraldic device for the new commonwealth, cleansed of the impurities of the past. To have been slaves was dirty. To be free is to be clean" to which Graham-Dixon adds: "The broom was not merely, then, a means to cleanliness, but the symbol of freedom from Spanish rule: of the new, purified Holland of the Republic" (*The Independent*, London, Tuesday, July 28, 1992, p. 12).

So, too, the Dutch artists attempted to achieve just this in their art.

Secondly, Alpers supports her claim that Dutch pictures called for close looking and not for "interpreting" by pointing out the accuracy of the pictures. A map which serves as the background for a Vermeer painting was so carefully drawn that the original of which it is a painting has recently been located in Paris (Alpers, p. 120). Another of Vermeer's paintings, one which Gombrich considers to be "one of the greatest masterpieces of all time," *The cook*, a woman pouring out milk

> is something of a miracle. One of its miraculous features ... is the way in which Vermeer achieves complete and painstaking precision in the rendering of textures, colours and forms without the picture ever looking laboured or harsh ... this strange and unique combination of mellowness and precision ... makes his best painting so unforgettable.
>
> (Gombrich, 1950, p. 340)

Unlike the Botticelli described above, the Vermeer neither recalls classical texts nor calls for interpretation, it is pure description (and of course no less beautiful for all that).

Thirdly, Alpers points out the close relation between picture and map making. A whole landscape tradition was developed by the Dutch in which factual map making held common cause with picture making. Even the Dutch word *landschap* was used to refer to both what the surveyor measured and the artist painted. Northern map makers and artists conceived of a picture as a "surface to inscribe the world" rather than for the portrayal of significant human action. They provide "disinterested" observation, what Alpers calls a "mapped landscape."

The close relation between maps and landscapes is also indicated by the fact that the point of view from which the artist viewed the landscape was often similar to that assumed in a map – the view from nowhere. Alpers points out that for the Dutch of the period, there was no strict distinction between maps and art, between knowledge and decoration, for "pictures challenged texts as a central way of under-standing the world" (p. 126).

When words appeared in such pictures, as they often did, they were offered not as explorations of meaning so much as for something more to look at. She points out that the Dutch artists believed they could carry the text by means of the picture.

Alpers notes two extremely interesting aspects of these drawings which, in my way of thinking, are crucial to determining whether pictures are seen as symbols or as representations (see Foucault, 1970, p. 57). She notes first that pictures represent ideas, but not ideas in the early Renaissance sense of ideals, but ideas (*oog te bedriegen*) as mental pictures. Secondly, they are representations in the sense that the pictures now represent particulars. Alpers writes:

Italian art was based on an intentional turning away from individuality in the name of general human traits and general truths ... Portraiture, since it must attend to individuals, was considered inferior to works that engaged higher, more general truths. The Dutch ... privileging of portraiture, which is the centre of their entire pictorial tradition, is connected on the other hand to a desire to preserve the identity of each person and each thing in the world.

(1983, p. 78)

The important point is that these Dutch paintings demonstrate a close correspondence with the assumptions of the Early Modern Scientists, with their strict attention to the appearances of things, their descriptions of the visible surfaces of things, their attempt at constructing correct representations rather than, as Alpers says, "as objects of interpretation" (p. 207). These pictures, like the texts they wrote and read, were to wear their meanings on their shirt-sleeves.

If more evidence is required to prove the Dutch artist's choice of the true testimony of the eye over subjective and misleading interpretations, we may cite Alpers' analysis of a print by Pieter Saendredam made in 1628 of the cross-section of an old apple tree. He made the drawing to repudiate the widely held belief that the dark wood at the core of the apple tree contained the miraculous images of Catholic clergy. In Protestant Holland, recently at war with Catholic Spain, there were important social reasons for contesting the belief. But Saendredam's method is indicative. He identifies which tree he has cut down, draws the core with great accuracy, dates the drawing and publishes an etching of it to repudiate the false picture. His strategy is to "separate the object seen from those beliefs or interpretations to which it had given rise" (p. 81). The drawing should reflect a close reading of nature and avoid interpretation. Again we may note that the notion of interpretation is now a pejorative one.

Figure 10.1   Etching by Saendredam of the 'false picture'

While Alpers' purpose is to demonstrate the close relation between the strategy of Dutch artists of the seventeenth century and their British scientific colleagues, an undertaking in which I believe she succeeds, my purpose is to suggest that both are by-products of the new ways of reading scripture, according to the sense, that is, according to the literal meanings, and of avoiding "interpretations," those interpolations, digressions, accretions, and "swellings of style" which, in the view of the Protestants, had interfered with the correct reading of scripture.

Representing the world in maps

In 1665 the Royal Society published a volume of "Directions for seamen, bound for far voyages." Such "voyages of discovery" were by now common but the impact of such voyages and the compilation of information that they allowed, provided the basis for a new world picture. An explorer, unlike other voyagers, works:

in the service of an organized vision of what might be found [and seeks] to relate it to what is known. Unlike the wanderer . . . the explorer sees himself as contributing to a sum of knowledge he has assessed beforehand.

(Hale, 1968, p. 9; cited by Eisenstein, 1979, p. 477)

The "organized vision" which generated the voyages of discovery was a theoretical conception of the world as represented by maps. Maps which could serve both the needs of navigation and provide a comprehensible view of the planet were the most conspicuous examples of the attempt to put the world on paper and to think about the world in terms of those representations.

Ptolemy's *Geography*, a massive achievement, combining both local geographical knowledge and a world picture based on the geometry of the sphere, was written in the third century. Ptolemy knew the world was round and could therefore be thought about in terms of the properties of a geometric sphere. As there are 360 degrees in a circle and the sun "travels" one complete circuit each twenty-four hours, it was possible to assess the number of miles covered by the sun in an hour and use this figure to compute the number of miles per degree and thence the circumference of the earth. Ptolemy's estimate of some sixty miles per degree is close to the now known value of some seventy miles per degree.

The earliest surviving manuscripts of Ptolemy's work are from the twelfth century. As Ptolemy's theory was highly mathematical, it was understood only by scholars. Furthermore, although the text could be readily copied, maps and drawings in the hands of copyists tended to lose their distinctive properties. I myself have seen the earliest copy of Ptolemy's map of the world, now in the British Museum, which provides an impressive representation of Europe, part of Asia and Africa but which shows the Indian Ocean as enclosed by land mass. Ptolemy's interests ran not only to natural science; he was far better known through the Middle Ages for his book on astrology, the *Tetrabiblos*.

Medieval world maps, *mappae mundi*, generally featured a sphere, surrounded by other spheres representing the heavens, or discs the circumference of which is surrounded by mythical beings. Skelton (1965) one time the Curator of Maps at the British Museum, pointed out that world maps of the Middle Ages, in most part kept in the

scriptoria of monasteries, reflected the conventional patterns of the
Christian view of the world:

Until the second half of the fifteenth century the habitable world continued to
be represented as a circular disc surrounded by the ocean sea, with Jerusalem
at the centre and east (with the Earthly Paradise) to the top; and the
symmetrical pattern of the T-O diagrams was still reflected in the more
elaborate mappae mundi.

(p. 111; cited by Eisenstein, 1979, p. 515)

One such map, the only one found in a manuscript of Marco Polo's
Book recounting his thirteenth-century trip to and stay in the Orient,
and now in the Royal Library of Stockholm, depicts a disc with the
Orient marked at the top and the Occident at the bottom with the
north and south hemispheres depicted as huge islands in a circular sea.
The Northern Hemisphere (on the left) is said to represent the three
known continents of Europe, Asia and Africa divided up by the
Mediterranean and the Nile.

Marco Polo's descriptions, on the other hand, are full of bearings
(directions) and distances and long land journeys are described along a
straight transverse line (Skelton, 1958, p. 12).

The 600 or so maps which have survived from the period before
1300 show no sign of general developmental progression towards a
comprehensive map of the world (Sarton, 1955; Eisenstein, 1979,
p. 479). The principal stumbling block to such a map was the lack of
reliable means of duplicating maps, an obstacle overcome only with
the invention of printing and engraving, and the invention of a
common, mathematical, frame of reference which would permit the
integration and synthesis of information being accumulated on the
voyages of discovery.

Although the availability of identical, widely distributed charts was
sufficiently dependent upon printing to lead Sarton, a historian of
science, to claim that "The main event separating the period we call
Renaissance from the Middle Ages was the double invention, typog-
raphy for the text and engraving for the images" (1955, p. xi) a view
importantly documented, if qualified, by Eisenstein (1979), our
primary concern is with the relation between the development of
representations of the world and our conception of the world. The

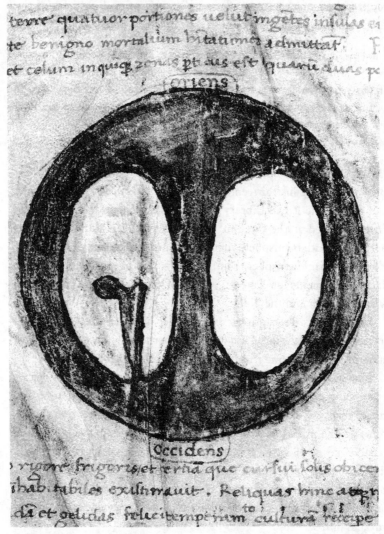

Figure 10.2   Mappa mundi, in a manuscript of Marco Polo

problem of representation was one of inventing and standardizing a system of projection of a round sphere on to a flat representational surface suitable for the integration of new information.

Although numerous local maps existed, describing the route from say, London to Paris or from Portugal to the Grand Banks of Newfoundland, these maps and charts (maps designed as aids to navigation on land or water) related particulars without integrating these particulars into a general scheme. Such "plane charts" treated the spherical earth as if it were a flat plane and so could be represented on a flat chart. Such charts were commonly used for navigation in the fifteenth and sixteenth centuries. (See Figure 10.3.)

The problem with such charts became obvious when they were used to represent a large area. The meridians (lines of longitude) which in fact converge at the poles were represented on a plane chart as parallel to one another, introducing large errors in representation of distance at high latitudes.

Some problems of representation were relatively trivial, such as developing a convention for putting North at the top of a map. Others were much more serious, like inventing a mathematical grid of lines of latitude and longitude for specifying locations. This abstract grid was what allowed the integration of detailed cartographic knowledge into a "world picture."

The mathematization of geographical space began as mentioned with Ptolemy's *Geography* which was translated into Arabic and later re-translated into Latin during the Renaissance. The important step was to see the world not only as round or as a sphere but as a sphere with the mathematical properties of a sphere, namely, that it could be represented by the 360 degrees of the circle. The degrees of the circle could provide the lines of latitude and longitude for the earth, providing a common frame of reference into which *any* newly discovered territory could be inserted. Only then, did the paper world become the conceptual scheme in terms of which the perceptual world could be understood.

Once recognized as a sphere there was the second problem of representing a spherical object on a flat surface, the so-called projection problem. Ptolemy had "solved" this problem by thinking of the hemisphere as a cone. (Think of the earth as being a pair of cones rather than as two hemispheres meeting at the equator with the base of the cone at the equator and the points of the cones at or over the poles, then transferring the lines and points of the globe on to the cone and then opening up the cone to make a roughly triangular surface.) A cone has the advantage of being representable as a flat surface with parallel, if curved lines for the equator and the other lines of latitude

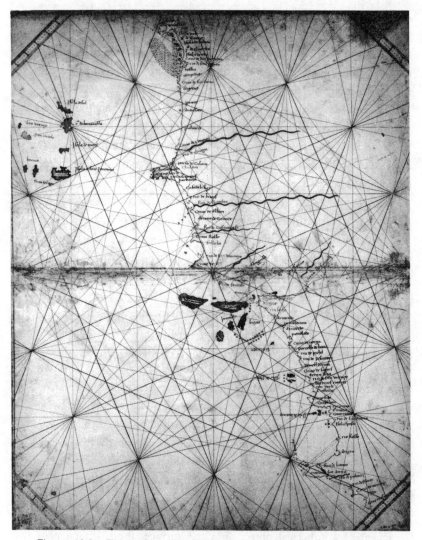

Figure 10.3   The west coast of Africa, in a MS portolan chart by
G. Benincasa, 1468

and straight, converging lines for the meridians. Such a representation
gave a good fit to regions near the equator but considerable distortion
at the middle latitudes, the area in which much of the fourteenth- and
fifteenth-century navigation took place.

A second solution to representing the spherical world on paper was
the invention of the globe, the most famous of which, made by Martin

Behaim of Nuremberg, was completed in the year of Columbus' discovery of America, 1492. Globes, however, while providing an admirable world picture could not accommodate details of any particular area. To provide details of a particular area they would have to be huge; hence globes were not useful for navigation.

A third solution was a Mercator-type projection, familiar to all school children. Nuñez, a Portuguese mathematician had discovered that on a globe, a rhumb line, the line defined by holding a constant compass heading, produced a spiral ending at the pole. This was the problem facing Gerard Mercator (1512–1594), a Dutch Protestant. He devised means for printing maps to be affixed to globes and a world map of 1569 with meridians spaced out towards the poles, amplifying the representation of the space in that region. It is Mercator's projection that makes Canada appear to have such a vast north land. His solution involved representing a sphere not as a cone but as a cylinder for a cylinder can also be represented on a flat surface. (Think of removing a label from a cylindrical can.) Wright, an Englishman, writing in 1599 provided an explicit account of how this could be done. He explained that if the earth were a spherical balloon with all the meridians and parallels drawn on it and it were placed in a cylinder with a diameter and a length equal to that of the balloon and the balloon then inflated until it fills the cylinder, all the meridians will be parallel. The images transferred from the balloon to the cylinder will be a Mercator projection. Not only can the earth then be represented on a flat surface, visible at a single glance, but also the rhumb lines will be straight lines, such that a fixed compass course can be drawn with a ruler (Boas, 1962, pp. 206–209). Furthermore, smaller charts representing the details of a particular area can be "mapped" into the world map for these will share the same frame of reference. These more detailed charts were suitable for navigation.

A map or a chart is of little use unless you can also solve the problem of reference, which for maps, consists of precise methods for relating positions on the map to positions in the world. This is particularly important if one is to navigate by means of a chart. How is one to determine present location on a chart if there are no visible landmarks to serve as a guide?

Navigational methods since the thirteenth century when the

compass was introduced into Europe perhaps from China had been based on the use of portolan charts, charts indicating distance and direction between ports and destinations, first of the Mediterranean and in the fifteenth century of the Atlantic coasts of Europe. These charts provided a careful outline of sea coast and ports. Their main feature was the series of *rhumb* lines radiating from a series of compass roses emanating from the "points of the compass," NNE and the like. Navigators could work out a course by locating themselves on one of these rhumb lines leading to a desired destination. And they kept track of their progress by "dead reckoning," working out the direction and distance sailed (Boas, 1962, p. 31). (See Figure 10.3.)

Such methods were completely inadequate for exploring the unknown oceans to search for new sea routes to Cathay (China) or the Spice Islands (Indonesia), possibilities that were coming into consciousness as the world image became more articulated. These new methods included the application of astronomical knowledge to navigation, an enterprise initiated by Henry the Navigator, a Portuguese prince in mid-fifteenth century. The altitude of the sun and stars could be used to determine the latitude on the surface of the earth if one had a device for measuring that altitude and tables to allow one to take into account the date and time of the measurement; only the North Star, Polaris, holds its position in the night sky.

The instrument most commonly used in the fifteenth century for measurement of altitude was the quadrant. A short moveable cross piece was slid back and forth along a calibrated "bow" aimed at one point, say the horizon, until the other end of the cross piece just covered the measured object, say a star. The distance the cross piece was down the bow indicated the angle of the star from the horizon. This value could then be compared to a table specifying the predicted altitude of that star for a given time and date for the navigator's home port and, if one knew the longitude, sail down the appropriate rhumb line. More often, longitude was "known" only by dead reckoning, that is, on the basis of speed multiplied by time, so the safer strategy was simply to sail to the latitude of the home port and then "run down the latitude" (Boas, p. 38). Precise measurement of longitude would depend upon the invention of the mechanical clock which allowed one to tell what time it was in Greenwich, at which the Prime Meridian was set early in the seventeenth century, when it was mid-day on board ship as measured by the quadrant. With latitude and longitude both measurable it was possible to integrate information for all locations into a single picture of the world. One's location was no longer the deictic "Here" but a point on a map.

The importance of these new representations of the world and new sophistication in navigation was that they could serve as a theory to generate novel predictions. Columbus' westward voyage was representative. Columbus knew that, being a sphere, the earth could be represented as 360 degrees. Further he concluded on the basis of reading Ptolemy, that each degree corresponded to some fifty miles, somewhat less than Ptolemy himself had concluded (a nautical mile is 1 degree of latitude at the equator, later found to be slightly greater than a linear mile). He also estimated, on the basis of information provided by Marco Polo's excursion to Cathay (China), that the extent of the old, known world was between 225 and 255 degrees. If the world is only 360 degrees that left only some 100 degrees, at most 5000 miles, between China and Spain, sailing westward. He also knew that Cipangu (Japan) was some 1500 miles east of China so he could infer that sailing due west for 3500 miles, some thirty-five days, he would arrive in Japan. All these were inferences from a paper world. Indeed, when Columbus arrived in Cuba, a voyage that took some thirty-five days, he took it to be Indo-China and a few days of sail from the Ganges River of India! (Skelton, 1958, p. 55). In fact, some 120 degrees of the globe, some one-third of the earth including the Americas and the Pacific, had yet to be admitted into the new world picture.

Perhaps even more impressive illustrations of the conceptual importance of the paper world, was the search for the "Southern Continent." By mid-sixteenth century the Pacific Ocean had become not only a trade route but subject of a second grand illusion sponsored by the paper world. The concept of a vast, inhabited continent, reaching from the South Pole to the Tropics and being bounded by the Atlantic, Pacific and Indian Oceans seemed obvious. Something must fill the void on the charts and in addition it was believed that if the earth was to remain in equilibrium there must be a southern continent to balance the northern one. Marco Polo's world map had shown both the northern continent and a globular, unknown, southern one. Mercator wrote on his world chart of 1569:

under the Antarctic Pole [lies] a continent so great that, with the southern parts of Asia, and the new India or America, it should be a weight equal to the other lands.

(Skelton, 1958, pp. 193–194)

The conjecture was not easily disproved for sailing ships ran with the trade winds from east to west on the equator side of the Tropic of Capricorn. But this left unexplored the southern side of the Tropic, a vast ocean which could be explored only by sailing from the West. In 1768, the British Admiralty commissioned James Cook, recently returned from five years of surveying the coast of Newfoundland, and a good mathematician, to command a bark, the *Endeavour* to take Royal Society astronomers to Tahiti. In addition, Cook's secret instructions required him to search for the continent which "there is reason to imagine ... may be found to the Southward" (Skelton, 1958, p. 233).

He reached Tahiti via the Cape Horn, then sailed south, circumnavigated New Zealand, proving it to be an island, discovered the east coast of New Holland (Australia), and after being nearly shipwrecked three times on the Great Barrier Reef returned, via the Torres Straits into the Indian Ocean. On his second search for the Southern Continent, he sailed from West to East from New Zealand to Cape Horn, three times crossing the Antarctic Circle (60 degrees S) and one time reaching 71 degrees S (roughly equivalent to mid-Greenland) thereby satisfying himself that if there is a southern continent "it must lie within the polar circle" and "would not be worthy of discovery" (Skelton, 1958, p. 241).

Skelton (1958) concludes that "Cook's may without exaggeration be called the first scientific voyages of discovery. They mark an epoch no less in the mapping of the world than in its exploration" (p. 243). Cook's voyages are, therefore, not to be seen simply as putting the world on paper but of exploring the world *from the map's point of view*. The map is the model or theory of which the voyages are the empirical tests. The maps have become representations. Since the seventeenth century to be completely lost is to be, in the words of our epigram, "mapless leagues from nowhere."

Mental maps

That this representation of the world is a paper world, not an intuitive one, may be shown by contrasting this representation with others which are equally impressive but which are not based on maps and charts but on personal knowledge, which in cognitive science circles is thought of as a mental model. The Micronesians and the Polynesians navigated thousands of miles in the South Pacific between Samoa, Hawaii and Easter Islands arriving at destinations visible from as little as ten miles away after days of sailing in an unmarked, uncharted sea. Tupaia, the navigator-chief from the Caroline Islands whom Captain Cook took aboard the *Endeavour* in 1769 knew all of the major island groups in Polynesia except for Hawaii and New Zealand, a span of some 2,600 miles. On the voyage with Cook he was able, day after day, Cook reports, to point, correctly, in the direction of Tahiti.

But only recently have we begun to understand the sophistication of the mental activities that go into such achievements. Gladwin (1970) studied the navigational practices still employed in the Caroline Islands. The navigator visualizes himself as the fixed centre of two moving frames of reference, one provided by the islands among which he sails and the other provided by the pattern of stars which wheel overhead from east to west.

Oatley (1977) has depicted these frames of reference in a helpful illustration (Figure 10.4). The boat is represented at the centre of a circle defined by the horizon. The navigator thinks of the boat as stationary while the point of embarkation recedes and the destination approaches; other islands move by in the same direction. At the same time a succession of stars rise over the horizon each of which bears a fixed, known relation to the destination and provides a heading for the boat. To keep track of distance made, one particular island, well off the ship's track and beyond the horizon, the so-called *Etak* or imaginary island, is held in mind. This Etak island, too, moves past the boat occupying the series of positions designated by the setting positions of the stars which originally served as headings for the boat. This system of triangulations allows the navigator to determine when he has arrived in the area of the destination at which time he will begin to look for more local clues such as clouds, bird flight, wave patterns and

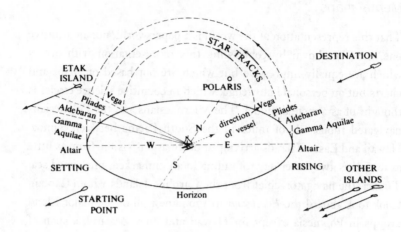

Figure 10.4   Pictorial representation of the Carolinian voyager's articulation of the moving spatial frames of islands and stars during an (imaginary) voyage

the like. Joshua Slocum (1900), the first person to sail around the world single-handedly, tells how he could recognize when he had entered the latitudes of the trade winds simply by the sound of the waves lapping the boat's hull.

Hutchins (1983) has pointed out some of the ways that Micronesian navigation differs from map-governed navigation. The frame of reference we have already mentioned; for the map follower "here" is a place on the map; for the traditional navigator "here" is the directly perceived location of the boat. Secondly, for the map follower, current location is deduced by means of "dead reckoning." Initial location is specified on a chart and measures of two variables, direction headed and distance travelled can be marked on the chart to yield current position. The traditional navigator keeps a continuously updated model of where the passing islands and stars are relative to his boat.

Hutchins (1983) has pointed out that concepts like observation and inference are critical to the map follower but not to the traditional navigator. Both the representations and the mental operations performed on them are distinctive. Astronomical observations are critical to both but in the former case, they are used to determine latitude and longitude and hence location on a chart. For the traditional navigator, the path of the stars indicate location and destination directly. The one lives in the world, the other in a world on paper. Hutchins states this point this way:

When the navigator takes a compass bearing on a landmark from the bridge of a boat he is no longer conceptually on the boat, he is over the sea surface looking down on the position of his craft in a representation of the real local space.

(p. 207)

He continues:

In our tradition, the operations of observation, computation, and interpretation are each a different sort of activity and they are executed serially. The Micronesian navigator's tool box is in his mind ... The interpretation of the result (bearing of the reference island, for example) is embedded in the computation (construction of the horizon image) which is itself embedded in the observation (time of day).

(p. 223)

Somewhat similar navigational prowess has recently been recognized in the establishment as fact of the Vikings' tenth-century voyages to "Vineland," the Norse name for the territory which included the northern tip of Newfoundland (*Macleans*, August 5, 1991, p. 41). The only records of how these navigational feats were achieved comes from the Norse Sagas (Mowat, 1965). The Sagas provide sailing instructions for distant voyages in terms of the *doegrs*, that is distances measured by how far a ship could run on an average day (roughly thirty-five miles), directions described in *airts*, and landmarks describing point of departure and point of destination. Although these navigators knew nothing of the geometrized world of latitudes and longitudes, they could measure the altitude of celestial objects and by comparing the present altitude of, say, the North Star and comparing it with the altitude of that star at the destination, manage the problem of latitude. Viking navigators could sail from Norway to North America observing landmarks at the Shetlands, the Faeroes, Iceland, Greenland and Baffin Island without losing sight of land for more than two hundred miles at any one time (Mowat, 1965, p. 356).

A final example of navigation without compass or chart comes from the long distance travel of the Inuit across the Arctic. Voyages of up to five hundred kilometres are communicated and remembered by memorizing a series of descriptive place names, direction is managed by such features as *sastrugi*, small ridges of hard snow which run parallel to the prevailing winds, and distances in terms of days of travel. Although such mental maps are route oriented, the Inuit are known to have remarkable ability for depicting local geography on maps. An impressive example of such a map is that which was prepared for the Danish explorer Knud Rasmussen, by the Inuit, Pukerluk, in 1922 to guide his travels in the Barrens west of Hudson's Bay. Pukerluk's map, in fact, corresponds very well to a modern map of the same territory indicating the precision of Pukerluk's experientially acquired knowledge (Pelly, 1991; see also Brody, 1981, 1987). Although maps are frequently drawn in the air or in the snow in the course of explaining a route, maps are rarely if ever carried or consulted on a voyage.

Although we are only now coming to acknowledge the complexity of the operations that can be carried out in the mind without the use of abstract representations and computational notations, whether for navigation or for theoretical speculation (Carruthers, 1990), it is nonetheless important to recognize the important stamp put on one's thinking about the world when one comes to think of it in terms of the explicit models which evolve in the attempt to represent it. The Inuit map serves only as a mnemonic for the already known; the world map of Columbus or Cook served as a theoretical model for thinking about the unknown.

Ong has admirably anticipated our conclusion:

Only after print and the extensive experience with maps that print implemented would human beings, when they thought about the cosmos or universe or 'world', think primarily of something laid out before their eyes, as in a modern printed atlas, a vast surface or assemblage of surfaces ... ready to be 'explored.' The ancient oral world knew few 'explorers,' though it did know many itinerants, travellers, voyagers, adventurers, and pilgrims.

(1982, p. 73)

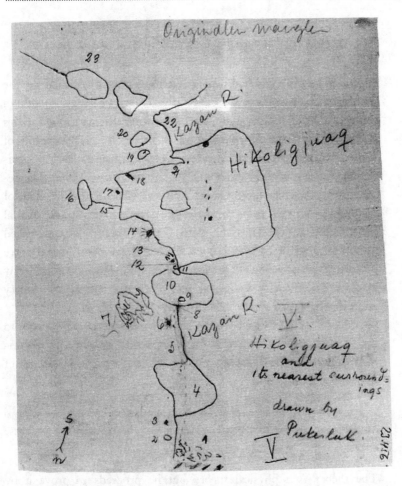

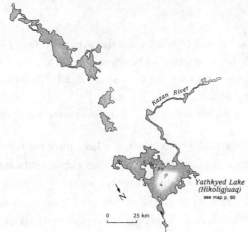

Figure 10.5
Modern map of Arabic
region compared to
Pukerluk map drawn
for Rasmussen.

Representation of nature: Galileo's mathematization of motion

Although geographers had taken the critical step of representing the physical world by means of an abstract geometry – seeing the world in terms of a geometrical sphere with its known mathematical properties – the more dramatic achievement was to see non-spatial properties of nature, motion in particular, in terms of such geometrical representations. Galileo is justly celebrated for just this achievement (Haugeland, 1987). We may recall Galileo's celebrated claim that the Book of Nature was written in mathematics. His method was to take logical propositions as postulates, the truth of which were to be established "when we find that the inferences from it correspond to and agree perfectly with experiment" (1638/1954, p. 172). The view is perfectly modern. The theory has a logical form, the implications of the theory are tested by experiment.

Galileo's strategy was to use the deductive properties of geometry to derive predictions which could be confirmed, if possible, by experiment. Consider his Theorem 1, Proposition 1 on the properties of uniform motion:

If a moving particle, carried uniformly at a constant speed, traverses two distances the time-intervals required are to each other in the ratio of these distances.

The theory is a physical theory but he proceeds to prove it by geometrical methods:

Let a particle move uniformly with constant speed through two distances AB, BC, and let the time required to traverse AB be represented by DE; the time required to traverse BC, by EF; then I say that the distance AB is to the distance BC as the time DE is to the time EF.

(Galilei, 1638/1954, p. 155)

Distance is readily represented by the length of a line; but time is now represented spatially by a similar line. The relations between distance and time are then represented by constant ratios: AB/BC = DE/EF.

Naturally accelerated motion required a somewhat more complex set of geometrical representations. Theorem 1, Proposition 1 states:

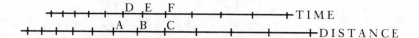

Figure 10.6   Drawing after Galileo. The formulaic expression D = V x T
is a modern convenience. Galileo would have objected to the
multiplication of incommensurables, preferring to express the relation
in terms of ratios.

The time in which any space is traversed by a body starting from rest and
uniformly accelerated is equal to the time in which that same space would be
traversed by the same body moving at a uniform speed whose value is the
mean of the highest speed and the speed just before acceleration began.

And the proof (as in Figure 10.7):

Let us represent by the line AB the time in which the space CD is traversed by a
body which starts from rest at C and is uniformly accelerated; let the final and
highest value of the speed gained during the interval AB be represented by the
line EB drawn at right angles to AB; draw the line AE, then all lines drawn from
equidistant points on AB and parallel to BE will represent the increasing values
of the speed beginning with the instant A. Let the point F bisect the line EB;
draw FG parallel to BA, and GA parallel to FB, thus forming a parallelogram
AGFB which will be equal in area to the triangle AEB, since the side GF bisects
the side AE at the point I; if the parallel lines in the triangle AEB are extended to
GI, then the sum of all the parallels contained in the quadrilateral is equal to
the sum of those contained in the triangle AEB; for those in the triangle IEF are
equal to those contained in the triangle GIA; while those included in the
trapezium AIFB are common. Since each and every instant of time in the
time-interval AB has its corresponding point on the line AB, from which points
parallels drawn in and limited by the triangle AEB represent the increasing
values of the growing velocity, and since parallels contained within the
rectangle represent the values of a speed which is not increasing, but constant,
it appears, in like manner, that the momenta [velocity] assumed by the
moving body may also be represented, in the case of the accelerated motion,
by the increasing parallels of the triangle AEB, and, in the case of the uniform
motion, by the parallels of the rectangle GB. For, what the momenta may lack
in the first part of the accelerated motion (the deficiency of the momenta being
represented by the parallels of the triangle AGI) is made up by the momenta
represented by the parallels of the triangle IEF.

Hence it is clear that equal spaces will be traversed in equal times by two
bodies, one of which, starting from rest, moves with a uniform acceleration,

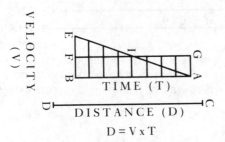

$$D = V \times T$$

Figure 10.7   Drawing after Galileo

while the momentum of the other, moving with uniform speed, is one-half its maximum momentum under accelerated motion Q. E. D.

(Galilei, 1638/1954, pp. 172–173)

Time is represented by a line in space, distance by an aggregate area and the proof of the relation between uniform and accelerated motion reduces to the proof that the area of a triangle with twice the base and equal height to that of a parallelogram has the same area. Geometry with known laws, rules and properties, serves as a model for representing the properties of motion. Nature is seen in terms of this mathematical model, represented on paper.

Note too that geometry is not merely a metaphor for acceleration but a representation of acceleration. The difference is not simply terminological. The representation specifies in a precise way how each of the features in the representation map on to the features of the objects in question and how the rules for interpretation of the representation – geometrical deductions – represent possible states of those objects. The statements of the model are to be interpreted as literally true of the represented world. Thus theories are to be interpreted as literally as the factual statements that provide evidence for those theories.

The importance of the "representation" problem in scientific advance is the concern of Bellone (1980, p. 141) who asks why the mathematization of a physical theory should be such a lengthy and laborious process rather than a routine translation into symbols of what is already known through experience. Illustrative of his point is the surprising fact that the equations representing Newton's laws of motion were actually written by the mathematician Leonhard Euler some sixty years after the publication of Newton's *Principia*. Newton expressed his laws in terms of ratios much as Galileo had done. While incommensurable properties such as space and time could be represented by lines, it was inconceivable that such incommensurables could be multiplied or divided. What would it mean to multiply velocity by time or mass by acceleration? Euler did just that; the product was the now universally accepted formula $F = ma$. Bellone argues that:

a process of mathematization is neither a translation, faithful or unfaithful, nor a purely formal substitution of the logic pre-existing in empirical laws ... [but rather that] the logical structure established between descriptive statements about facts ... is subject to sometimes radical modifications that not only change the form of the theory but affect the empirical evidence itself, and thus force us to give a different interpretation to the observations and to the relationships between measurements.

(p. 141)

Thus, representing the properties of motion in the form of geometric proofs and algebraic equations was not merely putting down what was known. Rather it was to reconstruct those properties in terms of the structures available in formalized, written languages. The thinking is done by means of the representations; the product of those computations is then compared to the observed facts. The world thought about is no longer simply the world but the world as represented on paper.

Representing the world of plants: botanical iconography

If twenty minutes with a gardener is not sufficient to convince one of the wealth of knowledge of plants possessed by a devoted practitioner, we may recall Levi-Strauss' (1966) account of the complex knowledge which was required for the successful domestication of plants and animals in paleolithic times. Not only is practical knowledge acquired, many cultures without writing have complex botanical taxonomies (Berlin, 1974; Atran, 1990, p. 73). Indeed, by the time they are four or five years of age Mayan children are reported to be able to classify over 100 botanical kinds by taxonomic rank (Stross, 1973; cited by Atran, 1990, p. 73.)

Without minimizing these achievements, it may be a mistake, as Atran has noted, to identify traditional classifications with scientific theory. While the practice of sorting plants and animals into sometimes elaborate taxonomies on the basis of some presumed underlying nature – all birds have properties in common, for example – those classes are often based on morphological aspect and ecological function rather than consistent principles such as reproductive lines of descent. Thus folk taxonomies honor categories such as trees and sparrows even if these do not constitute scientific taxa. Trees do not constitute either a species, a genus, or a family. Indeed, the family of legumes includes herbs, vines, trees, and bushes. Furthermore, folk taxonomies make no attempt to relate all such classes to a unified conception of Nature, the major concern of science since Aristotle (Atran, 1990, pp. 7, 78–80.) Our purpose in this chapter is to trace the ways in which botanical knowledge was affected by the attempt to represent systematically this knowledge in pictures and texts.

Robert Hooke's *Micrographia* is a record of seventeenth-century investigations with a microscope and represented by a series of drawings, reproduced by means of etchings, which were incorporated into a text. Those of a louse and a fly, for example, were published on sheets 12" by 16" folded so as to fit neatly within a bound, printed text. But the beginnings of scientific drawings of plants and animals goes back, as does all western science, to the Greeks.

The ideas of the ancients on natural history, especially on plants and animals is best represented in the work of Aristotle, Theophrastos, Dioscorides, all Greeks, and Pliny, The Elder, a Roman who wrote in the first century (Sarton, 1955). Each of these classical scholars had a number of sixteenth-century disciples who translated, edited and in some cases updated their works. In many cases no early Greek or Latin texts existed, access to this knowledge coming only through Latin translations of such Arabic texts as Avicenna's *Canon*.

Words are limited means for describing the visual details of hundreds of species of plants and animals. Renaissance scholars were often dismayed at the fact that they could not identify the plants described by ancient writers. Nor were pictures ideal as they are not readily copied; successive recopying of unfamiliar forms often loses their distinguishing features as Bartlett (1932), much more recently, demonstrated. While a few copies of these early botanical drawings remain; the earliest is in a sixth-century copy of Dioscorides' first-century manuscript which is filled with illustrations of plants (the volume is said to be the most valuable in the library of Vienna) (Sarton, 1955, p. 69) – later copies of copies were progressively debased and often unrecognizable (Boas, 1962, p. 52).

An interesting example of this problem may be seen in the first English translation of Dioscorides' herbal written in 1655 (Gunther, 1655/1934). The editor writes "Many of the figures seem hopeless of interpretation. Nevertheless we have printed them in the hope that field botanists ... may recognize a few of the plants which through mistaken features it has been impossible to identify in a herbarium of dried plants" (p. viii). The descriptions are unstandardized and include with the description some of the medical uses:

Linozostis. It hath leaves, like to Ocimum, suitable to those of Helxina but smaller, little boughs with 2 joints, having many wings, & those thin, but the seed, of the female growing in clusters & abounding, but of the male as for ye boughs small, round, as it were two little stones lying together, but ye whole shrub is a span long, or more: but both do move ye belly, being used as potherbs, & eaten. But being sodden in water & ye water drank up they expel choler & watery stuff. And it is thought also that ye leaves of ye female beaten small & drank & laid after the menstrual cleansing to ye privities, do cause ye conception of a femail, & that ye leaves of ye male being ordered after ye like sort, it comes to pass that a male is born.

(p. 593)

The corresponding drawing, made in Byzantium in AD 512, shown below, is labelled "Linozostis" but the editor adds a footnote saying that the identification is "doubtful." For such reasons Eisenstein (1979) argues that printing and engraving were in part responsible for the revolution in the sciences in the sixteenth and seventeenth centuries; original drawings made by a master could now be faithfully duplicated and, furthermore, checked against the experience of hundreds of readers. In fact, after the advent of printing, the growth of such herbals proceeded rapidly.

Yet botanical drawings had begun to change significantly in the Renaissance even before the development of printing. Sarton points out that the ancients had been satisfied to describe plants primarily in

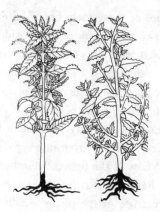

Figure 10.8   Linozostis, a medicinal herb as
depicted in Dioscorides' sixth-century herbal

words. When drawings were included they were primarily artistic;
they "had no desire to imitate natural forms too closely" (Sarton,
1955, p. 87). Drawings were often so discrepant from reality that they
would not permit recognition of the real plant. The delicate illustrations made by the medieval Cybo of Hyeres, Sarton describes as
realistic but religious rather than scientific: "it was artistic and
perhaps religious, for the beauty and loveliness of his creatures, even
the humblest, help us to love God" (pp. 87–88). By the fifteenth
century painters were including realistic depictions of plants in their
paintings; Botticelli's "Spring" has thirty recognizable species of
plants in it (p. 88).

There is no doubt that printing and etching had a dramatic impact
on the accumulation of knowledge of plants and animals. Most important of these early printed books of natural history were the descriptions of herbs that could be grown and harvested for medical purposes. In fact medical schools, beginning in Padua in 1542, created
herb gardens, to be used for training physicians in the recognition and
cultivation of such herbs. This activity was greatly enhanced by the
publication of a new generation of herbals in which descriptions of
plants accompanied by drawings were prepared for medical uses but
also to meet the interests of the common reader. Sarton argues that
advances in botanical drawings and in the distribution and standardization of those drawings which resulted from advances in etching and

printing led to a rejection of earlier drawings and a rewriting of the texts themselves.

The products, the new Herbals of the sixteenth century, were produced by Brunfels, Fuchs, Boch and Cordus, all German and all Lutheran, between 1530 and 1550. What made them new was the fact that rather than being copies, both texts and drawings, from earlier books by Dioscorides or Pliny, they were based on first-hand observation and drawing "from nature" of some five hundred plants. As in other domains of knowledge the transformation was sometimes thought of as a move away from "words," the ancient authorities, to "things"; in fact, it was no such thing. It was a systematic attempt to capture in representations the particular properties and uses of the plants, an activity greatly facilitated by the new style of art and the new means of reproduction of texts and illustrations.

Boas (1962) notes that:

illustrations delighted the eye and supplemented the text; but in botany and anatomy they did more, for they could convey what words, as yet insufficiently subordinated to technical needs, could not. There was as yet no technical language accurate in meaning and universally known, fit to explain in detail the necessary description of form; in fact botany dispensed with pictures when, in the eighteenth century, such a technical language was developed.

(p. 54)

The separation of the technical functions of the drawing from the aesthetic functions was worked out only slowly in the seventeenth century. Brunfels' *Portraits of living plants* incorporated drawings by Hans Weiditz which, while far superior to the text, included what for a modern botanist is irrelevant detail such as broken leaves, wilted flowers and signs of destruction by insects. These factual drawings, like the Dutch art of the seventeenth century, captured the visible properties of the plants separated from their symbolic or mythological associations. When Gesner included his "bishopfish" in his *History of animals* he was careful to add "Whether they truly exist or not, I neither affirm nor deny" (Boas, 1962, p. 58). In the representation of the natural world, depictions rapidly outran verbal descriptions, descriptions, as mentioned, taking their modern role only when an appropriate vocabulary for the nomination of the visible evolved.

Figure 10.9   The Bishop Fish, as depicted in
Gesner's sixteenth-century *History of animals*

Pictures provided the medium in which knowledge of the natural
world could be represented.

Only when drawing was coordinated with scientific description, as
in the work of the Swedish botanist Linnaeus in the eighteenth
century, did botanical drawings become diagrams and did botany
become a science. For Linnaeus the fundamental task of natural
history was that of "arrangement and designation" (Linnaeus, 1735/
1767; 1751; Foucault, 1970, p. 141). Only those features that were
visually recognizable by everyone and which could be given a name
that everyone could understand were allowed to enter botanical
description. Utility and significance, like resemblances and "simili-
tudes," and individual differences were abandoned. Descriptions were
tied to the visible, the nameable and the depictable features of plants.
Each part of the plant – roots, stem, leaves, flowers, fruits – was seen to
be a product of four variables: form, quantity, manner of relation and
magnitude. For example, for the flower, one was to note the form – are
the stamens and pistil arranged in a circle? – the quantity – how many
are there? – the relation – are they below, above, beside the pistil? – and
the magnitude – are they taller or shorter than the pistil? Such
taxonomic descriptions allowed the formation of orders and families,
groups sharing one or more significant features; genera, groups sharing
a large number of basic features; and species, groups with identical

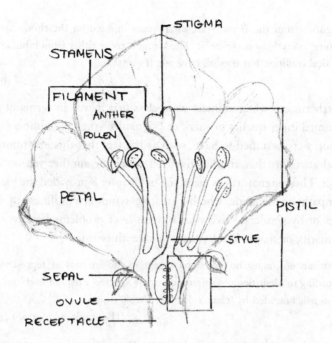

Figure 10.10   Student representation of a generic flower

values on the variables mentioned above. These accounts, of course, make up the introduction to plants that all children are introduced to and taught to draw in the middle school years.

Not only does such analysis reveal a pattern in the world, it is a kind of analysis that ties these patterns to the nameable and the depictable, ignoring all differences that do not fall on to the selected dimensions. In diagrams as in maps, information is exchanged for verisimilitude. A school-book illustration of the parts of a flower looks nothing like any real flower. Yet the pictured flower, the representation, becomes the conceptual entity in terms of which real flowers are perceived and classified. Botanical drawings, like maps, become the conceptual models in terms of which we experience the world. To adopt a metaphor of Gombrich's (1960); knowledge becomes a kind of formulary in terms of which any real event is represented. The formulary, like the map, provides the frame of reference in terms of which events are experienced.

The transformation in the structure of knowledge was dramatic. In medieval times, as Dom Leclercq (1961) noted:

allegories from the *Bestiary* are often superimposed on the things seen. In Nature, everything is symbolic. The symbols come either from biblical ... or classical tradition but they all have moral overtones.

(p. 137)

Furthermore, when animals were classified it was in terms of some assumed inner quality or mark or "signature" that all members of the group were assumed to have, such as the fact that this one hunted its food at night, that another lived on water, or another fed on living flesh. These signatures as we noted in Chapter 8 provided the basis for sympathetic medicine, whether treating symptoms of illness by opposites or by similars – liverwort to treat liver problems because of the similarity of shape. But by the seventeenth century:

there can no longer be any signs except in the analysis of representations according to identities and differences ... [a species] exists in itself only in so far as it is bounded by what is distinguishable from it.

(Foucault, 1970, pp. 144–145)

The relation between folk biology, the biology of commonsense experience, and scientific biology is not merely one of detail and explicitness. It is a matter of translating local knowledge into a general theoretical scheme. Folk biological classifications of plants into flowers, fruits and vegetables are expressions of a social function – a fruit is something one eats for dessert. Scientific botany sees the fruit from, so to speak, the plant's point of view, as an instrument of seed dispersal. The general theoretical scheme involves the attempt to integrate all botanical knowledge into "an overall view of biological nature" (Atran, 1990, p. 75). It is this attempt to construct a general frame of reference (think of the invention of latitude and longitude as devices for integrating geographical knowledge) for all such biological knowledge that turns folk biology into a science. The attempt to capture universal properties of plants by means of a proscribed set of distinguishing features, first in drawing and later in a technical descriptive vocabulary were important steps in that achievement.

So just as reading the Book of Nature required reading according to its visible appearances, so writing the Book of Nature required capturing in words and drawings the visible properties of the objects themselves independently of the social or symbolic function of those objects, an activity that required the invention of new ways of both drawing and describing in the attempt to nominate the visible.

Representing imagined worlds: the beginnings of fiction

Students of literature are familiar with the distinctive literary forms that characterize the modern era. The beginnings of prose (Kittay, 1991; Kittay & Godzich, 1987), the beginnings of fiction (Sanders, 1991), the rise of the novel (Watt, 1957), and the rise of utopian novels are identified with this era. In this section I will simply note how once a representational format had been developed for factual description, as exemplified by Boyle, for example, that form could be exploited for literary purposes. Jonathan Swift's *A modest proposal* gives no indication that it is irony; it adopts all of the features of an honest proposal. Even more impressive are the imaginative accounts of imaginary voyages such as those of Defoe's *Robinson Crusoe*.

Fiction is a new kind of allegorical writing in which literal meanings, that is, meanings which normally report truth, are used to report things known to be false. Medieval allegorical writing, such as *Pilgrim's Progress*, made prominent the fact that the writing was allegorical by providing characters with names like Pilgrim and Envy; the story never pretended to be factually true. Fiction, on the other hand, often pretends to tell the truth. There is nothing in the fiction to indicate that the account is not factually correct. Fiction remains allegorical in the sense that the reader comes away thinking he or she has learned something about reality but the reader knows that, counter to its appearance, it is not a factual narrative report. Consequently, some literary sophistication is required to see truth, now allegorical truth, not factual truth, in fiction; to the uninitiated it appears to be a lie. Defoe heightened the effect by stating in the Preface that the story of Robinson Crusoe was "a just history of fact; neither is there any appearance of fiction in it." Furthermore, his report of how he captured a goat is almost identical in style to that of Boyle or Hooke in reporting an experiment:

I observ'd if they saw me in the Valleys, tho' they were upon the Rocks, they would run away as in a terrible Fright; but if they were feeding in the Valleys, and I was upon the Rocks, they took no Notice of me, from whence I concluded, that by the Position of their Opticks, their Sight was so directed downward, that they did not readily see Objects that were above them ...

(1719/1930, p. 61)

Here is a comparable sample from Robert Hooke's *Micrographia*:

We will begin these our Inquiries therefore with the Observations of Bodies of the most simple nature first ... of which kind the Point of a Needle is commonly reckon'd for one; and is indeed, for the most part made so sharp, that the naked eye cannot distinguish any parts of it. ... But if viewed with a very good Microscope, we may find that the top of a Needle (though as to the sense very sharp) appears a broad, blunt, and very irregular end.

Now though this point be commonly accounted the sharpest ... yet the Microscope can afford us hundreds of Instances of Points many thousand times sharper: such as those of the hairs, and bristles, and claws of multitudes of Insects ...

(pp. 1–2)

What is distinctive about such simple narratives? They are first person, they report factual observation and report it in such a way that anyone else in the same position could have seen the same thing and they appeal for their authority to the reader who could have seen for him or herself the same things. Scientific discourse relies on just such a factual reporting style which lays its meanings open for all to see, a kind of literal meaning of signs, chosen to represent the world precisely. Fiction exploits the same kind of literal representational discourse, but now employed in a non-representational context.

Concluding comment: representations

The important development in the explicit representation of the world, the world on paper, was the new form of discourse involved. The firm distinction between what Sarton calls the artistic and the technical or what Alpers calls the descriptive and the interpretive is a product of the new way of reading texts and nature, according to their detectable, surface properties. Texts, including drawings and charts, neither mean nor imply anything; they purport simply to describe. They state what is available for anyone to see; they assert, insist, imply nothing. Even links in the discourse are not seen as conclusions or inferences made by a writer. They are seen as simply "following" from what went before. They excise the presence of the writer.

They achieve this by a new management of illocutionary force. The writer or artist moves from being an orator with a persuasive message to being a mere reporter who simply tells what we would see *if we were there ourselves*. Even Galileo's demonstrative proofs regarding motion were presented as logical inferences that even the innocent interlocutor, Simplicio, could follow. To serve this representational function, language itself has to be reformed so that it can present the object to the reader and by naming, represent it. For this reason, as both Foucault (1970) and Hacking (1975a) point out, in the seventeenth century there was no theory of meaning. Terms did not have to be seen as meaning anything; they simply pointed to and thereby represented the world. Even when the problem of meaning did again emerge in the nineteenth century, it was not the old style as commentary on meaning and significance, but "in a mode that was to be considered as positive, as objective, as that of natural history" (Foucault, 1970, p. 131).

This optimistic view of the objectivity of representation is no longer so appealing. J. L. Austin's (1962) central insight was that even the most neutral reports of facts have an illocutionary force as well as a propositional content. Even simple descriptions which purport to point to "the things themselves" are, at base, assertions which express a proposition with an illocutionary force. The factual description "Grass is green" or "Two plus two are four" are, he suggests, abridged versions of "I assert that grass is green" and "I claim that two plus two are four." Statements express both a content and the speaker's attitude to that content, the latter of which indicates to the listener how that content is to be taken. Consequently, the presumably simple verbal art of describing is one in which that force is not eliminated but rather hidden.

Pictures are to be analyzed in a similar way. The achievement of the Dutch masters was, as Alpers pointed out, to represent the visible world free from the beliefs and assumptions traditionally read into it; they could represent without "meaning" or symbolizing anything. Yet, as we now know, pictures do not, contra the Dutch masters, simply depict things as they are. Even if the intentions of the artist seem to be neutral, they represent a stance of the describer (Schama,

1987) within a "vocabulary of forms" (Gombrich, 1950). Visual descriptions, too, are disguised assertions. But they are assertions with a new warrant as to their truthfulness. The warrant for the truthfulness of the depiction is the assumption that if the viewer were present at the time the picture was made, the viewer would have seen just what the artist depicted. Just as Boyle turned his readers into "virtual witnesses" of his experiments (Shapin, 1984), so too did the Dutch artists of the seventeenth century.

Now, in the twentieth century, we realize that all observation is, as we say, theory driven, and we need to revise our interpretation of the seventeenth-century achievement. We realize that a "sincere eye and a faithful hand" is not enough to see all that is there; it requires, in addition, a prepared mind. It was the great task of our present generation to discover, report, and thereby bring into consciousness the attitudes implicit in these simple objective reports.

But the seventeenth-century representations we have surveyed, whether in Dutch art, in cartography, or in natural history, indeed, the very attempt at representation, yielded a new understanding of the world. In the case of herbals we noted that improved drawings of plants led to the improvement of verbal descriptions, that is, the selection of the critical discriminating features of the plants themselves. This is not merely putting down what one already knew – almost anyone could, for example, recognize a radish – but of finding the significant features and their relations and articulating them both in words and images so that they could provide a "world picture" of all plants and so that they became part of the public store of knowledge. The paper world, therefore, did not simply provide a means for accumulating and storing what everyone knew. Rather it was a matter of inventing the conceptual means for coordinating the bits of geographical, biological, mechanical, and other forms of knowledge acquired from many sources into an adequate and common frame of reference. This common frame of reference became the theoretical model into which local knowledge was inserted and reorganized. This is the sense, I believe, in which western science of that period acquired the distinctive property of being theoretical science.

And the Dutch artists of the seventeenth century knew that the visible world was not of interest only because it carried a hidden narrative or a moral tale. It was worthy of representation in its own right. What they along with everyone else failed to note was that different representational formats bring still different properties of the world into view. Consequently, the Dutch achievement, while it marked a new stage, did not mark the final or ultimate or only way of representing, and thereby thinking about, the world.

But their attempts at objectivity had a second set of implications. As the distinction between what was "in the world" to be seen and what was sometimes "seen" as being in the world became sharpened, it not only produced more objective accounts of the world but provided a ground for ascribing other aspects of knowledge to the mind. It provided a new understanding of subjectivity. That is the topic of the next chapter.

REPRESENTING THE MIND:
THE ORIGINS OF SUBJECTIVITY

....

> I resolved to seek no other knowledge than that which I might
> find within myself, or perhaps in the great book of nature.
>
> (Descartes, 1637–41/1960, p. 8)

"Subjective," according to The Oxford English Dictionary, means "existing in a person's mind, not objective." Subjectivity as I shall use the term here goes one step further; it is the *recognition* that what is in the mind is in the mind. Subjectivity has a reflexive property; it is the recognition of one's own and others' mental states as mental states. Furthermore, it involves the attempt to construct a first-person perspective to one's own mental states and the mental states of others (Thornton, 1989). That is, it involves an understanding of how those states are regarded by their holders. Subjectivity, then, shows up in several ways. If I regard someone else as not knowing something or falsely believing something, that is not, by my definition, to understand their subjectivity. But if I understand their attitude to their beliefs, for example, that they think they know the truth, then I understand their subjectivity. Similarly, if I understand my attitudes, my ways of holding my own beliefs, I understand something of my own subjectivity. Subjectivity opens the door to introspection. To take another example, if I regard my interpretation of a text as given by or intrinsic to the text I fail to recognize it as my interpretation of a text; I fail to recognize the subjectivity of interpretation. Similarly, if I regard my representation of the world as given by the world I fail to recognize the subjectivity of my own view. I achieve subjectivity when I recognize that even my cherished beliefs, my "truths" are possibly mistaken. Subjectivity, then, is tied to consciousness, not to consciousness generally but to consciousness of mind and the vulnerability of one's own beliefs. While we may have little hope of explaining the origins of consciousness (but see Dennett, 1991) we may have some hope of explaining the origins of subjectivity in a new way of reading and writing and a new understanding of language and thought.

The development of subjectivity may be approached in at least two ways. We shall examine how beliefs and mental states are ascribed to oneself and others both in real life and in literate situations and in this way chart the development of subjectivity. We shall do this by reference to recent work on children's understanding of mental states and their ascription of those states to themselves and others, in particular in the context of reading and writing texts. Secondly, we shall look at conceptions of mind or theory of mind or the science of mind – psychology – to see how the mind is represented in various cultural and historical contexts. Our concern is with the role that writing and reading may have played, not so much in coming to understand intentionality as in the cultural ways invented for thinking about the mind. We begin with the historical perspective.

The discovery of mind

Folk psychology, the pervasive commonsensical view that behavior is to be explained by reference to personally held beliefs and desires, is generally assumed to be a common possession of mankind and perhaps even shared with other primates. Such understanding, dubbed "Theory of Mind," is a topic of much recent research interest.

Fodor (1985, 1987, 1992) has argued that the understanding of mental states of others is probably innate and therefore universal in humans. Certainly the ability to recognize others as intentional beings – as wanting, thinking, trying – appears quite early in children's developmental history (Shultz & Wells, 1985; Astington, Harris & Olson, 1988). Notions like "doing," "trying," which indicate a recognition that behavior is directed at something, that it is purposeful, indicate some understanding of intentionality. Further, young children's understanding of the possibility of false belief and deception indicate that they understand something of the role of such mental states as beliefs and intentions in action and communication.

A failure to understand such mental states is not merely a weakness but characteristic of a serious abnormality. Autistic subjects fail to ascribe beliefs or intentions to others and yet have been shown to cope with conceptual problems of some complexity (Baron-Cohen, 1991; Frith, 1989). Thus, some understanding of mind seems an essential part of human cognition.

Studies of non-human primates also indicate some limited understanding of the mental state of what others want if not what others think (Whiten, 1991). Premack and Dasser (1991) summarize much of the recent research by saying that while there is clear evidence for chimpanzees' ability to attribute motivational states, there is a lack of evidence for their ability to attribute informational, that is, belief states to others. Cheney and Seyfarth (1991), too, suggest that it is more likely that the Vervet monkeys they studied were adept at monitoring others' behavior and attention rather than recognizing mental states such as beliefs and intentions. This competence is grounded in the perception of attention in others.

Neurophysiological studies (Parret, 1990) indicate that a part of the visual cortex of chimpanzees is devoted to the detection of others' gaze, presumably a precursor of the recognition of the intentions of others. Monitoring the direction of gaze of others is an ability which is also lacking in autistic subjects (Baron-Cohen, 1991).

Thus while it appears that the ability to recognize oneself and others as intentional is a fundamental part of being human, the attempts to conceptualize these relations between action and intention, belief and desire are more complex and do appear to have a cultural history. A fascinating part of this history comes from the study of the Greek invention of the concept of mind, an invention that is thought to have occurred between the time of the oral poet Homer, "author" of *The Iliad* and *The Odyssey*, and the time of the Greek philosophers Socrates, Plato and Aristotle.

The Homeric epics recount in great detail the ways of living and thinking of the pre-literate ancestors of the classical Greeks. They are by far the earliest accounts of life and thought in Europe. These poems are universally granted to be literary masterpieces. So much so that many critics, struck by their outstanding aesthetic qualities, have been sceptical of the attempts to account for their literary structure on bases other than aesthetic ones. Yet Parry (1971) and his student Lord (1960; see Havelock, 1991 for a first-hand version of this development) were able to demonstrate that these poems were the product of "oral" composition produced for live audiences by bards, who like their audiences, could neither read or write. Before they were written down, around the seventh century BC, there was no fixed text but rather renditions were generated anew on each performance on the basis of a fixed theme, fixed metrical structure and a stock of formulaic phrases. Recent scholarship has tempered these conclusions somewhat. Goody (1987) argued that the written version shows some signs of literate editing and Lynn-George (1988) argued that the mode of composition of "oral" poetry did not importantly alter either form or meaning.

Several scholars have used these texts to reconstruct the mental lives of the Homeric Greeks. Onians (1954) provides a colourful introduction:

The manliest warriors weep copiously and publicly. Because the Achaeans are driven back, imperial Agamemnon stands unashamed before the assembled host, 'weeping like a fountain of black water that from a beetling crag pours its dark stream'. Priam, pleading with Hector to retire, first beats his head with his hands and then plucks out his hair. When Hector dies, he rolls in dung, and, gathering it up, befouls his head and neck with it and stays in the midst of it for twelve days, inconsolable.

The noblest behave like savages in battle. Agamemnon, after slaying the suppliant son of treacherous Antimachos, cuts off his arms and head, then sends the trunk rolling. ... Telemachos, the wise and good ... twists the hands and feet of the unfaithful Melantheus behind his back, and by a cord fastened to them, hangs him up so 'that he may long remain alive and suffer torments.' Later they took him down still alive, led him through the court, 'cut off his nostrils and ears with the pitiless bronze, plucked out his genitals for the dogs to devour raw, and hacked his hands and feet with vengeful spirit', then left him.

Women are an avowed aim and approved prize of war. It is to save their wives that men fight. When a city is taken, the men are slain, the children are dashed to death or enslaved, and the women violently dragged away to serve as slaves and concubines of their married or unmarried conquerors.

(pp. 3–5)

Little sign here of the tender emotions of shame, embarrassment, sympathy, forgiveness, anger (as opposed to rage), or the form of self-consciousness I earlier referred to as subjectivity. Nor is there much evidence of praise or blame or feelings of personal responsibility

(Onians, 1954, p. 51). Yet there is a shared and coherent tradition and the individuals are at times brave, resourceful, planful and cooperative and at other times crafty, wily, and deceitful. The understanding of deception is usually taken as criterial in ascribing a "theory of mind" to children and non-human primates and to that extent at least, the Homeric Greeks had an understanding of mind.

But, that understanding was seriously limited it seems by their limited understanding of subjectivity. We get a better picture of their psychology by an examination of their ways of referring to knowledge and speech. The most striking feature of the Homeric conception of mind is that they had none. There is no evidence of a concept of mind as distinguished from body and there is an absence of such terms as "decided," "thought," "believed," "doubted" or "equivocated." Homer's characters, of course, do all of these things (at least we feel comfortable in ascribing such states and activities to them) but Homer reports them in a quite different way. For example, Homer reports that King Agamemnon was *told by his voices* to take the fair-cheeked Briseis away from Achilles. This is not merely a quaint, poetic way of speaking; it is their way of speaking and, presumably, their way of thinking about those activities (Havelock, 1982, p. 224). Making a decision was represented, and hence experienced, as hearing voices dictate what one was to do.

The Homeric vocabulary included terms for referring to talk and feelings but whereas for their literate descendants, the Classical Greeks, such terms refer to internal, mental events, for the Homeric Greeks, they referred to external, bodily, objective events. For the Homeric Greeks, what we refer to as thinking is usually described as speaking, an activity originating in the organs of speaking, the lungs. Pondering is conversations addressed to those internal organs. Thus Odysseus "smote his breast and rebuked his heart with words: 'Endure, O heart'; ... and his heart enduring abode fast. But Odysseus himself rolled this way and that pondering ..." (Homer, *The Odyssey*, xx, 6, 1946).

Since thinking is an aspect of speaking to one's organs or hearing voices there is no notion of a separate domain of "thoughts" or "ideas." Only later does the same root word come to be distinguished into two distinctive concepts, *ratio*, rationality, and *oratio*, speech

(Onians, 1954). Similarly the word *logos* only later comes to be differentiated into the concepts of *word* and *idea* (Havelock, 1982).

Jaynes (1976), who worked through these Homeric materials as well as the more ancient parts of the Bible, noted that Homer represented what we think of as mental states as bodily states or activities. Feelings and emotions are referred to as the palpitating heart or panting breath or uttering cries. *Thumos* is the experience of stress which moves one to action: "it is not Ajax who is zealous to fight but his *thumos*, nor is it Aeneas who rejoices but his *thumos*. . . . a man may speak to his *thumos* and hear from it what he is to say" (pp. 262–263).

Phrenes, lungs, provide a place for retaining words, fears, and even wine which beclouds *thumos*. *Noos* derives from the verb "to see," resides in the chest, and is used to refer to information obtained from the senses. Thus Zeus keeps Hector in his *noos* and later, Odysseus turns over deceitful thoughts in his *noos*. *Psyche*, the Greek word that we now translate as mind, refers simply to life. When a warrior is speared, his *psyche* is destroyed or dissolved or is coughed out or bled out through a wound. No one in the *Iliad* decides, thinks, knows, fears, or remembers anything in his *psyche* (Jaynes, 1976, p. 271). Only in the Classical period do *psyche*, *thumos* and *noos* come to be united in a general concept of mind as a mental organ located in the head (Snell, 1960) and only then does mind come to be seen as contrastive to, and in control of, the body.

As Padel (1992) shows, the pre-Aristotelian Greeks did not make a strict distinction between literal and metaphorical usage and hence it is inappropriate to force our distinctions on their language for describing mental states. Pre-Socratic Greeks did not feel it necessary to state clearly whether *noos* was a vessel, an organ or a force. What seems clear is that they had not adopted the now-familiar view of mind as the organ of belief, desire and intention.

The Homeric Greek poems, then, provide little evidence of thinking about the mind as the instrument of the self employed in controlling the body and in carrying out intentional actions. There is little evidence of a concept resembling the Cartesian ego. The model of action, rather, is that of telling and doing. Penelope sets up a great loom to weave a robe because "some god breathed into my lungs that I should" (Homer, *The Odyssey*, XIX, 138). If the gods tell a warrior that he will die in battle, he simply lays down his arms and awaits death. We see the characters in the epics as lacking in some aspects of self-consciousness because they do not see beliefs, desires and intentions originating in themselves.

The Homeric folk psychology was therefore quite different from ours in at least one way. Like us, they understood lies and deception – the competence that distinguishes children under four years, autistic adults and non-human primates from normal humans – yet they lacked a vocabulary and its corresponding concepts for thinking about the mind. Representing one's thoughts and actions as originating other than in the self indicates a limited notion of responsibility, deliberateness, and intentionality. Seeing actions as the expression of one's thoughts, it may be argued, is what allows them to be seen as subject to deliberation and control. Agamemnon, for example, claimed that he was not to blame for stealing fair-haired Briseis from Achilles for he had been made to do so by the god Zeus:

But I am not to blame!
Zeus and Fate and the furies stalking through the night
They are the ones who drove the savage madness in my heart
That day in assembly when I seized Achilles prize –
On my own authority, true, but what could I do?

(Homer, *The Iliad*, Book 19, 100–104)

Bruner (1990; Bruner & Weisser, 1991) has recently argued that self-consciousness arises through autobiographical story-telling in which one interprets a variety of experiences from the perspective of the narrative "I." The public, communal narratives of the Homeric Greeks appeared to allow less opportunity for the formation of such personal narratives. Action, for them, appears to reside in the collective which included the gods rather than in the individuals and their minds.

By the Classical period the mind is thought of, much as we do today, as the storehouse of thoughts and ideas; the theory of the passions, subjective mental and emotional states, is essentially unsurpassed (Nussbaum, 1986; de Sousa, 1980). Aristotle's theory of formal cause is little different from modern theories of intentionality as formulated, for example, by Searle (1983). But did the theory of mind of the Classical Greeks with its increased articulation of the mental and its almost glaring self-consciousness have anything to do with the invention of writing or the growth of literacy?

Havelock (1976, p. 2) has argued that it does. His argument, we may recall, is that an oral culture preserves information by making it memorable. Both form and content reflected that need; the language must be poetic and the content must be of action not reflection (1982, p. 8). Writing, he suggested, released cognition from the constraint of memorability allowing a new form of discourse, the discourse of principles, statements, and definitions. That general claim is somewhat undercut by recent work showing that most if not all philosophical discourse both then and in the Middle Ages was oral in form (Carruthers, 1990; Finnegan, 1988; W. Harris, 1989). Some of these arguments were reviewed in Chapter 3.

Havelock's second argument is less vulnerable and it corresponds to the general notion developed in Chapter 4, namely, that writing provides the model for speech and thereby makes aspects of language, including words, into objects of consciousness. All speakers are conscious of what is said but not conscious of those linguistic constituents we think of as words. As Havelock puts it, when language is written down it comes to be seen as an object in its own right. Words can be distinguished from the content or meanings expressed which then "come to be objectified as thoughts, ideas, notions existing in their own right. ... As separate entities, [ideas] seem to require a separate source, not a linguistic one associated with the speaker's tongue or mouth, but a mental one of a different order located in his consciousness" (Havelock, 1982, p. 290). Ideas are the counterpart of words; when words are seen as objects, so too are ideas. It is writing rather than speech which encourages consciousness of the distinction between what I say and what I meant to say. It is "what was meant" which comes to be seen as the mental.

Here, then, is a possible literate source of the concepts of mental – words become distinguished from ideas, what is said is distinguished from what is thought, the thing from the idea or representation of a thing, and the mind from the body. The concept of idea, a mental object, is central to all literate-based theories of mind from Plato to Descartes to Fodor although, as we shall see, the idea of an idea was to undergo some important conceptual shifts long after it was first introduced.

To recap briefly. The Homeric Greeks experienced or represented speaking, thinking, feeling and acting as originating outside the self, typically in the speech of the gods: they "had to" act rather than "decide to" act. The Classical Greeks came to see speech and action as originating in the mind and progressively under the control of the self. It is this new way of seeing speech and action which allowed for the increased control and responsibility that we speak of as the rise of self-consciousness. The proposed route to this self-consciousness is the experience of writing. Writing provided a model for one's speech. The very possibility of inventorying the lexical resources of the language arises only when writing provides a model for such entities. Consciousness of words permits their distinction from the ideas that words express. Writing, therefore, gives rise to the idea of an idea and the mind becomes the storehouse of those ideas. Thus it is at least plausible that the discovery of the mind was part of the legacy of writing.

The making of the modern mind

As our concern is with the conceptual implications of writing rather than with the history of ideas, we may perhaps be excused for simply jumping to another period in which forms of reading and writing arguably influenced conceptions of mind. A number of philosophers and literary theorists have noted the new awareness of and concern with subjective mental states that appeared in the Early Modern period. Foucault (1970, p. 213) referred to "the great crisis of the Western experience of subjectivity" which was expressed in the need "to take a direct part in spiritual life, in the work of salvation, in the truth which lies in the Book." Stock (1983) noted the new concern with personal beliefs, doubts, understandings and interpretations and with "meaning" that began first in the eleventh and twelfth centuries. LePan (1989) noted the shift in literary sensitivities as when Shake-speare's *Othello* explored the implications not, as did the Greeks, of action, but of beliefs, as when Othello falsely believes Desdemona to be unfaithful.

The modern conception of mind and modern notions of subjectivity are usually traced to Descartes and his famous dictum: "Cogito ergo sum": I think therefore I am. Since the seventeenth century, thinking rather than knowing has been the central function of mind. Descartes helped to show that our access to knowledge and truth was, at base, psychological. The criterion of truth, for example, was not simply "what is," but that which I cannot doubt; doubt, a psychological state, became central to the judgment of truth. With Descartes, we see modern consciousness of mind erupt on to the stage (Vendler, 1972, p. 205).

I prefer to think of Descartes' achievement as one of establishing the autonomy of the mental. Whereas Plato had seen ideas as "ideal forms" existing in the world and Aristotle has seen ideas as abstractions from classes of objects in the world, Descartes advanced the notion that ideas may be pure inventions of mind so much so that he postulated a form of dualism of mind and body. Both were parts of a person but there was nothing in common to thought and extension (things). In thinking about things, the mental was prior.

Descartes established the priority of the mental by his method of doubt. He found that he could doubt everything: he may be mistaken about objects or bodies in the world – as when he took a distant square object to be round; he may be mistaken about the sensible qualities of objects – things which look small may only be distant; or, indeed, he may be mistaken that there is a real world at all – he may be dreaming. But of one thing there could be no possible mistake, namely, that he thought or that he doubted. In a celebrated passage, Descartes wrote:

What then am I? A thinking being. What is a thinking being? It is a being which doubts, which understands, which conceives, which affirms, which denies, which wills, which rejects, which imagines also, and which perceives.

(1637–41/1960, p. 85)

We could add: which remembers, believes, forgets, pretends, and imagines, all of which are subjects of modern psychological theory. Vendler (1972) re-examined Descartes' list of mental activities and found that they correspond to what are now referred to as Speech Act Verbs – affirm, deny – and Mental Verbs – think, doubt, understand. The relation between the two is that the latter, mental verbs, provide the "sincerity condition" for speech act verbs. Thus, to assert something sincerely one must believe that something; to deny sincerely one must at least doubt; and to promise sincerely one must intend to do something (Searle, 1983). These close relations between saying and thinking have become apparent only in this century (see Chapter 5).

Ideas for Descartes are clearly distinguished from reality. The relation is one of representation. Ideas have three sources: some are born with me, others come from without, and the rest are made and invented by myself (Descartes, 1637–41/1960, p. 94). Most ideas come from the third source, myself. Those from without can all be doubted:

As far as the ideas of corporeal objects are concerned, I recognize nothing in them [that could not] arise from myself. I find that there are only a few elements in them which I conceive clearly and distinctly – namely, size or extension; shape; location and movement. As for other elements such as light, colors, sounds, odors, tastes, heat, cold . . . occur in my thought with so much obscurity and confusion . . . it is not necessary for me to attribute to such ideas any other source than myself . . . [Even] my clear and distinct ideas of corporeal things . . . might be contained in my nature. . . . I do not see why they could not be produced by myself and why I could not be their author.

(pp. 99–101)

Ideas, then, originate primarily in oneself not in the world: "The principle and most common error . . . consists in judging that the ideas which are in myself are similar to the things outside myself" (p. 94). Consequently, "we know very little with certainty about corporeal things and . . . we know much more about the human mind" (p. 109).

But this is the familiar theme that we explored in Chapters 8 and 9 when we discussed the new way of reading in which a new set of strictures as to what a text meant allowed a clear distinction between what was in a text and what was read into a text whether the text at issue was the Book of Scripture or the Book of Nature. For the scientists and philosophers of the seventeenth century, the problem was to disentangle what was in the world from the construals, inventions and interpretations provided by the mind. Francis Bacon attempted to set out rules for correctly reading or interpreting the book of God's work primarily by removing the impediments to correct interpretation, what he called the idols of the tribe, the received opinions, the tendency to form vague abstract generalizations, and the biasing effects of will and affections, "for affections color and infect the understanding" (Aphorism 49). True understanding was possible only through unmixing "the dreams of the imagination" from the "patterns in the world" (p. 323).

For Bacon the interest in the mind was primarily one of bringing it under submission to the patterns in the world. One must control the overactive intellect for it "mixes up its own nature with the nature of things" (p. 317). The human understanding is a distorting mirror which "distorts and discolours the nature of things by mingling its own nature with it" (Aphorism 41). It is subject to "vain imaginings" (p. 326), it has a tendency to "imagine and suppose" (Aphorism 10), to make "pretty and probable conjectures" (p. 329), and to "represent worlds of [its] own creation" (Aphorism 44). Hence, "the understanding must not therefore be supplied with wings, but rather hung with weights to keep it from leaping and flying" (Aphorism 104). Indeed, the ideal forms discussed by Plato and the Scholastics were now seen as "figments of the human mind" (Aphorism 51).

For scientists such as Boyle and Hooke working in the Baconian model, the concern was to eliminate the mental by focusing on the "observed facts." The product was Early Modern Science. But for Descartes and the British Empiricist philosophers the concern was in characterizing the contributions of the mental. The product was a psychology, a science of the mind. Descartes, as we saw, found the mental ineliminable, believing that most ideas originate in the mind. And the British Empiricist philosophers Locke, Hume and Berkeley advanced a series of proposals as to the role of the mind in the formation of knowledge. Only by subtracting the contributions of the mind could one see nature as it really was.

As Locke acknowledged in the preface to *An essay concerning human understanding*, (1690/1961, p. 4), his analysis of the nature of ideas and their role in human understanding was provoked by a discussion with friends whose scientific work, they felt, would be hindered until they could sort out the limits of the understanding. The result, completed some twenty years later, was the celebrated *Essay*. Locke proposed to distinguish the properties of the things themselves – properties such as figure and extension – which he called primary qualities, from secondary qualities, such as taste and color, which were added by the perceiver. In this, Locke followed Galileo who in *The Assayer* had written:

tastes, odours, colours, and so on are no more than mere names so far as the object in which we place them is concerned and reside only in the consciousness. Hence, if the living creature were removed, all these qualities would be wiped away and annihilated.

(Galilei, 1623/1957, p. 274)

Hume (1748/1962) distinguished two levels of mental activity, sense impressions, our "more lively perceptions," from the less direct and less lively "thoughts and ideas." The powers of the mind "amount to no more than the faculty of compounding, transposing, augmenting, or diminishing the materials afforded by the senses" (p. 34). Because ideas are products of the mind, they are "naturally faint and obscure" (p. 36). No ideas are "given" by nature. They are all products of the activities of the mind: "In all reasonings from experience there is a step taken by the mind which is not supported by any argument or process of the understanding" (p. 60). Even the idea of God is not apprehended directly but "arises from reflecting on the operations of our own mind" (p. 35). Hume's most celebrated claim was that causality exists neither in nature nor in logical necessity but merely in custom or habit of the mind; causality is an idea inferred from sequence, not something given in nature. In general, "all inferences from experience, therefore, are effects of custom, not of reasoning" (p. 61).

It was Bishop Berkeley (1709–10/1975), however, who took the major step in building a theory in which interpretation figures as a central part of perception. In the end, for Berkeley, nothing is free from interpretation: "To be is to be perceived." But how Berkeley gets to this position is our concern, for it demonstrates the hermeneutical basis of this theory of mind.

To see how radical Berkeley's view was it is useful to contrast it with the Platonic and Scholastic view of ideas. Both sensible species and intelligible species, as Aquinas called them, were regarded as given by nature. The working of the mind was to capture these species, that is, these concepts or ideas. Reformation theology insisted upon a division between what was given by Scripture and what were the mere accretions of habit, tradition and invention. That distinction between the given and the interpreted when applied to reading the Book of Nature came out as one of distinguishing observed facts from probable conjectures. But when the issue was attacked systematically by the Empiricist philosophers, they were unable to find a satisfactory distinction between that given to observation and that imposed by the mind.

Berkeley's solution was to treat observations as themselves inferences from simpler or more primitive "immediate, proper or direct objects of vision." What we actually see, Berkeley claimed, were colours, relative sizes, sequences and other sensory "qualia" or sense-data which were signs from which one could infer, on the basis of past experience, the presence of objects in the world. He provides an example:

> ... the passions which are in the mind of another are of themselves to me invisible. I may nevertheless perceive them by sight, though not immediately, yet by means of the colours they produce in the countenance. We often see shame or fear in the looks of a man, by perceiving the changes of his countenance to red or pale.
>
> (p. 10, no. 9)

The redness or paleness are the "immediate objects of perception" while the shame or fear are inferred from those features. Similarly we do not perceive a man directly but only the colour, size, figure, and motions from which we infer a man (p. 124, no. 148). And further, we perceive God by inference from "manifest tokens of divinity" (p. 124, no. 148).

That objects are inferred from the data of sense rather than directly perceived is a view shared by Locke, Hume and Berkeley. But Berkeley takes these ideas in two new directions, one his idealism, the other his model of perception as a kind of reading.

Whereas Locke had claimed that at least primary qualities existed in the world, Berkeley argued that all qualities existed in the mind: "those arguments, which are thought manifestly to prove that colours and tastes exist only in the mind ... may with equal force be brought to prove the same thing of extension, figure and motion" (p. 81, no. 15). And again, "Extension, figure and motion are only ideas existing in the mind" (p. 79, no. 9). On Berkeley's view, all properties are secondary properties.

Berkeley's idealism is a direct implication of this denial of primary qualities. He denied any material reality independent of perception or knowledge of it: "all those bodies which compose the mighty frame of the world, have not any subsistence without a mind, . . . their being is to be perceived" (p. 78, no. 6).

Berkeley's idealism was advanced as an argument against the skepticism of Hume. Hume had argued that if knowledge was made up by the mind, one could not be certain of anything. Berkeley's argument was not to deny that the mind makes up knowledge but rather that just because the mind made it up, it does not follow that knowledge is not true. What the mind can perceive does indeed exist but its existence is dependent upon its being perceived. Thus Berkeley completes what Descartes began, namely, putting the mind at the centre of knowledge.

That Berkeley's theory of vision is in fact a theory of reading is less well known and perhaps more equivocal. For Berkeley, the immediate objects of perception are better regarded as signs than as properties of objects. One reads signs and infers objects just as one reads letters and infers meaning. Visible signs only suggest their meanings to the understanding just as words do: "The manner wherein [objects of vision] signify and mark unto us the objects which are at a distance is the same . . . [as] that of languages and signs of human appointment" (p. 52, no. 147). The relation is one of sign (or representation) to thing signified, an argument Berkeley spells out in detail (pp. 54–55, no. 159). The only difference between seeing and reading is that natural signs are given in nature whereas the latter depend upon convention. Visible signs signify tangible objects by virtue of a "language of nature" which "doth not vary in different ages or nations" (p. 49, no. 140) whereas human languages are of human invention and are therefore arbitrary. "The voice of the Author of Nature, which speaks to our eyes, is not liable to that misinterpretation and ambiguity that languages of human contrivance are unavoidably subject to" (p. 53, no. 152).

Just because Berkeley's model of perception was at base a model of reading does not prove that mental philosophy generally was a by-product of a new way of reading. So let us reconsider, briefly, that relation.

Reformation hermeneutics distinguished itself by tying interpretation to textual properties, what perhaps somewhat misleadingly I have referred to as its literal meaning. Tying interpretation to textual structures allowed seventeenth-century readers to distinguish the meaning of a text from the "amplifications, digressions, and swellings of style" which Medieval rhetorical procedures had accepted as part of valid reading. This new austere mode of reading assigned to the "bin" the creative, inventive and active constructions of the mind of the reader or interpreter.

But excluding the mind was not a simple matter. Once the quest began it turned out that almost no matter how deeply one cut one could find the imprint of the mind on perception and knowledge. The alternative to eliminating the mind was to acknowledge the various ways in which the mind was involved. One way was to distinguish observed facts – those which could be "witnessed" by anyone – from hypothetical conjectures as Boyle and his contemporaries did (Shapin, 1984). The other was simply to bite the bullet as both Descartes and Berkeley did in their different ways and to admit that knowledge was at best a set of beliefs which could not be doubted.

Seen this way, what these philosophers were attempting to do was to cope with those aspects of interpretation that had been problematical in reading, namely, those related to illocutionary force – how utterances and events were to be taken. Just as the central problem of reading scripture was that of determining not so much what was said as how it was to be taken, so, too, the problem of the mentalistic philosophers was to sort out these "ways of taking." They did not deny the "texts" or the structures of those texts. What they debated was precisely what was in those texts and how to get from those texts to interpretations. Their proffered solution was an applied hermeneutics. Nature was a kind of a book which could be read but one must exercise judgment in order not to ascribe too much to the "book." Much of what earlier generations had seen in both scripture and nature was now judged to be if not an outright invention at least an inference by the mind. An austere hermeneutics produced an austere ontology; the world was not as complex as it had seemed. It required careful reading and diligent observation to sort out fact from fiction.

On the other hand by establishing the autonomy of the mental, that is, the independence of ideas from the things they were ideas of, they established the possibility of genuine theoretical knowledge, often taken as the hallmark of modern science. What makes the knowledge theoretical is the understanding that one may consider the logic, the coherence and the simplicity of the theory, independently of the evidence that may count for or against the theory. This is just what the new understanding of representations made possible.

Children's theories of mind

Children growing up in any culture acquire the folk-ways of that culture including its ways of talking and thinking about talk, action and its consequences, and feelings. Any understanding of the speech and actions of oneself and of others requires some understanding of needs, desires, goals, feelings, and beliefs. Children acquire such basic understanding quite early in life (Astington, Harris, & Olson, 1988; Perner, 1991; Wellman, 1990). In western cultures, at least, we tend to think of such understandings as an understanding of the mind. Indeed, children are said to have a "theory of mind" if they can use ascriptions of beliefs and desires as means of interpreting or explaining the sayings and actions of themselves or others.

A pivotal achievement in this understanding is the recognition of beliefs. Beliefs are special in that they may be false and yet "held" or "entertained" by a person. Misdirected actions, for example, may be explained by noting or postulating that the actor holds a false belief. Impressive experimental work on the highest non-human species, the chimpanzee (Premack & Woodruff, 1978) yields at best ambiguous evidence of an understanding of false belief (Dennett, 1978). Experiments with young children are much more conclusive. Wimmer and Perner (1983) provided evidence, now widely replicated, that children under four years of age are unable to recognize the very possibility of a false belief. By age four or five they understand that someone could hold a false belief and that such a belief would lead the holder to fail to reach his goal. That understanding underlies a host of "mental" activities such as introspection (Gopnik & Astington, 1988), the understanding of surprise (Hadwin & Perner, 1991; MacLaren & Olson, 1993), deception (Chandler, Fritz, & Hala, 1989; Peskin, 1992), the interpretation of ambiguity (Ruffman, Olson, & Astington, 1991) as well as a variety of childhood games such as hide-and-seek.

In western cultures, the acquisition of an understanding of beliefs, desires and intentions is completely tied up with the acquisition of a mentalistic language for talking about these events. Four-year-old children correctly use such expressions as "think," "know," "surprise," "guess" and the like before they begin school (Dunn, 1988). Even where this language is meagre, children appear to grasp the basic understanding of the possibility of false belief in that they understand the possibility of tricking or misleading someone (Avis & Harris, 1991).

Yet there is some indication that mental states, including false beliefs, may be thought about in a less mentalistic way at least in some cultures. McCormick (1994) collected folk tales from the Quechua in remote regions of Peru. These tales are recognizable in almost any culture. One tale told of "Wily Coyote" who saw the moon reflected in a lake and mistook it for a cheese. Failing to persuade Owl to retrieve the "cheese" for him, Coyote dived into the lake to retrieve the cheese for himself and drowned. For the Quechua, the mistaking is described in terms of appearances – "the moon appeared to be a cheese" rather than false belief – "Coyote thought it was a cheese." Interestingly, when McCormick (1994) read the same story to Canadian university students, without exception, they reported the story as saying that the fox "thought" it was a cheese. (Readers may note that in my telling of the story I used the verb "mistook" and I put quotation marks around the word cheese to indicate that it was not really a cheese.) Both ways of telling cover much the same ground; but English speakers are socialized into a discourse of mental states whereas the Quechua are socialized into a language of appearance and illusion. These ways of talking appear to fit into the general cultural ways of experiencing actions and events. Cultural differences between Western and Indian children in understanding of mental life has also been reported by Kakar (1978).

Even after children acquire some rudimentary understanding of the mental states of themselves and others they may understand relatively little of the subjectivity of mental states, that is, how those states are experienced by their holders. To return to a case described in Chapter 6, five- and six-year-old children are led to understand that a certain character, say John, falsely believes that a piece of candy is in a drawer. The children are then asked: "What will John say if we ask him: 'John, do you know where your candy is?'" They incorrectly reply "No." They do understand that John does not know where the candy is but they fail to understand that from John's point of view, he thinks he knows. They fail, we infer, to understand the subjectivity of belief (Olson, Howes, & Torrance, in preparation; Perner & Howes, 1992).

Similarly, right into the school years they continue to have difficulty understanding irony. Sarcasm presents less difficulty presumably because it is marked by a strong, sneering intonation. Sarcasm without intonation is irony. Children tend to take ironic utterances either as literally true or as lies (see Keenan, in preparation; Lucariello, 1989; Winner, 1988). To interpret an utterance as ironic requires that the listener or reader grant both that the utterance is not true and that the speaker does not believe it to be true nor want the listener to take it as true and yet that it be taken as informative. Thus, understanding irony requires some sophistication in understanding both language and the mental states of the speaker. Sorting out these complex intentions presents problems for even eight and ten year olds and some adults.

We may conclude that some understanding of mind is necessary for understanding action and communication. The elaboration of this understanding and the invention of distinctive concepts for referring to these states both has a cultural history and a developmental history. The complexity that these states take in literate cultures is readily demonstrated by noting the complex ways in which expressions can be taken and the elaborate language for distinguishing these ways in literate discourse.

Literacy and mental states

In the discussion of what writing does not represent (Chapter 5) we noted that scripts do not capture stress, intonation and paralinguistic properties of speech nor the context of the expression. These features are critical to illocutionary force, how the speaker or writer intends the utterance to be taken – as statement or command, as literal or metaphorical. Such features also indicate more subtle distinctions such as suggestion versus command or conjecture versus assertion. Intonation also carried markers of structural cohesion, that is markers of how propositions are to be related. Main points, subordinate points, asides, digressions and the like can often be recognized from non-lexical clues (Tannen, 1985).

In reading texts children have to learn a new set of devices for managing both illocutionary force and textual structure. Often no indication of how a text is to be taken is present and the reader is expected to infer it from the textual context. To read a text the reader has to learn to recognize the clues that indicate how texts are to be taken and in writing they must learn to bring these very devices under deliberate control (Herriman, 1986).

Some of these properties may be learned independently of learning to read and write. Children of bookish parents may learn to speak with subordinate clauses, parentheticals, and the like, marking structure lexically by means of subordinating conjunctions, relative pronouns, and speech act verbs. Such bookish parents can do so because writing can and does provide a model for their speech. Other children's primary opportunity for acquisition of such literate knowledge comes through the school.

Reading and writing provide opportunities for sustained practice in assigning force and structure to texts both when it is explicit in those texts and when it has to be inferred. Because this point is little discussed in either educational theory or in guides for practice it is worth elaborating briefly.

Consider these two statements which are grammatically identical:

The box is light because it is empty.
The box is light because I can lift it up.

The first uses the conjunction "because" to express a causal relation; the second to express an evidence relation (Donaldson, 1986; Feider, 1970). The reader is expected to infer the appropriate construal on the basis of prior knowledge. But prior knowledge of any advanced domain is often sufficiently limited that children have no grounds for automatically filling in the kind of relation intended. For this purpose they have to learn to rely on explicit markings of these relations. "Because" has to be narrowed to mean only "is caused by" and the second meaning has to be replaced by such expressions as "I know that," "is evidence for," "is the reason for," "it follows logically," and so on. In one sense, nothing is learned, for children understand these relations in simple contexts such as lifting light boxes. But in another sense, in explicating these relations children are learning to think systematically and to convey, systematically, their thinking to others.

There is evidence that children acquire a specialized vocabulary for marking illocutionary force relatively late in their school career if they acquire it at all. Astington (1988) found that children well into the middle school years had difficulties in sorting out the differences between promises, assertions and predictions. In another study, Olson and Astington (1990) found that only students in the more academic streams had a working knowledge of such concepts as *concede, imply, infer, hypothesize, interpret* and the like. One explanation comes readily to hand. Such terms rarely occurred in the textbooks studied by these children – the concepts had been sacrificed in the interest of "readability." Informal discussions with teachers revealed two contrasting attitudes. Some teachers said they never used such terms because the children did not understand them; other teachers said they were essential to teaching.

A more formidable problem lies in the fact that written texts rarely indicate how a proposition is to be taken. Chemistry textbooks in the same "breath" state that the atomic number of oxygen is 16 and that it is a colourless gas. The first indicates a location in a periodic table which is a matter of theory; the second an empirical fact. The students' task is to sort out the assumptions of the discipline, the definitions, the theoretical frameworks, the supporting evidence, the plausible conjectures and inferences. In our terms, that is to say that each of the propositions encountered has a status or a force – it is to be taken a certain way – yet those ways are often left for the student to sort out for him or herself.

Opportunities for discussion of how expressions are to be taken are more often seized in the field of literary studies where problems of interpretation are central than in science. One must judge whether a statement is to be taken literally or metaphorically, or as strictly speaking or loosely speaking or as a statement, a suggestion, a conjecture, an impossible ideal or a realistic claim and so on. How does one know that Swift in *A modest proposal* is writing ironically? Even here many such opportunities are lost because of the drive for the one best or conventionally accepted answer.

The failure to recognize that science is a branch of literature (*pace* Popper) leads many teachers to overlook opportunities for discussing how to take statements and hold beliefs and is as much a concern of science education as of literary studies.

Developing subjectivity

The relation between children's early understanding of the mind and a more advanced knowledge of mental states and attitudes to propositions may be viewed from either of two perspectives which are often seen as contradictory. The first, a naturalistic perspective associated with Piaget, would emphasize how complex concepts arise from the more primitive ones. *Interpret* could arise from coordinating the concepts *think* and *mean* to yield *think it means*. We considered these aspects of development in Chapter 6.

The second, a more social perspective, is associated with Vygotsky (1962). Whether in reading, being read to, writing, or even in talking about texts children learn to recognize the clues that indicate that one statement is asserted as true, another as an analogy, another as an inference from some other statement, another a construal or an interpretation of some utterance or event. As they become more sophisticated in determining the ways of taking textual statements they also come to understand that their own utterances are intended to be taken in a certain way – as claims, inferences, examples, digressions – that their interpretations are in fact interpretations, and that what they had previously taken as pure "knowledge" is in fact composed of sets of beliefs held with varying attitudes and degrees of commitment. With any luck they will begin to recognize that any content can be entertained with almost any attitude; today's conjecture may be turned into tomorrow's belief by means of amassing the critical evidence. In learning to make these distinctions children will be

learning what the British Empiricists had earlier learned, namely, that
"some of the things previously taken to be features of the universe
around us are really characteristics of our own internal constitution"
(Flew, 1962, p. 7).

This second perspective has the advantage that it is in line with the
history of writing and reading developed earlier in this book. Language and knowledge have frequently been seen in terms of the models
of language and interpretation served up by writing. Thinking about
thinking may be no exception. Children may have to be shown how to
take a text just as they have to be shown how to look at a picture if they
are to recognize just what the writer or painter has done and with what
intended effect.

Research is only beginning on the question of how these elementary
mentalistic concepts continue to develop through the school years or
what impact reading and writing have on their development. Consequently the evidence reviewed and the conjectures as to the nature of
this development should be seen as merely setting out a line of inquiry
rather than as settling the issues involved.

The comprehension and production of texts requires the management of both content and force – what is said and how it is to be taken.
The experienced reader and writer is conscious of both. The experienced reader can recognize the mind behind the writing and the mind
of the putative reader that the writer has in mind. These two minds
the reader must coordinate with his or her own. Subjectivity is the
recognition that each of these minds may have a different perspective
on the world. Coordinating them is what initiates the internal mental
dialogue which both Plato and Hobbes (1651/1958) took to be
thinking.

· ·

It seems clear enough that there are cultural, historical and developmental differences in the ways in which people think about themselves and their world. Not only are there differences in what they know but more importantly, they think about what they know and how they came to know it in quite different ways. Butterfield's metaphor of "putting on a new kind of thinking cap" aptly describes the transformation we have examined in thinking about language, the world and the mind.

In this volume we have examined the role that writing, reading and literacy in general played in these conceptual changes in the West. We considered a number of factors including the type of script, the ways of reading scripts and interpreting texts and the application of principles of reading text to "reading" the natural world. As we have seen there are many different writing systems, employed in many different cultures, for many different purposes, in importantly different ways with quite different levels of competence and with quite different consequences and implications. Research in this field has done little more than begin to map out this diversity.

In order to understand the conceptual and cognitive implications of writing and reading we have had to differentiate the cognitive resources involved in perception, speech and action – processes whose origins have to be explained evolutionarily – from those cognitive processes involved in the creation, storage and use of artifacts and symbols which serve representational functions – processes and products whose origins have to be explained culturally and historically. For it is these technical resources that have given literate thought at least some of its distinctive properties in the West.

Just how these technical resources do so is, of course, the big theoretical puzzle. The proposals I have advanced herein are quite different from those suggested by Finnegan (1988) who suggested that we seek an explanation not in a technical property of writing but rather in aspects of control and use. My concern, rather, is in identifying the indelible conceptual stamp which a reliance upon

writing has put on our cultural and cognitive activities. My proposals
are also quite different from those recently offered by Donald (1991)
who suggested that symbols and artifacts have their impact on cognition by extending memory. I have argued, rather, that the cognitive
implications of cultural artifacts are a product of the new concepts
invented in dealing with these symbols and artifacts. Our graphic
systems not only preserve information but also provide models which
allow us to see our language, our world and our minds in a new way.

Even if there is important diversity in the graphic systems involved
and the functions they serve, the primary concern of this volume has
been to extract some general principles, a theory if you will, that may
help to explain some of the available evidence and point us in fruitful
new directions of research. The explanations we have discussed may
be summarized in eight principles. The first four of them arise from
reversing the traditional assumption about the relation between
speech and writing. Contrary to writers from Aristotle to Saussure I
have argued that writing is not transcription of speech but rather
provides a model for speech; we introspect language in terms laid
down by our scripts. The remaining four address how models of
language then serve as models for the world and for the mind.

Principle one: writing was responsible for bringing aspects of
spoken language into consciousness, that is, for turning aspects of
language into objects of reflection, analysis and design. This is why the
history of writing is necessarily a part of understanding the cognitive
implications of writing, for different writing systems brought different
aspects of language into consciousness. The earliest uses of graphic
devices in the form of pictures and emblems, like the oral or memorial
tradition of which they are a part, provided a notion of saying the same
thing each time they were scanned or recited. But "the same thing" in
this case is the meaning, what the picture, emblem or story is about.

The first general writing systems evolved some four thousand years
ago in Mesopotamia, in Egypt, in China and somewhat later in Central
America (Gaur, 1984/1987). The distinctive property of such writing
systems was the possession of a syntax for combining signs so as to
express propositions; it is the first type of script that can be taken as a
model for the verbal form rather than the content of an expression.
Thus this type of writing provides a new criterion for the notion of

"saying the same thing," one in which the actual words are relevant as subjects and predicates of propositions. Such scripts were responsible for bringing linguistic entities such as words into consciousness. Furthermore, as these scripts represented propositions they were the first capable of representing negative statements: How would you represent "Thou shalt not kill" in a picture? Such writing, I have argued, was basic to the formulation of a clear distinction between what was said and what was meant or intended by it, a distinction elaborated in quite different ways in literate than in non-literate cultures.

Later scripts brought other linguistic segments into consciousness: Syllabic scripts made syllables into objects of consciousness and alphabets provided the model for thinking of speech as composed of sub-syllabic constituents, close to but not identical with, phonemes.

The general relation between writing and consciousness, then, may be expressed by extending Whorf's notion of the relation between language and thought; writing provides a set of categories for thinking about language. This is not to say that the only consciousness of language is script induced but rather that in learning to write and read one comes to think of speech in terms of the entities in the representational system. Writing provides a series of models for, and thereby brings into consciousness, the lexical, syntactic and logical properties of what is said.

This principle would help to explain how literacy contributes to the writing of grammars and the formation of dictionaries as well as the discovery of logic and the invention of theories of rhetoric. These are metalinguistic activities in which the categories of the system depend upon the properties of speech that the script can be seen as representing. It does not imply that speech without writing lacks grammar, a lexicon, logic or rhetoric. What it does imply is that the formulation of a theory of grammar or of logic is constructed in terms of the categories brought into consciousness by means of the script. Once explicitly formulated, grammar and logic may be intentionally employed in the formation of sentences or of arguments. To illustrate, once an argument is seen to have a deductive structure, one can search for premises from which necessary inferences can be drawn. And once a sentence is seen to have a grammatical form, one can reject sentences that fail to fit the model. It would be inappropriate, of course, to think that this deliberateness emerged simply because one could read and write a few words; it is a reflectiveness that would occur only with the growing consciousness of the structure of speech in terms of the structure served up by the writing system. Systematic analysis of that speech, now "heard" in terms of the writing system, would be required to isolate the grammar from the meanings usually expressed in the language. This took some time historically and it takes some time and effort to develop in children.

Principle two: no writing system, including the alphabet, brings all aspects of what is said into awareness. Emblems and totems do not bring words into consciousness; logographs do not bring syllables, nor syllabics, phonemes. And, most importantly, even scripts such as the alphabet, which may be taken as representing the verbal form of an expression, fail to provide an explicit representation for the illocutionary force of an utterance. To the extent that they transcribe *what* was said, they fail to transcribe *how* it was said, and with it the indicators of how the speaker intended for the listener to take what was said. What is lost in the act of transcription is precisely what is so difficult to recover in the act of reading, namely, how the expression is to be taken. When Empedocles said that the salt sea is the sweat of the earth, was he speaking literally or metaphorically? The written record gives no indication.

This principle implies that it is inappropriate to think that any writing system has the same effect on one's awareness of language as any other, or, indeed, to think of "metalinguistic awareness" as a unitary phenomenon. A writing system can be taken as a model of some properties of a language. Some levels of reading competence may be attained without adopting the script as a model of all that it could be a model of. Some readers of alphabets may not realize that the alphabet provides a rough model of phonology. Such readers would, presumably, represent a fairly low level of competence. Higher levels of competence including the ability to write rather than simply to read would require grasping the graphic system as a model of sound patterns of the language. Indeed, successful readers grasp this relation relatively early in their careers.

Principle three: what the script-as-model does not represent is difficult, perhaps impossible, to bring into consciousness. What is represented tends to be seen as a complete model of what there is or, stated another way, whatever model of language a person holds, that model is taken as a complete model of what is said. Several anthropologists have reported the difficulty they had in convincing their non-literate informants that they should use "the same words" on each retelling of a song or story; as far as the informant was concerned the tellings *were* in the same words (Finnegan, 1977; Goody, 1987). Their model of "what was said" did not, it seems, apply to the very words. Elegant studies of the phonological awareness of non-readers which we reviewed in Chapter 4 have shown that it is knowledge of the alphabet that brings phonemes into awareness; for those unfamiliar with an alphabet, the phonemes are simply not heard. Similarly readers skilled in the reading of Chinese characters find it difficult or impossible to delete phonetic segments from spoken words, a difficulty not experienced by readers of Chinese written in alphabetic Pinyin.

The same appears to be true of the meaning of expressions. Recall the discussion in Chapter 9 of meanings we judge to be metaphorical but which their users do not. Levy-Bruhl's analysis of the belief held by the Huichol Indians of Mexico, namely, that corn is deer or Evans-Pritchard's analysis of the Nuer belief that twins are birds are cases in point. To the Huichol and the Nuer the expressions meant just what they said. If the writing/reading system makes no allowance for the distinction between what an expression literally means and what it metaphorically means, the users of those expressions fail to see those as alternatives.

Even after the literal–metaphorical distinction was securely in place, writers had difficulty in granting that texts did not completely determine the ways readers interpreted them. Thomas Cranmer, Archbishop of Canterbury under Henry VIII, wrote the *Book of Common Prayer* under the conviction that everyone who read it would come up with the same meaning; he thought of the text as a complete representation of what was said. Even modern readers and writers have difficulty recognizing that texts, no matter how well written, never provide more than an indication of a speaker's or writer's audience-directed intention. Alphabetic scripts represent verbal form, what was said, not the attitude of the speaker to that verbal form, what was meant by it. Consequently, the illocutionary force of an utterance has been difficult to resolve theoretically just as it has been difficult to manage practically in reading and writing.

Principle four: once a script-as-model has been assimilated it is extremely difficult to unthink that model and see how someone not familiar with that model would perceive language. Alphabetic literates find it astonishing when someone else fails to hear "alphabetic" constituents in their speech; to the literate, those distinctions are simply there. Similarly, modern readers accustomed to a strict distinction between literal meaning and metaphor, cannot imagine what the world is like to someone for whom that is not a primary distinction. When modern anthropologists encounter expressions such as "Twins are birds," they tend either to claim that the Nuer are speaking literally and hence are guilty of self-contradiction (Beattie, 1970) or that they are merely speaking figuratively (Hutchins, 1980). But why should they be forced to take one side or the other of what, for us, is a great divide? And medieval clerics could not grant that Jesus may have meant what he said when he said "I am the door." Only such modern scholars as Frye (1982) are comfortable in saying that for New Testament discourse, the metaphorical meaning may be the literal meaning. The difficulty is in seeing our written model of language as one model among others. The structures represented by the model tend to be taken as objectively given facts whether words, syllables, letter sounds, or literal meanings. Once detected such structures tend to be seen as being in the text and another's failure to see them is often misinterpreted as a form of blindness.

The third and fourth principles imply that in learning to "detect" sound-letter relations, the so called "phonetic" principle, the child is not learning to associate two knowns, sounds and letters, but rather is learning a model. If that is the case it would seem inappropriate to stress the learning of the model before one had any clear understanding of what the model is a model of, namely, what is said. Although the ongoing debate about children's learning to read is as much a matter of attitudes to children as it is about optimal pedagogy, it is worth affirming both of the two principles that are sometimes seen as contradictory. First, writing systems are not expressions of phonological or grammatical knowledge, rather they provide models for those constituents and hence are secondary; meaningful expressions are primary at the first stage. On the other hand, learning to read skillfully and especially learning to spell requires that one understand the graphic model as a model of speech; thus the model is primary at a second stage. The fourth principle in particular implies that teachers and policy makers may err in seeing learning to read as a "skill" that can be trained rather than as an intellectual achievement – coming to understand how what is said can be represented by a set of graphic symbols (Ferreiro, 1991).

The notion that scripts provide a model for speech rather than express linguistic structure warrants an additional comment. We oversimplify when we say that scripts "represent" implicit structures of speech, phonemes for example, in a graphic medium. My suggestion has been that scripts represent linguistic structures only in the sense of providing a model for them. The difference is important for what each view assumes. The former assumes that phonemes are available to consciousness and so directly expressible in the new medium. The latter assumes that the script is responsible for *bringing them into consciousness*. If the script provides the model then it is the script which defines the categories and the sound properties will come to be heard in terms of those categories. Evidence for this view, which we considered in Chapter 4, is the fact that children learn to hear both long /a/ and short /a/, which are phonemically different, as a single sound represented by the letter *a*. The category is given by the script not by the pre-existing consciousness of the phonological system. Speech may even come to be shaped by orthographic conventions as when the highly literate pronounce the "silent" /t/ in the word "often" or when children come to believe, falsely, when they learn to spell, that the word "pitch" is longer than the word "rich" and that the former, but not the latter, contains a /t/ sound (Ehri, 1985.) Thus we say that scripts, rather than expressing linguistic knowledge, provide a model for that knowledge. If this is true it is obvious that writing is important *to speech*; it changes us from speakers into language users.

These first four principles are not to be taken as reducible to either the conservative or the radical views of interpretation. It should provide no comfort either to those who believe that the meaning is in the text ready to be excavated by an ardent reader nor those who think that meaning is in the reader and brought or applied to the text. The literacy story I have been telling cuts the problem in a quite different way. The history of writing is one of inventing devices which serve as models for what is said. But what even the most explicit writing systems succeed in representing is what was said, not how it was said, that is, how the speaker or writer intended it to be taken. What is said is rarely ambiguous; how it was to be taken, on the other hand, is almost impossible to determine with certainty.

How expressions and texts are to be taken can be analyzed in terms of the distinction between locutionary act – saying something – and illocutionary force – intending something in saying it (Austin, 1962). In much, indeed most, oral discourse we get by with the expression of the content; force is left to be picked up from tone of voice, intonation, gesture and context. Thus a listener hearing "Dinner is at eight" would not, from the words themselves, know whether that is a promise, a prediction, an invitation or merely an observation. Moreover, the listener would not know, from the words themselves, whether "eight" meant *eight*, or eight for *eight-thirty*, or *roughly eight* and so on. The listener would rely upon tone and context to determine how it was to be taken, that is, the force of the utterance.

A written transcription of what was said fails to represent illocutionary force. Austin's original insight was that so-called constative utterances, roughly factual descriptive statements – do in fact have a force. The utterance "Grass is green" if fully expressed would be something like "I assert/state/claim/deny *that* grass is green." The baldest factual "authorless" statement in fact is an expression of an audience-directed intention. It is the recovery of that unmentioned illocutionary force which is hard to conceptualize – it awaited recent theory of speech acts – and it is that illocutionary force which has been difficult to represent in writing and to recover in reading. Indeed, I argued that the history of reading and writing was in large part a matter of learning to compensate for what scripts failed to provide a model for, namely, how expressions were to be taken – as loose or precise, as literal or metaphorical, as a command or a suggestion, and so on.

Principle five: the expressive and reflective powers of speech and writing are complementary rather than similar. Traditionally it had been assumed that writing was the medium appropriate to rational discourse. But at least since de Saussure (1916/1983), speech has been seen as primary, writing as mere transcription. The arguments on either side misfire in that much of the history of reading and writing is the attempt to make up for what is lost in transcribing speech. Hence, speech is primary in expressive power. But what writing provides is consciousness of the implicit structure of speech. Hence, writing is primary in linguistic consciousness. Neither is, overall, primary.

The advantage of speech, it was argued, is that it has adequate devices for expressing illocutionary force through stress and intonation along with body stance, tone of voice and the like. "You are going home," depending upon intonation, could be a question or a command. Ironic utterances, too, may be recognized, in part, through sarcastic intonation (but see Winner & Leekam, 1991). Difficulties arise particularly when one is faced with a mere transcript of what was said, in which case illocutionary force must be inferred. Inferring the communicative intention, its putative audience, its context, its relevance to new audiences, and other such questions make the issue of determining how to take a text one of those open questions that dominates contemporary thought. Learning to read is, in part, learning how to cope with the unexpressed.

When we grasp the principle that a written, decontextualized expression frequently fails to indicate how that expression is to be taken we are in a position to recognize the difficulties faced by those unfamiliar with literate conventions for taking texts. Recall our earlier analysis of Luria's (1976) syllogism task presented to non-literate peasants in a remote area of the Soviet Union in the 1930s. What the psychologist intended as a premise was "taken" by the subject as an implausible factual claim. There is no reason to believe that "ways of taking" are cultural universals.

Principle six: an important implication of literacy derives from the attempt to compensate for what was lost in the act of transcription. As we have seen, while scripts well represent lexical and syntactic properties of speech they do not adequately represent the author's audience-directed intentions – how the author means his text to be taken. But this lapse should not be seen as merely a loss, a poverty of writing as some have implied, but as an indirect contributor to the significance of writing. For if writing cannot capture speaker's stance, gaze, tone of voice, stress and intonation, reading such texts calls for a whole new world of interpretive discourse, of commentary and argument as to how, precisely, an utterance, now transcribed, was to be taken. Conversely, it called for the elaboration and systematization of a set of more complex speech act and mental state verbs such as *stating* versus *implying* as well as more precise notions of literal meaning, metaphorical meaning, speaking "largely" as opposed to speaking precisely, and the like.

Furthermore, quantitative dimensions embodied in tone of voice which express degree of commitment to a proposition, came to be represented lexically as assumptions, observations, conjectures, inferences, these categories turning out to have important epistemological functions. The evolution of such concepts, I argued, was a result of the attempt to recover or compensate for what was lost in the simple transcription of the words of the speaker. They were attempts to control how a reader took a statement. We may recall Boyle's worry about distinguishing facts, visible to all, from mere conjectures.

Such concepts, of course, do not spring from nowhere. Oral discourse, including that in traditional societies, has some concepts for indicating the manner in which utterances are to be taken. We may recall the Ilongot distinction between "straight" and "crooked" speech. What the interpretation of written texts calls for is the reorganization of these concepts into strict distinctions between the literal and the metaphorical and the reorganization of simple concepts into more complex forms such as *assume* and *infer* and their nominal equivalents *assumption* and *inference*. Talk and thought about assumptions, inferences, and conjectures, concepts which depend critically upon the concept of literal meaning, is distinctive of literate discourse.

This too, formed the basis of our analysis of those beliefs Levy-Bruhl took as indicative of primitive, pre-logical thought. We now see that such beliefs as "Corn is deer" lack nothing in logical inference. The gods require deer for sacrifice. But corn is deer. Therefore, the gods will accept corn as a sacrifice. What is deviant, from our perspective, is the absence of a strict notion of literality, that strictly speaking, corn is not deer. For us, logical inference is confined to the literal meaning of expressions. Informal reasoning, of course, is not tied to such univocality.

This sixth principle formed the basis for the formulation of a history of reading and writing viewed as the attempt to come to grips with the illocutionary aspects of the meaning of written texts, especially sacred texts. On this view the theory of literal meaning was a major achievement of the medieval period. The theory of literal meaning was an extremely important solution to the problems of interpreting not only scripture but other things as well.

That solution, which we traced through the influential twelfth- and thirteenth-century writers such as Andrew of St. Victor and Thomas Aquinas, was to sort out the communicative intention of statements in scripture, that is, to sort out clear and defensible ways of determining what a text meant, which is to say the way in which a text *was to be taken* by its primary audience. Equally importantly, it provided grounds for rejecting meanings that historically had been read into a text, but which textual analysis showed to be unwarranted. The solution was to think of the literal meaning not merely as the thoughts that came to mind as one meditated on the words but as what the writer intended the listener or reader to think by what he or she said or wrote. Readers began to distinguish themselves as readers from the primary intended audience; they became concerned with the putative intended reader – the audience envisioned by the original speaker or writer. They became concerned with the specific author, the context in which the author wrote, and with the authorial intention. A clearer notion of literal meaning was sufficient to "disenchant" text; by providing clear criteria for determining what texts meant, they were able to exclude the adventitious interpretations that had earlier been seen as legitimate. Texts meant what they said and that meaning was open to all to see, if not through simple inspection, at least through careful study.

This was a far cry from the simple distinction between the "letter" and the "spirit" of a text; the spirit was now to be recovered by careful analysis of the letter. The theory of literal meaning provided a means for harnessing the interpretation to the very form of the text; no gift of the spirit or internalizing the text was required to arrive at the meaning. Meaning was seen to be in the text, derivable by textual means. Interpretation was, so to speak, naturalized.

This new theory of literal meaning was not a kind of fundamental-ism; it was the recovery or management of intentionality. It was a new understanding of how to determine how the author intended his or her text to be taken. The route from text to interpretation could, for the first time, be seen as mechanical as the route from sound to letter had seemed. I called such reading "algorithmical," depending, as it seemed, upon purely mechanical procedures applied to the properties of the text itself.

The solution was neither simple nor ultimately satisfactory, but it was sufficient to form the basis for a new community of readers and writers who shared the belief in its feasibility and validity. These communities of readers of scripture, what Stock (1983) describes as "textual communities," as long as they were unsuccessful politically were thought of as heretical movements, but when they were finally successful formed the basis of the Protestant Reformation. What had seemed to be a workable strategy to Aquinas became an article of faith to the reformers. For Aquinas the literal meaning of scripture could never be seen as anything more than the first stage of interpretation; for Luther, it was all that there was.

As could be predicted from the fourth principle, once the "literal meaning," which was now seen as the intended meaning, incorporat-ing both the content and attitude of the utterance, was seen in the text, that meaning was seen as being completely represented by the text. Consequently, these new readers, Archbishop Cranmer being our example, believed that anyone reading *The Book of Common Prayer* carefully would see the same meanings in the text that he had seen. This, of course, was the blind spot of both heretical movements and evangelical protestant sects each of which justify their formation with the claims of going "back to the text" (Goody, 1987).

Principle seven: once texts are read in a certain new way, nature is "read" in an analogous new way. A number of theories have been advanced to explain the link between Protestantism and the rise of Early Modern Science. The celebrated Merton thesis sought the link in Puritanism, a humble attitude to truth and the value of hard work. Gellner (1988) advanced a similar argument suggesting that "scriptu-ralism is conducive to a high level of literacy; scripturalism and an individualist theology lead naturally to an individualist theory of knowledge" (p. 107). My hypothesis was that the categories evolved for reading the Book of Scripture were equally appropriate for "reading" the Book of Nature. Epistemology was applied hermeneutics. It consisted of systematic means for determining how to "take" expressions – as assumptions, hypotheses, inferences – how to take texts – literally, metaphorically and so on – and how to take natural signs – as evidence or data suitable for establishing the truth of beliefs.

Certainly the writings of British empirical philosophers Bacon, Boyle, Hooke, and Harvey fit this model. They set out to read the book of nature according to its literal meanings, those meanings that were plain for all to see. These literal meanings were the observable facts of nature. Boyle learned the languages of the Middle East so that he could read scripture correctly and he devised scrupulous experimental methods so that he could examine the facts of nature directly. Literal meanings like observed facts were the things that could be taken as "given" in their respective domains. Boyle, like Galileo, made a clear distinction between the "facts" which could be seen by all, and the "causes" which might be inferred or postulated in the mind and which could be matters of dispute (Shapin, 1984, p. 500).

A possible counter-argument to the relation between reading scripture and nature advanced here is the quite different attitude to intentionality in the two cases. Just at the moment that readers came to grips with intentionality as the key to the interpretation of texts, they began to avoid appeals to intentionality in their interpretation of nature. Aristotle explained motion by appeal to intention which he called "formal cause"; we employ an Aristotelian argot when we say that water *seeks* its own level. But those were the very causes that the seventeenth-century scientists abandoned. In my view that is not too surprising; to understand intentionality in a text as an audience-directed intention on the part of the author, is to see a personal undertaking in saying something rather than to seeing every utterance as a part of a divine plan. Similarly, in observing nature one was to see the properties of immediate events and not see those events as signs of some divine plan. Justifications in both cases were to be based on available evidence. Thus, the attitude to intentionality is quite consistent in interpreting texts and interpreting nature; inferences to purpose or intention had to be marked as inferences and justified by appeals to evidence.

The facts of nature like the meanings of scripture were thought to be available to all who read or looked carefully and sincerely. Just as Cranmer believed that scripture could be read only one way, Boyle believed that everyone who witnessed his experiments with the vacuum jar would see just what he had seen. Although scripture and nature were read in much the same way, when scripture and science came into conflict, the conflict was resolved by claiming that science speaks "exactly" while scripture speaks "largely" (Willey, cited by Eisenstein, 1979, p. 471).

I say they did not solve the problem of illocutionary force because they assumed that facts could be stated directly. They failed to acknowledge, as did everyone until J. L. Austin pointed it out, that stated facts, too, have an illocutionary force; they have the force of an assertion. As I mentioned above, every factual statement can be expanded to say "I assert that ..." Factual statements express an audience-directed intention too, and criticism of such statements requires that we recognize that intention. That is not an easy task; even honor students mistakenly take written statements as direct expressions of objective facts rather than as expressions of the beliefs of the writers (Wineburg, 1991). Only in the twentieth century and then only with considerable experience as readers and writers do we see statements as assertions and facts as theory dependent.

Principle eight: once the illocutionary force of a text is recognized as the expression of a personal, private intentionality, the concepts for representing how a text is to be taken provide just the concepts necessary for the representation of mind. The theory of mind is nothing other than the set of mental concepts which correspond to the expression of the illocutionary force of utterances. What are beliefs? Beliefs are the states one is in when one asserts a statement sincerely. What are intentions? Intentions are the states one is in when one promises sincerely to do something. What are desires? Desires are the states one is in when one requests sincerely. As Searle (1983) has pointed out, mental states are simply the sincerity conditions for speech acts. An account of the manners of saying things is, therefore, an account of the ways of thinking things. The stage is set for a new understanding of mind. Descartes' *Res cogitans*, the thing which thinks, and which also believes, doubts, remembers, is the model for the new understanding of mind derived from the new understanding of how to take utterances and texts. That understanding was sufficient for a new naturalistic model of the mind.

These eight principles relating the understanding and use of the variety of the world's scripts to the understanding of language, the world and the mind are advanced as aspects of a theory relating literacy and thought. In the course of sorting out these principles the original notions of writing, reading, literacy and thinking have all undergone radical revision and I conclude with a general discussion of these concepts.

What is reading?

Speaking generally, writing systems must be seen as devices for visual communication as both Gaur (1984/1987) and Harris (1986) insist rather than as devices for the exact representation of what is said – a goal which no script achieves. Scripts can vary enormously in their external structure and still be efficient graphic means of communication. There are none-the-less important watersheds. The most important one is in the invention of graphic systems which have a syntax and hence can express propositions. Gombrich tells of the vain attempt by some city fathers to portray pictorially their city as one which had never been captured. Only a script with a syntax can express such a proposition. Word signs, syllable signs, letter signs, each have their advantages and disadvantages but the possibility of explaining cultural change simply by appeal to the script seems to be unpromising. Even the Chinese script which has been disparaged by many from Samuel Johnson to Douglas MacArthur's advisers, is now thought to be no impediment to Chinese science (Needham, 1954–59.)

Yet the history of cultural and conceptual change that we have examined is at base a theory of reading. Reading, most generally construed, is a matter of rendering visible marks into a linguistic form. Almost anything can be "read" in this most general sense; as we saw Paracelsus read his patients illnesses by examining both their physical symptoms and the position of the planets. Even our much admired seventeenth-century scientists "read" the Book of Nature. Our twentieth-century notion of reading would limit the concept of reading to rendering man-made marks created with the intention of conveying a meaning. So we read scripts, shorthand, musical scores but not sermons in stone and books in brooks.

But a verbal rendering of a written script is only a part of reading – the rendering recovers what was said but not how it was to be taken, that is, what the writer meant by it. Consider the lapidary statement "Columbus discovered America in 1492," a putative fact known to every schoolchild. The truth of the matter is that it was Rodrigo de Triana, lookout on the *Pinto*'s forecastle, who was the first to spot the white sand cliffs of Guanahani, now thought to be San Salvador. Does that make the original statement false? Or would it indicate that the meaning of the statement was not absolutely precise? Would someone who read the statement in such a way as to exclude that possibility be misreading the text?

Or consider an earlier example: *Dinner is at eight*. The text in one sense can be read in only one way "Dinner is at eight." But in another sense it can be read in more than one way, as a prediction, a statement, an invitation, a promise and so on. Would someone who took what was intended as an invitation as a prediction have mis-read the text?

Reading, we may conclude is a matter of recovering or inferring authorial intentions by means of recognition of graphic symbols. Neither recognizing words nor recognizing intentions alone constitute reading. The meanings or intentions recognized have to be those compatible with the graphic evidence.

Writing systems differ in the aspects of speech they represent graphically. Learning to read is a matter of learning to recognize the aspects represented graphically and to infer those aspects of meaning which are not represented graphically at all.

Reading competence takes many forms. Reading is usefully seen as a transitive verb; in saying someone can read or not read we are obliged to say what can be read whether racing programs, computer manuals or literary texts. Furthermore, reading is purposive; a reader concerned with the gist sets a different criterion for reading than one concerned with literary form. Again, what readers see in a text depends upon the level of competence of the reader. Greater knowledge allows a reader to see more in a text than a novice does while at the same time allowing the reader to exclude meanings not warranted by the text.

Just as many practices may be included within the concept of reading so too quite different activities may make up skilled reading of particular texts for particular purposes. No set of categories such as basic skill or functional literacy captures this variability. As a provisional definition, which has some of the properties of an ideal, we may say that reading is the recovery/postulation of an audience-directed intention for a text which is justifiable on the basis of the available graphic evidence.

What is literacy?

As with the concept of reading, so too, the concept of literacy requires reconsideration. A host of definitions such as basic literacy, functional literacy, scribal literacy, critical literacy, restricted literacy and the like run through the literature. Sometimes literacy is contrasted with orality. These concepts, like the general concept of literacy, have limited theoretical value. But again we may identify some criteria for the use of the term. Literacy is, of course, competence with a script; different scripts recruit different competencies. Literacy is functionally oriented; one may be competent in using a script for some purposes but not others. Barton (1991) described one person who identified himself as not "literate" and yet he used writing to keep track of times and distances travelled by his pigeons! Literacy is a social condition; in reading and writing texts one participates in a "textual community" a group of readers (and writers and auditors) who share a way of reading and interpreting a body of texts (Stock, 1983). To become literate in a domain is to learn to share a "paradigm." Kuhn (1962) advanced this notion to describe a scientific community which shares a set of texts, a set of interpretations and a set of beliefs as to what poses a problem for further research and discussion. To be literate it is not enough to know the words; one must learn how to participate in the discourse of some textual community. And that implies knowing which texts are important, how they are to be read and interpreted, and how they are to be applied in talk and action.

While an individual may have the competence required to participate in any number of such literate or textual communities, we must
also acknowledge the fact that any society is organized around a body
of beliefs, sometimes expressed in textual form, access to which is a
source of power and prestige. In a bureaucratic society the issues of
law, religion, politics, science and literature make up this privileged
domain and access to, and participation in, those domains defines a
particular form of literacy. This is the kind of literacy that public
institutions, educational institutions in particular, are concerned with.
Literacy, from this perspective, is the competence required for participation in these privileged domains.

Faced with such complexity critics of literacy have tended to go in
either of two directions. One is to abandon the notion of literacy as an
explanatory term and as a viable educational goal. In its place goals are
stated which are suitable to specialized domain-specific knowledge,
overlooking anything that may be general to the activities of reading
and criticizing texts. The other is to pick rather arbitrary criteria for
defining "basic" literacy or "functional" literacy. This strategy leads,
on the one hand, to a focus on activities of dubious relevance to
understanding texts such as reading nonsense words and spelling
tests, and on the other, to the identification as functional of whatever
strikes the testers as relevant "to daily life" – bankers think that
deposit slips define functional literacy, advertisers think it the ability
to read ads, clerics think it the ability to read the Lord's prayer, and so
on. No one set of activities is functional for everyone and the diversity
of ways of creating and using texts has only begun to be grasped by
students of literacy.

But an understanding of the role of reading and writing in a culture,
both in the personal lives of individuals and in the diversity of textual
communities in which they participate, including participation in the
dominant institutions of the society whether legal, scientific, religious
or whatever, should allow us to nuance the notion of literacy. Again as
a tentative definition, which again serves as an ideal as much as a
description, we may think of literacy as both a cognitive and a social
condition, the ability to participate actively in a community of readers
who have agreed on some principles of reading, a hermeneutics if you
will, a set of texts to be treated as significant, and a working agreement

on the appropriate or valid interpretation(s) of those texts. That definition helps us to understand how the kind of literacy developed and shared by a community of readers towards the end of the medieval period and the beginning of early modern period could provide both a new way of reading texts and a new way of looking at and thinking about the world. And that definition may assist both teachers and testers in seeing classrooms as one type of literate community, thereby clarifying just what they are doing when they pursue the goal of a high level of literate competence.

Two caveats must be added. One is that culturally significant uses of writing have traditionally been defined too narrowly by defining literacy in terms of the dominant public culture – science, literature, history and the like. Only now are we beginning to recognize the enormous range of uses made of writing for different purposes in different cultures and different segments within one culture. Secondly, competence is often defined too narrowly. Students are reported to be quite successful in summarizing, remembering and reporting the gist of what they read but they are sometimes described as lacking in critical abilities. Criticism of texts, I shall argue presently, is an important part of thinking and an important link between literacy and thought.

What is thinking?

Since neither reading nor literacy are unitary phenomena, we cannot state a general rule relating literacy to cognition. As we have seen different scripts serve up different aspects of language to consciousness and different ways of reading the same script bring different aspects of meaning into consciousness. But by examining the diversity of scripts and the ways they are used and what they provide models of, we have been able to specify a set of relations between literacy and cognition. The relation was this: every script can be verbalized or read out, thus every script serves as a model for speech. *Ergo*, every script has cognitive implications. But scripts which could be taken as representing the lexical and syntactical properties of what was said were the ones which provided the levels of awareness necessary to the formation of dictionaries, grammars, logics and rhetorics. No script provides an adequate model for illocutionary force. Learning how to cope with what was lost in the act of transcriptions was, I suggested, a major achievement of the Early Modern period. It made possible the "protestant" reading of scripture and the "objective" representation of nature. As this is critical to the theory of literacy and thinking let us review the argument briefly.

Thinking systematically about how an author intended a text to be taken posed a major hurdle in the history of reading. Medieval rhetorical theory treated texts as deep wells from which one could take an inexhaustible supply of meanings. One category, "Amplification," specified four ways of taking a text: historically, allegorically, morally, and anagogically. An example:

Jerusalem which is built as a city may be taken historically about the Church on earth; allegorically about the Church militant; morally about any faithful soul; anagogically, about the Church triumphant.

(Basevorn, 1322/1971, p. 183)

The method could start interpretation; what it lacked was a clear means for stopping it or for privileging any one interpretation. As long as the Church was the arbiter of interpretation, there was an official means of deciding such issues. But by the fourteenth century a new way of reading and thinking about texts was seen as defensible. The new way of reading was exploited by several church fathers and various heretical movements but became institutionalized only with the Reformation.

Perhaps because of a revival of the Greek and Latin classics, perhaps because of increased availability of texts and increased numbers of readers, or perhaps because of improved writing technology and more readable scripts (Morrison, 1987; Saenger, 1991), the tradition of reading strictly, that is, reading according to the literal meanings of the text had attained a new prestige. The new prestige was based, in part on that fact that such an interpretation *could be justified by the lexical, syntactic, contextual evidence*. Interpretation had become a science and the science was the art of thinking.

But what was it that all that lexical, syntactic and contextual evidence was used to derive? It was, I argued, the illocutionary force of an expression, that is, how the author intended that his or her utterance be taken. Not only could that force be reconstructed in reading, it could be, and was, managed in writing. We may recall Bacon's injunction not to confuse a "dream of the imagination" with a "pattern in the world" and Boyle's determination to leave a "conspicuous interval" between the factual descriptions of his experimental findings and his occasional "discourses" upon their interpretation (Boyle, *Works*, Vol. 1, notes 1, 2; see Shapin, 1984).

All thought consists of the formation, updating and revision of beliefs. We see, and think about, the world in terms of our beliefs. Our beliefs make us conscious *of the world*. What literacy contributes to thought is that it turns the thoughts themselves into worthy objects of contemplation. It becomes worthwhile to try to determine the meanings of words and provide definitions for them. It turns ideas into hypotheses, inferences, assumptions which can then be turned into knowledge by the accumulation of evidence. And it does this, I have argued, by first turning words and propositions into objects of knowledge and secondly by turning the force of an utterance – the issue of intentionality – into objects of discourse.

Literate thought is premised on a self-consciousness about language, for it is modern writing that provides a relatively explicit model for the intentional aspects of our language and so renders them conscious. This is the final topic of this book, and we, like the early navigators, having fixed our course, will "run down the latitudes" to our destination.

So what is the form of thinking that evolved in the western literate tradition? The major feature of literate thought is that it is about representations such as explicit statements, equations, maps, and diagrams rather than about the world. The first problem to be solved if one is to think by means of such representations is to make a precise and categorical distinction between the representation and the thing it is a representation of. This understanding makes it clear that anything can be used to represent anything else – geometry to represent motion and words to represent rather than to name things.

Having granted representation this autonomy, the second problem is to determine how such representations are to be taken. This point is critical in that what is to be inferred from an expressed proposition depends upon how that proposition is to be taken. What follows from the Huichol expression "Corn is deer" is not that corn has antlers but that corn may be offered to the gods as a sacrifice if deer is not available. What follows from "All men are created equal" depends upon whether "all men" is to be taken as referring to all men or only to all free men, thereby excluding slaves, and on whether "all men" is taken as referring to all men or to all men and women. The issue is whether a representation is to be taken literally or metaphorically, as a factual claim or a relational model, as a cause or an effect, as a claim or as evidence for a claim. How is one to determine how any utterance or expression to be taken? Can the ability to make such a determination constitute a mode of thought?

Cognitive psychological theories of thinking and reasoning, theories which focus on how subjects derive inferences, have undergone an important shift in the past decade, a shift which has moved the issue of how expressions are to be taken on to centre stage. Until recently, the psychology of reasoning has been based on Aristotle's view that logic provides an account of valid inference. The syllogism is a logical form in which the truth of an inference follows from the truth of the premise. Advances in thinking, whether across cultures or within a child, could be described in terms of mastery of the rules of logic. This was the view that gave rise to the notion of primitive or pre-logical thought.

Recent research on human reasoning has shown that logic provides at best an ideal account of reasoning and not what thinkers actually do. Henle (1962) showed that even educated adults tend to follow the rules of logic only insofar as they generate conclusions with which they happen to agree! Others (Johnson-Laird, 1983; Kahneman and Tversky, 1982) have shown that while subjects show some understanding of logical rules, the same rule may be violated in one problem context and not in another. It appears that people lack a general rule for deriving valid inferences.

The problem, it seems, is just the one we have been examining. Inferences are not, perhaps cannot be, derived from statements themselves but are derived from particular ways of "taking" those statements. This is nicely shown in a study by Cheng and Holyoak (1985) which explored the ways subjects examined the implications of a logical rule. Rather then test the strict logical implications of the rule, subjects tended to translate or "take" what the researchers had intended as a logical premise, *if p then q*, into a pragmatic permission statement. Consequently, instead of examining the logical implication, *if not q then not p*, they examined the implications that would derive from a statement granting permission. Thus if asked to judge the validity of the rule expressed in the form of a permission statement such as "If one is to drink alcohol, then one must be over eighteen," subjects were likely to think of two implications, one valid, namely, *p only if q* (one can drink alcohol only if one is eighteen) and one invalid, namely, *if q then (one can) p* (if eighteen then one can drink alcohol). The latter, while pragmatically plausible, makes the logical error of affirming the consequent: as *If p then q* entailed *If q then p*.

The second concern of literate thinking, then, is consciously to assign an appropriate illocutionary force to an expression or other representation. Expressions themselves do not have implications; speech acts do. What follows from "Corn is deer" depends upon how the expression is taken. The Huichol knew how to take their expression; Levy-Bruhl did not. But why are such expressions problematic for us? And why was Empedocles' conjecture "The salt sea is the sweat of the earth" rejected by Aristotle as mere metaphor? What had come into place was a strict conception of literal meaning of an expression and a belief in the appropriateness of such language for systematic thought. Literal meanings of expressions come to be preferred as the primary mode of scientific thinking because strict implications may be derived from them. In fact that constitutes a working definition of literal meaning; a statement is intended literally only if the author intends as well the logical entailments of the statement. Again, ordinary language rarely achieves such logical purity and as a consequence science prefers technical language and mathematical expression.

To summarize, the second problem to be overcome in the transformation from thinking to literate thinking is the awareness of the alternative ways in which statements can be taken with a particular awareness of taking statements "literally." Only utterances intended to be taken literally may play a deductive role in scientific knowledge.

The third problem to be overcome in developing literate thinking also presupposes the existence of the representation independent from the thoughts of the speaker or writer and from the world of which it is a representation. For once expressions are distinguished from the things they are representations of – recall how Galileo used geometry to think about motion – one is free to revise the status of those representations on the basis of evidence. The gap between knowledge and opinion thought to be unbridgeable before the seventeenth century (Hacking, 1975b) will have been closed. Thus evidence may be seen as a means for altering the probability of the truth of a claim. A shift in this probability is a shift in the illocutionary force of the expression; it is the difference between *suspecting, believing,* on one hand and *knowing that such and such is the case* on the other. Literate thinking, then, involves understanding the role of evidence in the assignment of illocutionary force to expressed propositions. Such thinking is essentially theoretical in that it consciously distinguishes the implications that follow logically from the theory from the evidence which bears on the truth of those implications. D. Kuhn (1989) has recently shown that school-aged children and even many adults fail systematically to honor these distinctions in their thinking. They typically fail to represent the evidence separately from the theory that it is to be used to criticize.

All thinking involves perception, expectancies, inference, generalization, description and judgment. Literate thought is the conscious representation and deliberate manipulation of those activities. Assumptions are universally made; literate thought is the recognition of an assumption *as an assumption.* Inferences are universally made; literate thought is the recognition of an inference *as an inference,* of a conclusion *as a conclusion.* But it is not enough merely to recognize the force of an utterance. Equally important is to see the relation among utterances. Assumptions, inferences and conclusions are statements differing only in their degrees of commitment to their truth. An assumption makes no claim to truth; assumptions have only to be acknowledged. Hypotheses make tentative claims; hypotheses have only to be testable. Inferences are derived from statements whether they are taken to be true or merely assumed; inferences have only to be valid. Theoretical knowledge claims have to be validly derived from a theory and to be sustained by available evidence. And so on.

It is important to note that the epistemological distinctions relevant

to systematic thinking and to the advance of knowledge are appropriate for, indeed in part derive from, the reading of a text. Interpretations of a text are subject to the same range of attitudes from
conjecture to belief and are revisable on the basis of evidence. Thinking about text requires that a reader learn how to take texts in various
ways and adjudicate those possible ways in the light of available
evidence. Critical reading is the recognition that a text could be taken
in more than one way and then deriving the implications suitable to
each of those ways of taking and testing those implications against
available evidence. There is no great gap between the "two cultures."

Even if literate thought is to a large extent ordinary thought
rendered self-conscious and deliberate it is not tied exclusively to the
practice of reading and writing. Literate thought can be, indeed is to
some degree, embedded in the oral discourse of a literate society. We
can talk of conjectures just as well as read and write about them.
Literate thought is not restricted to the medium of writing even if
writing and reading were critical in their evolution. Furthermore, the
concepts of relevance to literate thinking have their roots in ordinary
oral discourse. The concepts of *think, know, mean* as well as simple
modal verbs *might be, could be, must be* are part of the oral competence
of very young children. Complex concepts are built by integrating
these simple ones:

interpret	→	think it means
hypothesize	→	think it might be
infer	→	think it must be
deduce	→	think it is

Complex verbs such as *infer*, also have a nominal form, *inference*.
These nominal forms, however, are what turn processes into entities.
Attempts to formulate rules for evaluating arguments and otherwise
thinking critically are built upon just such nominal entities. The rule
that inferences should be justified or the rule that assumptions should
be acknowledged cannot even be formulated without this set of
concepts.

Furthermore, the elaboration of concepts such as *imply* and *infer*
problematize the interpretation of utterances earlier represented
unproblematically by a more basic and generic term such as *say* – did

the speaker actually say that p? or did the listener merely infer that p from what was said? Such distinctions are systematically applied only when one is deeply embedded in literate culture.

Thus, while in a sense these concepts are available to everyone, they tend to be acquired late in the school career if they are acquired at all. Perhaps because of the traditional emphasis on content knowledge, educational programs at all levels tend to underemphasize the significance of such concepts and often fail to provide opportunities for their acquisition.

Mind, in part, is a cultural artifact, a set of concepts, formed and shaped in dealing with the products of literate activities. These artifacts are as much a part of the world as the stars and stones with which they were once confused. Inventing these artifacts put an indelible stamp on the history of culture; learning to cope with them puts an indelible stamp on human cognition.

It would be a mistake to insist that intellectual uses of literacy all took the same form in all cultures. But there seems little doubt that writing and reading played a critical role in producing the shift from thinking about things to thinking about representations of those things, that is, thinking about thought. Our modern conception of the world and our modern conception of ourselves are, we may say, by-products of the invention of a world on paper.

REFERENCES

Aarsleff, H. (1982). *From Locke to Saussure*. Minneapolis: University of Minnesota Press.

Ackerman, B., Szymanski, J., & Silver, D. (1990). Children's use of the common ground in interpreting ambiguous referential utterances. *Developmental Psychology*, 26, 234–245.

Alpers, S. (1983). *The art of describing: Dutch art in the seventeenth century*. Chicago: University of Chicago Press.

Anderson, O. (1989). The significance of writing in early Greece. In K. Schousboe & M. T. Larsen (eds.), *Literacy and society*. Copenhagen: Centre for Research in Humanities.

Aquinas, St. T. (1964–81). *Summa theologica (Latin/English edition)*. London: Blackfriars/McGraw-Hill. (Original work published 1267–73)

Aries, P. (1962). *Centuries of childhood: A social history of family life* (R. Baldick, trans.). New York: Vintage Books.

Aristotle (1938). *De Interpretatione* (H. P. Cook, trans.). London: Loeb Classical Library.

Ash, T., MacLaren, R., Torrance, N., & Olson, D. R. (1991, June). *Being of two minds: Young children's understanding of another's possible thoughts*. Paper presented at the meeting of the Canadian Psychological Association, Calgary, AB.

Astington, J. W. (1988). Children's understanding of the speech act of promising. *Journal of Child Language*, 15, 157–173.

   & Gopnik, A. (1988). Knowing you've changed your mind: Children's understanding of representational change. In J. W. Astington, P. L. Harris, & D. R. Olson (eds.), *Developing theories of mind* (pp. 193–206). Cambridge: Cambridge University Press.

   Harris, P. L., & Olson, D. R. (eds.). (1988). *Developing theories of mind*. Cambridge: Cambridge University Press.

   & Olson, D. R. (1990). Metacognitive and metalinguistic language: Learning to talk about thought. *Applied Psychology*, 39(1), 77–87.

Astle, T. (1784). *The origin and progress of writing*. London: Author.

Atran, S. (1990). *Cognitive foundations of natural history*. Cambridge: Cambridge University Press.

Austin, J. L. (1962). *How to do things with words*. Cambridge, MA: Harvard University Press.

Avis, J., & Harris, P. L. (1991). Belief-desire reasoning among Baka
    children: Evidence for a universal conception of mind. *Child
    Development*, 62(3), 460–467.
Bacon, F. (1857–64). The advancement of learning. In J. Spedding, R. Ellis,
    & D. Heath (eds.), *The works of Francis Bacon (Vols. 1–14)*. London:
    Longmans.
    (1964). Redargutio philosophiarum. In B. Farrington (ed.), *The philosophy
    of Francis Bacon*. Liverpool: Liverpool University Press. (Original work
    published 1608)
    (1965). The great instauration. In S. Warhaft (ed.), *Francis Bacon: A
    selection of his works* (pp. 298–324). Toronto: Macmillan. (Original work
    published 1620)
    (1965). The new organon. In S. Warhaft (ed.), *Francis Bacon: A selection
    of his works* (pp. 326–392). Toronto: Macmillan. (Original work
    published 1620)
Baker, S., Barzun, J., & Richards, I. A. (1971). *The written word*. Rowly,
    MA: Newbury House.
Baron-Cohen, S. (1991). Precursors to a theory of mind: Understanding
    attention in others. In A. Whiten (ed.), *Natural theories of mind:
    Evolution, development and simulation of everyday mindreading*
    (pp. 233–251). Oxford: Blackwell.
Barthes, R. (1977). *Image-music-text* (S. Heath, trans.). Glasgow: Fontana
    Collins.
Bartlett, F. (1932). *Remembering: An experimental and social study*.
    Cambridge: Cambridge University Press.
Barton, D. (1991). The social nature of writing. In D. Barton & R. Ivanic
    (eds.), *Writing in the community* (pp. 1–13). Newbury Park, CA: Sage.
Basevorn, R. (1971). The form of preaching. In J. Murphy (ed.), *Three
    medieval rhetorical arts*. Berkeley: University of California Press.
    (Original work published 1322)
Bäuml, F. (1980). Variety and consequences of Medieval literacy and
    illiteracy. *Speculum*, 55, 237–265.
Beaglehole, J. C. (ed.). (1967). *The journals of Captain James Cook*.
    Cambridge: Cambridge University Press, for the Hakluyt Society.
    (Original work published 1955)
Beal, C. R. (1990). Development of knowledge about the role of inference in
    text comprehension. *Child Development*, 61, 1011–1023.
Beattie, J. H. M. (1970). On understanding ritual. In B. R. Wilson (ed.),
    Rationality (pp. 240–268). Oxford: Blackwell.

Bell, B., & Torrance, N. (1986, April). *Learning to make and recognize inferences in the early grades.* Paper presented at the meeting of the American Educational Research Association, San Francisco, CA.

Bellone, E. (1980). *A world on paper: Studies on the second scientific revolution.* Cambridge, MA: MIT Press.

Bennett, J. O., & Berry, J. W. (1991). Cree literacy in the syllabic script. In D. R. Olson & N. Torrance (eds.), *Literacy and orality* (pp. 90–104). Cambridge: Cambridge University Press.

Berkeley, G. (1975). *Philosophical works: Including the works on vision.* London: Dent. (Original work published 1709–10)

Berlin, B. (1974). *Tseltzal plant classification.* New York: Academic Press.

Bertelson, P., de Gelder, B., Tfouni, L. V., & Morais, J. (1989). The metaphonological abilities of adult illiterates: New evidence of heterogeneity. *European Journal of Cognitive Psychology, 1*, 239–250.

Berthoud-Papandropoulou, I. (1978). An experimental study of children's ideas about language. In A. Sinclair, J. Jarvella, & W. Levelt (eds.), *The child's conception of language* (pp. 55–64). Berlin: Springer-Verlag.

Blixen, K. (1972). *Out of Africa.* New York: Random House.

Bloch, M. (1975). *Oratory and political language in traditional society.* London: Academic Press.

    (1989). Literacy and enlightenment. In K. Schousboe & M. T. Larsen (eds.), *Literacy and society.* Copenhagen: Centre for Research in Humanities.

    (in press). The uses of schooling and literacy in a Zafimaniry village. In B. Street (ed.), *Readings on literacy.* Cambridge: Cambridge University Press.

Bloomfield, L. (1933). *Language.* New York: Holt, Rinehart & Winston.

Boas, M. (1962). *The scientific Renaissance 1450–1630.* New York: Harper.

Bonitatibus, G. (1988). What is said and what is meant in referential communication. In J. W. Astington, P. L. Harris, & D. R. Olson (eds.), *Developing theories of mind* (pp. 326–338). Cambridge: Cambridge University Press.

Boorman, S. (1986). Early music printing: Working for a specialized market. In G. Tyson & S. Wagonheim (eds.), *Print and culture in the Renaissance: Essays on the advent of printing in Europe.* Newark: University of Delaware Press.

Boyle, R. (1772). New experiments physico-mechanical, touching the spring of the air. In T. Birch (ed.), *The works of the Honourable Robert Boyle. Volumes 1–6.* London: J. & F. Rivington.

Brody, H. (1981). *Maps and dreams*. Toronto: Douglas & McIntyre.

(1987). *Living Arctic: Hunters of the Canadian North*. Toronto: Douglas & McIntyre.

Browne, Sir T. (1972). *The prose of Sir Thomas Browne*. New York: Norton. (Original work published 1643)

Bruner, J. S. (1983). *Child's talk: Learning to use language*. New York: W. W. Norton.

(1986). *Actual minds, possible worlds*. Cambridge, MA: Harvard University Press.

(1990). *Acts of meaning*. Cambridge: Cambridge University Press.

& Weisser, S. (1991). The invention of self: Autobiography and its forms. In D. R. Olson & N. Torrance (eds.), *Literacy and orality* (pp. 129–148). Cambridge: Cambridge University Press.

Butterfield, H. (1965). *The origins of modern science 1300–1800*. London: G. Bell & Sons.

Bylebyl, J. J. (1979). *William Harvey and his age: The professional and social context of the discovery of the circulation*. Baltimore, MD: Johns Hopkins University Press.

Calvino, I. (1985). *Mr. Palomar* (W. Weaver, trans.). New York: Harcourt Brace Jovanovich. (Original work published 1983)

Camille, M. (1992). *Image on the edge: The margins of Medieval art*. Cambridge, MA: Harvard University Press.

Capelli, C. A., Nakagawa, N., & Madden, C. M. (1990). How children understand sarcasm: The role of context and intonation. *Child Development, 61*(6), 1824–1841.

Carruthers, M. J. (1990). *The book of memory: A study of memory in medieval culture*. Cambridge: Cambridge University Press.

Cassirer, E. (1951). *The philosophy of the Enlightenment* (F. Koelln & J. Pettegrove, trans.). Princeton, NJ: Princeton University Press.

(1957). *The philosophy of symbolic forms* (vol. 3). (R. Manheim, trans.). New Haven, CT: Yale University Press.

Chafe, W. (1985). Linguistic differences produced by differences between speaking and writing. In D. R. Olson, N. Torrance, & A. Hildyard (eds.), *Literacy, language, and learning: The nature and consequences of reading and writing* (pp. 105–123). Cambridge: Cambridge University Press.

(1991). Grammatical subjects in speaking and writing. *Text, 11*(1), 45–72.

Chandler, M., Fritz, A. S., & Hala, S. (1989). Small-scale deceit: Deception as a marker of two-, three-, and four-year-olds' early theories of mind. *Child Development, 60*(6), 1263–1277.

Chaytor, H. J. (1945). *From script to print: An introduction to medieval literature*. Cambridge: Cambridge University Press.

Cheney, D. L., & Seyfarth, R. M. (1991). Reading minds or reading behaviour? Tests for a theory of mind in monkeys. In A. Whiten (ed.), *Natural theories of mind: Evolution, development and simulation of everyday mindreading* (pp. 175–194). Oxford: Blackwell.

Cheng, P., & Holyoak, K. (1985). Pragmatic reasoning schemas. *Cognitive Psychology, 17*, 391–416.

Chomsky, N. (1980). *Rules and representations*. New York: Columbia University Press.

Cipolla, C. M. (1969). *Literacy and development in the West*. Harmondsworth: Penguin.

Clanchy, M. T. (1979). *From memory to written record: England, 1066–1307*. London: Edwin Arnold. (2nd edition: Blackwell, 1993)
    (1985). Literacy, law, and the power of the state. In *Culture and idéologie dans l'état moderne*. Rome: Collection de l'École Français de Rome, No. 82.

Coe, M. D. (1992). *Breaking the Maya code*. New York: Thames and Hudson.

Cohen, M. (1958). *La grande invention de l'écriture et son evolution*. Paris: Imprimerie nationale.

Cole, M., Gay, J., Glick, J., & Sharp, D. (1971). *The cultural context of learning and thinking*. New York: Basic Books.

Comte, A. (1830–42). *Cour de philosophie positive*. Paris: Bachelier.

Coulmas, F. (1989). *The writing systems of the world*. Oxford: Blackwell.

Dante, A. (1973). The letter to Can Grande. In R. S. Haller (ed.), *Literary criticism of Dante Alighieri*. Lincoln: University of Nebraska Press. (Original work published 1317)

de Castell, S., Luke, A., & Egan, K. (eds.). (1986). *Literacy, society and schooling*. Cambridge: Cambridge University Press.

de Sousa, R. (1980). The rationality of emotions. In A. O. Rorty (ed.), *Explaining emotions*. Berkeley: University of California Press.

Defoe, D. (1930). *The life and strange surprising adventures of Robinson Crusoe, of York Mariner*. New York: Limited Editions Club. (Original work published 1719)

DeFrancis, J. (1989). *Visible speech: The diverse oneness of writing systems*. Honolulu: University of Hawaii Press.

Dennett, D. C. (1978). Beliefs about beliefs. *Behavioral and Brain Sciences, 1*, 568–570.
    (1991). *Consciousness explained*. Boston: Little, Brown.

Derrida, J. (1976). *Of grammatology* (G. Spivak, trans.). Baltimore, MD: Johns Hopkins University Press.

Descartes, R. (1960). *Discourse on method and Meditations* (L. J. LaFleur, trans.). (The Library of Liberal Arts edn.). Indianapolis/New York: Bobbs-Merrill. (Original work published 1637–41)

(1968). *The philosophical works of Descartes* (E. S. Haldane & G. R. T. Ross, trans.). Cambridge: Cambridge University Press. (Original work published 1637–44)

Diringer, D. (1962). *Writing*. London: Thames and Hudson.

(1968). *The alphabet: A key to the history of mankind* (3rd edn.). New York: Funk & Wagnalls.

Donald, M. (1991). *Origins of the modern mind: Three stages in the evolution of culture and cognition.* Cambridge, MA: Harvard University Press.

Donaldson, M. (1978). *Children's minds.* Glasgow: Fontana/Collins.

(1986). *Children's explanation: A psycholinguistic study.* Cambridge: Cambridge University Press.

Downing, J. (1987). Comparative perspectives on world literacy. In D. Wagner (ed.), *The future of literacy in a changing world* (pp. 25–47). Oxford: Pergamon Press.

Dunn, J. (1988). *The beginnings of social understanding.* Cambridge, MA: Harvard University Press.

Duranti, A. (1985). Famous theories and local theories: The Samoans and Wittgenstein. *Quarterly Newsletter of the Laboratory of Comparative Human Cognition, 7,* 46–51.

Durkheim, E. (1948). *The elementary forms of religious life.* Glencoe, IL: The Free Press.

Ehri, L. C. (1985). Effects of printed language acquisition on speech. In D. R. Olson, N. Torrance, & A. Hildyard (eds.), *Literacy, language, and learning: The nature and consequences of reading and writing* (pp. 333–367). Cambridge: Cambridge University Press.

Eisenstein, E. (1979). *The printing press as an agent of change.* Cambridge: Cambridge University Press.

(1985). On the printing press as an agent of change. In D. R. Olson, N. Torrance, & A. Hildyard (eds.), *Literacy, language, and learning: The nature and consequences of reading and writing* (pp. 19–33). Cambridge: Cambridge University Press.

Evans-Pritchard, E. (1937). *Witchcraft, oracles, and magic among the Azande.* Oxford: Oxford University Press.

(1956). *Nuer religion.* Oxford: Oxford University Press.

Faulkner, W. (1955). *Big woods.* New York: Random House.

Febvre, L. (1982). *The problem of unbelief in the sixteenth century: The religion of Rabelais.* Cambridge, MA: Harvard University Press. (Original work published 1942)

& Martin, H.-J. (1976). *The coming of the book: The impact of printing 1450–1800* (D. Gerard, trans.). London: NLB. (Original work published 1958)

Feider, H. (1970). The grammar of assymetric relations in child language and cognition. *Glossa, 4*, 197–205.

Feld, S., & Schieffelin, B. (1982). Hard words: A formational basis for Kaluli discourse. In D. Tannen (ed.), *Analyzing discourse: Text and talk* (pp. 350–370). Washington, DC: Georgetown University Press.

Feldman, C. F. (1991). Oral metalanguage. In D. R. Olson & N. Torrance (eds.), *Literacy and orality* (pp. 47–65). Cambridge: Cambridge University Press.

Ferreiro, E. (1985). Literacy development: A psychogenetic perspective. In D. R. Olson, N. Torrance, & A. Hildyard (eds.), *Literacy, language, and learning: The nature and consequences of reading and writing* (pp. 217–228). Cambridge: Cambridge University Press.

(1991). Psychological and epistemological problems on written representation of language. In M. Carretero, M. Pope, R. J. Simons, & J. Pozo (eds.), *Learning and instruction: European research in international context*. Oxford: Pergamon Press.

& Teberosky, A. (1982). *Literacy before schooling (Los sistemas de escritura en el desarrollo del nino)*. Exeter, NH: Heinemann (English translation)/Mexico DF: Siglo Veintiuno Editors. (Original work published 1979)

Finnegan, R. (1973). Literacy versus non-literacy: The great divide? In R. Horton & R. Finnegan (eds.), *Modes of thought* (pp. 112–144). London: Faber.

(1977). *Oral poetry: Its nature, significance, and social context*. Cambridge: Cambridge University Press.

(1988). *Literacy and orality: Studies in the technology of communication*. Oxford: Blackwell.

Flew, A. (1962). Introduction. In D. Hume, *On human nature and the understanding*. New York: Macmillan.

Fodor, J. A. (1985). Fodor's guide to mental representation: The intelligent auntie's vade mecum. *Mind, 94*, 76–100.

(1987). *Psychosemantics: The problem of meaning in the philosophy of mind*. Cambridge, MA: Bradford Books/MIT Press.

(1992). A theory of the child's theory of mind. *Cognition, 44*, 283–296.

Foucault, M. (1970). *The order of things*. London: Tavistock.

Fox, B., & Routh, D. (1975). Analyzing spoken language into words, syllables, and phonemes: a developmental study. *Journal of Psycholinguistic Research, 4*, 331–342.

Francis, H. (1975). *Language in childhood: Form and function in language learning.* London: Paul Elek.

Frank, R. G. (1980). *Harvey and the Oxford physiologists: Scientific ideas and social interaction.* Berkeley: University of California Press.

Frazer, J. G. (1976). *The golden bough.* London: Tavistock. (Original work published 1911–15)

Frith, U. (1985). Beneath the surface of developmental dyslexia. In K. E. Patterson, J. C. Marshall, & M. Coltheart (eds.), *Surface dyslexia: Neuropsychological and cognitive studies in phonological reading.* London: Erlbaum.

(1989). *Autism.* Oxford: Blackwell.

Frye, N. (1982). *The great code.* Toronto: Academic Press.

Fuller, B., Edwards, J., & Gorman, K. (1987). Does rising literacy spark economic growth? Commercial expansion in Mexico. In D. Wagner (ed.), *The future of literacy in a changing world* (pp. 319–340). New York: Pergamon Press.

Gadamer, H.-G. (1975). *Truth and method.* London: Sheed & Ward.

Galilei, Galileo. (1954). *Dialogues concerning two new sciences* (H. Grew & A. de Salvio, trans.). (1914 edn.). New York: Dover. (Original work published 1638)

(1957). The assayer. In S. Drake (ed.), *Discoveries and opinions of Galileo.* Garden City, NY: Doubleday. (Original work published 1623)

(1957). Letter to the Grand Duchess Christiana. In S. Drake (ed.), *Discoveries and opinions of Galileo.* Garden City, NY: Doubleday. (Original work published 1615)

Gaur, A. (1987). *A history of writing* (Paperback edn.). London: The British Library. (Original work published 1984)

(in press). The history of writing systems. In I. Taylor & D. R. Olson (eds.), *Scripts and literacy: Reading and learning to read alphabets, syllabaries and characters.* Dordrecht: Kluwer.

Geertz, C. (1973). *The interpretation of cultures.* New York: Basic Books.

Gelb, I. J. (1963). *A study of writing* (2nd edn.). Chicago: University of Chicago Press.

Gellner, E. (1988). *Plough, sword and book: The structure of human history.* London: Collins Harvill.

Gibbon, E. (1896). *The history of the decline and fall of the Roman empire* (vol. 1). (J. B. Bury, ed.). London: Methuen. (Original work published 1776)

Gibson, W. (1950). Authors, speakers, readers, and mock readers. *College English, 11*(5), 265–269.

Gilson, E. (1957). *Painting and reality*. New York: Bollingen/Pantheon
    Books.
Ginzburg, C. (1982). *The cheese and the worms: The cosmos of a
    sixteenth-century miller*. Markham, ON: Penguin Books.
    (1986). The dovecote has opened its eyes: Popular conspiracy in
    seventeenth-century Italy. In G. Henningsen, J. Tedeschi, & C. Amiel
    (eds.), *The inquisition in early modern Europe: Studies on sources and
    methods*. Dekalb: Northern Illinois University Press.
Gladwin, T. (1970). *East is a big bird: Navigation and logic on a Pulawat Atoll*.
    Cambridge, MA: Harvard University Press.
Gombrich, E. H. (1950). *The story of art*. Oxford: Phaidon.
    (1960). *Art and illusion: A study in the psychology of pictorial representation*.
    New York: Bollingen/Pantheon Books.
Goody, E. N. (1978). Towards a theory of questions. In E. N. Goody (ed.),
    Questions and politeness (pp. 17–43). Cambridge: Cambridge University
    Press.
Goody, J. (1986). *The logic of writing and the organization of society*.
    Cambridge: Cambridge University Press.
    (1987). *The interface between the oral and the written*. Cambridge:
    Cambridge University Press.
    & Watt, I. (1968). The consequences of literacy. In J. Goody (Eds.),
    Literacy in traditional societies. Cambridge: Cambridge University Press.
    (Originally published 1963 in *Contemporary Studies in Society and
    History*, 5, 304–345)
Gopnik, A., & Astington, J. W. (1988). Children's understanding of
    representational change and its relation to the understanding of false
    belief and the appearance-reality distinction. *Child Development*, 59, 26–37.
Goswami, U., & Bryant, P. (1990). *Phonological skills and learning to read*.
    Hove, England/Hillsdale, NJ: Erlbaum.
Graff, H. (1979). *The literacy myth: Literacy and social structure in the
    nineteenth-century city*. New York: Academic Press.
    (1986). *The legacies of literacy: Continuities and contradictions in Western
    society and culture*. Bloomington: Indiana University Press.
Greenfield, P. M. (1983). Review of "The psychology of literacy" by
    Sylvia Scribner and Michael Cole. *Harvard Educational Review*, 53,
    216–220.
Grice, P. (1989). *Studies in the way of words*. Cambridge, MA: Harvard
    University Press.
Gunther, J. (Ed.). (1934). *The Greek herbal of Dioscorides (512 A.D)*. Oxford:
    Oxford University Press. (Original work published 1655)

Haas, C., & Flower, L. (1988). Rhetorical reading strategies and the construction of meaning. *College Composition and Communication*, 39, 30–47.

Hacking, I. (1975a) *Why does language matter to philosophy?* Cambridge: Cambridge University Press.

(1975b). *The emergence of probability: A philosophical study of early ideas about probability, induction and statistical inference.* Cambridge: Cambridge University Press.

(1990). *The taming of chance.* Cambridge: Cambridge University Press.

Hadwin, J., & Perner, J. (1991). Pleased and surprised: Children's cognitive theory of emotion. *British Journal of Developmental Psychology*, 9, 215–234.

Hale, J. R. (1968). *Renaissance exploration.* New York: Norton.

Halliday, M. A. K. (1985). *Spoken and written language.* Oxford: Oxford University Press.

(1990). Linguistic perspectives on literacy: A systemic-functional approach. In F. Christie & E. Jenkins (eds.), *Literacy in social processes.* Sidney: Literacy Technologies.

Hallpike, C. R. (1979). *The foundations of primitive thought.* Oxford: Clarendon.

Halverson, J. (1992). Goody and the implosion of the literacy thesis. *Man*, 301–317.

Hamilton, K. G. (1963). *The two harmonies: Poetry and prose in the seventeenth century.* Oxford: Clarendon.

Hanson, N. R. (1958). *Patterns of discovery.* Cambridge: Cambridge University Press.

Happé, F. G. E. (1993). Communicative competence and theory of mind in autism: A test of relevance theory. *Cognition*, 48(2), 101–119.

Harbsmeier, M. (1988). Inventions of writing. In J. Geldhill, B. Bender, & M. T. Larsen (eds.), *State and society: The emergence and development of social hierarchy and political centralization.* London: Unwin Hyman.

Harris, R. (1986). *The origin of writing.* London: Duckworth.

Harris, W. V. (1989). *Ancient literacy.* Cambridge: Cambridge University Press.

Haugeland, J. (1987). *Artificial intelligence: The very idea.* Cambridge: Cambridge University Press.

Havelock, E. (1963). *Preface to Plato.* Cambridge: Cambridge University Press.

(1976). *Origins of Western literacy.* Toronto: OISE Press.

(1982). *The literate revolution in Greece and its cultural consequences.* Princeton, NJ: Princeton University Press.

(1991). The oral-literate equation: A formula for the modern mind. In D. R. Olson & N. Torrance (eds.), *Literacy and orality* (pp. 11–27). Cambridge: Cambridge University Press.

Heath, S. B. (1983). *Ways with words: Language, life and work in communities and classrooms.* Cambridge: Cambridge University Press.

Hedelin, L., & Hjelmquist, E. (1988). Preschool children's mastery of the form/content distinction in spoken language. In K. Ekberg & P. E. Mjaavatn (eds.), *Growing into the modern world.* Trondheim: The University of Trondheim, Norwegian Centre for Child Research.

Heeschen, V. (1978). The metalinguistic vocabulary of a speech community in the highlands of Irian Jaya (West New Guinea). In A. Sinclair, R. Jarvella, & W. Levelt (eds.), *The child's conception of language* (pp. 155–187). Berlin: Springer-Verlag.

Hegel, G. W. (1967). *The phenomenology of mind.* New York: Harper and Row. (Original work published 1910).

Henle, M. (1962). On the relation between logic and thinking. *Psychological Review, 69(4),* 366–378.

Herriman, M. L. (1986). Metalinguistic awareness and the growth of literacy. In S. de Castell, A. Luke, & K. Egan (eds.), *Literacy, society and schooling.* Cambridge: Cambridge University Press.

Hobbes, T. (1958). *Leviathan.* Indianapolis: Bobbs-Merrill. (Original work published 1651)

Homer (1946). *The Odyssey* (R. V. Rieu, trans.). Harmondsworth: Penguin Books.

(1991). *The Iliad* (R. Fayles, trans.). New York: Penguin Classics.

Hooke, R. (1961). *Micrographia* (With a preface by R. T. Gunther, ed.). New York: Dover Publications. (Original work published 1665)

Householder, F. (1971). *Linguistic speculations.* Cambridge: Cambridge University Press.

Hume, D. (1962). *On human nature and the understanding.* New York: Macmillan. (Original work published 1748)

Hunter, I. M. L. (1985). Lengthy verbatim recall: The role of text. In A. Ellis (ed.), *Progress in the psychology of language.* Hillsdale, NJ: Erlbaum.

Hutchins, E. (1980). *Culture and inference: A Trobriand case study.* Cambridge: Cambridge University Press.

(1983). Understanding Micronesian navigation. In D. Gentner & A. Stevens (eds.), *Mental models.* Hillsdale, NJ: Erlbaum.

Illich, I. (1991). A plea for research on lay literacy. In D. R. Olson & N. Torrance (eds.), *Literacy and orality* (pp. 28–46). Cambridge: Cambridge University Press.

  & Sanders, B. (1989). *ABC: The alphabetization of the popular mind.* New York: Vintage Books.

Inhelder, B., & Piaget, J. (1964). *The early growth of logic in the child: Classification and seriation.* London: Routledge & Kegan Paul. (Original work published 1959)

Innis, H. (1950). *Empire and communications.* Oxford: Oxford University Press.

Jaynes, J. (1976). *The origin of consciousness in the breakdown of the bicameral mind.* Boston: Houghton Mifflin.

Johnson-Laird, P. N. (1983). *Mental models.* Cambridge: Cambridge University Press.

Kaestle, K., Damon-Moore, H., Stedman, L. C., Tinsley, K., & Trollinger, V. W. (1991). *Literacy in the United States.* New Haven, CT: Yale University Press.

Kahneman, D., & Tversky, A. (1982). On the study of statistical intuitions. In D. Kahneman, P. Slovic, & A. Tversky (eds.), *Judgement under uncertainty: Heuristics and biases* (pp. 493–507). Cambridge: Cambridge University Press.

Kakar, S. (1978). *The inner world: A psychoanalytic study of childhood and society in India.* Oxford: Oxford University Press.

Karmiloff-Smith, A. (1992). *Beyond modularity: A developmental perspective on cognitive science.* Cambridge, MA: Bradford Books/MIT Press.

Karpova, S. N. (1977). *The realization of verbal composition of speech by preschool children.* The Hague: Mouton.

Katz, M. B. (1968). *The irony of early school reform.* Boston: Beacon Press.

Keenan, T. (in preparation). *Children's understanding of irony.* Unpublished Ph.D. thesis, University of Toronto, Toronto.

  Olson, D. R., & Torrance, N. (1990). *Children's understanding of the invariance of text.* Unpublished paper, Centre for Applied Cognitive Science, Ontario Institute for Studies in Education.

Keightley, D. (1989). The origins of writing in China: Scripts and cultural contexts. In W. M. Senner (ed.), *The origins of writing.* Lincoln: University of Nebraska Press.

Kiparsky, P., & Kiparsky, C. (1970). Fact. In M. Bierwisch & K. Heidolph (eds.), *Progress in linguistics* (pp. 143–173). The Hague: Mouton.

Kittay, J. (1991). Thinking through literacies. In D. R. Olson & N. Torrance (eds.), *Literacy and orality* (pp. 165–173). Cambridge: Cambridge University Press.

& Godzich, W. (1987). *The emergence of prose: An essay in prosaics.*
Minneapolis, MN: University of Minnesota Press.

Klima, E., & Bellugi, U. (1979). *The signs of language.* Cambridge, MA:
Harvard University Press.

Kuhn, D. (1989). Children and adults as intuitive scientists. *Psychological
Review, 96*(4), 674–689.

Kuhn, T. S. (1962). *The structure of scientific revolutions.* Chicago: The
University of Chicago Press.

(1977). *The essential tension.* Chicago: University of Chicago Press.

Larsen, M. T. (1989). What they wrote on clay. In K. Schousboe & M. T.
Larsen (eds.), *Literacy and society.* Copenhagen: Copenhagen
University, Centre for Research in the Humanities.

Latour, B., & Woolgar, S. (1986). *Laboratory life: The construction of scientific
facts.* Princeton, NJ: Princeton University Press.

Leach, E. (1982). *Social anthropology.* Oxford: Oxford University Press.

Leclercq, J. (1961). *The love of learning and the desire for God* (C. Misrahi,
trans.). New York: Fordham University Press.

Leech, G. N. (1983). *Principles of pragmatics.* London: Longmans.

LePan, D. (1989). *The cognitive revolution in Western Culture, Vol. 1. The birth
of expectation.* London: Macmillan.

Levi-Strauss, C. (1961). *Tristes Tropiques.* New York: Atheneum.

(1966). *The savage mind.* Chicago: University of Chicago Press.

Levy-Bruhl, L. (1923). *Primitive mentality.* London: George Allen & Unwin.

(1926). *How natives think.* London: George Allen & Unwin. (Original
work published 1910)

Linnaeus, C. (1751). *Plant philosophy.*

(1767). *Systema naturae.* Leiden: Hook. (Original work published 1735)

Lloyd, G. E. R. (1979). *Magic, reason and experience.* Cambridge: Cambridge
University Press.

(1983). *Science, folklore and ideology: Studies in the life sciences in ancient
Greece.* Cambridge: Cambridge University Press.

(1990). *Demystifying mentalities.* Cambridge: Cambridge University Press.

Locke, J. (1961). *An essay concerning human understanding.* London: Dent.
(Original work published 1690)

Long, A. A., & Sedley, D. N. (1987). *The Hellenistic philosophers.*
Cambridge: Cambridge University Press.

Lord, A. (1960). *The singer of tales.* Cambridge, MA: Harvard University Press.

Lucariello, J. (1989). *Situational irony.* Unpublished paper, New School for
Social Research, New York.

Lukes, S. (1973). *Emile Durkheim: His life and work.* Markham, ON: Penguin
Books.

Luria, A. (1976). *Cognitive development: Its cultural and social foundations.* Cambridge: Cambridge University Press.

Lynn-George, M. (1988). *Epos: Word, narrative and the Iliad.* Atlantic Highlands, NJ: Humanities Press International.

Lyons, J. (1977). *Semantics* (Vols. 1 & 2). Cambridge: Cambridge University Press.

Macaulay, M. (1990). *Processing varieties in English: An examination of oral and written speech across genres.* Vancouver, BC: University of British Columbia Press.

MacLaren, R., & Olson, D. R. (1993). Trick or treat: Children's understanding of surprise. *Cognitive Development*, 8, 27–46.

Macleans Magazine, Toronto. (1991, August 5). p. 41.

Maimonides, M. (1963). *The guide for the perplexed* (S. Pines, trans.). Chicago: University of Chicago Press. (Original work published 1190)

Marx, K. (1906). *Capital.* Chicago: C. H. Kerr.

Masonheimer, P., Drum, P., & Ehri, L. (1984). Does environment print identification lead children into word reading? *Journal of Reading Behavior, 16*, 257–271.

Mattingly, I. G. (1972). Reading, the linguistic process, and linguistic awareness. In J. Kavanagh & I. Mattingly (eds.), *Language by eye and by ear.* Cambridge, MA: MIT Press.

McCarthy, S. (1991). *The Cree syllabary and the writing system riddle: A paradigm in crisis.* Unpublished paper, Centre for Applied Cognitive Science, Ontario Institute for Studies in Education, Toronto.

McCormick, P. (1989). Intentionality and language: Is belief possible without the language of belief? *Periodically: The newsletter of the McLuhan Program in Culture and Technology and the Consortium on Literacy* (12), 4–5.

(1994). *Children's understanding of mind: A case for cultural diversity.* Unpublished Ph.D. thesis, University of Toronto, Toronto.

McKellin, W. H. (1990). Allegory and inference: Intentional ambiguity in Managalase negotiations. In K. Watson-Gegeo & G. White (eds.), *Disentangling: Conflict discourse in Pacific societies* (pp. 335–370). Stanford, CA: Stanford University Press.

McKitterick, R. (1990). Conclusion. In R. McKitterick (ed.), *The uses of literacy in early mediaeval Europe.* Cambridge: Cambridge University Press.

McLuhan, M. (1962). *The Gutenberg galaxy.* Toronto: University of Toronto Press.

Merton, R. K. (1970). *Science, technology and society in seventeenth century England* (1st American edn.). New York: H. Fertig.

Michaels, S., & Collins, J. (1984). Oral discourse style: Classroom interaction and the acquisition of literacy. In D. Tannen (ed.), *Coherence in spoken and written discourse*. Norwood, NJ: Ablex.

Mitchell-Kernan, C., & Kernan, K. T. (1977). Pragmatics of directive choice among children. In S. Ervin-Tripp & C. Mitchell-Kernan (eds.), *Child discourse*. New York: Academic Press.

Morais, J., Alegria, J., & Content, A. (1987). The relationships between segmental analysis and alphabetic literacy: An interactive view. *Cahiers de Psychologie Cognitive, 7*, 415–438.

Bertelson, P., Cary, L., & Alegria, J. (1986). Literacy training and speech segmentation. *Cognition, 24*, 45–64.

Morris, C. (1938). Foundations of the theory of signs. In *International encyclopedia of unified science. Vol. 1, No. 2*. Chicago, IL: University of Chicago Press.

Morrison, K. F. (1982). *The mimetic tradition of reform in the West*. Princeton, NJ: Princeton University Press.

(1987). Stabilizing the text: The institutionalization of knowledge in historical and philosophical forms of argument. *Canadian Journal of Sociology, 12*, 242–274.

(1988). *I am you: The hermeneutics of empathy in western literature*. Princeton, NJ: Princeton University Press.

(1990). *History as a visual art in the twelfth-century Renaissance*. Princeton, NJ: Princeton University Press.

Morrison, S. E. (1942). *Admiral of the ocean sea: A life of Christopher Columbus*. Boston: Little, Brown.

Mowat, F. (1965). *Westviking: The ancient Norse in Greenland and North America*. Boston: Little, Brown.

Murphy, J. (ed.). (1971). *Three medieval rhetorical arts*. Berkeley: University of California Press.

Needham, J. (1954–59). *Science and civilization in China*. Cambridge: Cambridge University Press.

(1969). *The grand titration: Science and society in East and West*. Toronto: University of Toronto Press.

Newman, D. (1982). Perspective taking versus content in understanding lies. *The Quarterly Newsletter of the Laboratory of Comparative Human Cognition, 4*, 26–29.

Nicholson, G. (1984). *Seeing and reading*. Atlantic Highlands, NJ: Humanities Press.

Nissen, H. J. (1986). The archaic texts from Uruk. *World Archeology*, *17*(3), 318–334.

Norris, S. P., & Phillips, L. M. (1987). Explanations of reading comprehension: Schema theory and critical thinking theory. *Teachers College Record*, *89*, 281–306.

Nussbaum, M. C. (1986). *The fragility of goodness: Luck and ethics in Greek tragedy and philosophy*. Cambridge: Cambridge University Press.

Oatley, K. (1977). Inference, navigation, and cognitive maps. In P. Johnson-Laird & P. Wason (eds.), *Thinking: Readings in cognitive science* (pp. 537–547). Cambridge: Cambridge University Press.

Olson, D. R. (1977). From utterance to text: The bias of language in speech and writing. *Harvard Educational Review*, *47*(3), 257–281.

(1980). Some social aspects of meaning in oral and written language. In D. R. Olson (ed.), *The social foundations of language and thought*. New York: W. W. Norton.

(1990). Possible minds: Some reflections on Jerome S. Bruner's recent writings on mind and self. *Human Development*, *33*(6), 339–343.

& Astington, J. W. (1990). Talking about text: How literacy contributes to thought. *Journal of Pragmatics*, *14*(5), 557–573.

Howes, D., & Torrance, N. (in preparation). *What will the listener think? Children's understanding of interpretation and misinterpretation*. Unpublished paper, Centre for Applied Cognitive Science, Ontario Institute for Studies in Education, Toronto.

Ong, W. (1976). *The presence of the word*. New Haven, CT: Yale University Press.

(1982). *Orality and literacy: The technologizing of the word*. London: Methuen.

Onians, R. B. (1954). *The origins of European thought*. Cambridge: Cambridge University Press.

Ozment, S. (1980). *The age of reform 1250–1550: An intellectual and religious history of Late Medieval and Reformation Europe*. New Haven, CT: Yale University Press.

Padel, R. (1992). *In and out of the mind: Greek images of the tragic self*. Princeton, NJ: Princeton University Press.

Palmer, L. (1980). *The Greek language*. Atlantic Highlands, NJ: Humanities Press.

Paracelsus. (1958). *Paracelsus: Selected writings* (J. Jacobi, ed.; N. Guterman, trans.), (2nd edn.). Princeton, NJ: Princeton University Press.

Parkes, M. (1992). *Pause and effect: An introduction to the history of punctuation in the West*. Aldershot, England: Scholar Press.

Parret, D. (1990). *Chimpanzees' attention to direction of gaze of others*. Paper presented at the meeting of the Canadian Psychological Association, Halifax, NS.

Parry, E. (ed.). (1971). *The collected papers of Milman Parry.* Oxford: Oxford University Press.

Pattanayak, D. P. (1991). Literacy: An instrument of oppression. In D. R. Olson & N. Torrance (eds.), *Literacy and orality* (pp. 105–108). Cambridge: Cambridge University Press.

Pelly, D. (1991). How Inuit find their way in the trackless Arctic. *Canadian Geographic, 3*(4), 58–64.

Perner, J. (1991). *Understanding the representational mind.* Cambridge, MA: Bradford Books/MIT Press.

& Howes, D. (1992). "He thinks he knows": And more developmental evidence against the simulation (role taking) theory. *Language and Mind, 7*(1 & 2), 72–86.

Peskin, J. (1992). Ruse and representations: On children's ability to conceal information. *Developmental Psychology, 28*(1), 84–89.

Pilkington, R. (1959). *Robert Boyle, father of chemistry.* London: J. Murray.

Pinker, S. (1989). Language acquisition. In M. I. Posner (ed.), *Foundations of cognitive science* (pp. 359–399). Cambridge, MA: Bradford Books/MIT Press.

Polanyi, M. (1958). *Personal knowledge.* London: Routledge & Kegan Paul.

Pollock, F., & Maitland, F. (1898). *The history of English law before the time of Edward I* (2nd edn.). Cambridge: Cambridge University Press.

Popper, K. (1972). *Objective knowledge: An evolutionary approach.* Oxford: Clarendon.

Premack, D., & Dasser, V. (1991). Perceptual origins and conceptual evidence for theory of mind in apes and children. In A. Whiten (ed.), *Natural theories of mind: Evolution, development and simulation of everyday mindreading* (pp. 253–266). Oxford: Blackwell.

& Woodruff, G. (1978). Does the chimpanzee have a theory of mind? *Behavioral and Brain Sciences, 1,* 515–526.

Ptolemy. *Almagest.*
Geography.

Rawski, E. (1978). *Education and popular literacy in Ch'ing China.* Ann Arbor: University of Michigan Press.

Read, C. A., Zhang, Y., Nie, H., & Ding, B. (1986). The ability to manipulate speech sounds depends on knowing alphabetic reading. *Cognition, 24,* 31–44.

Reid, J. F. (1966). Learning to think about reading. *Educational Research, 9,* 56–62.

Reiss, T. J. (1982). *The discourse of modernism*. Ithaca, NY: Cornell University Press.

Robinson, E., Goelman, H., & Olson, D. R. (1983). Children's relationship between expressions (what was said) and intentions (what was meant). *British Journal of Developmental Psychology*, *1*, 75–86.

Rosaldo, M. Z. (1982). The things we do with words: Ilongot speech acts and speech act theory in philosophy. *Language in Society*, *2*, 203–237.

Rousseau, J.-J. (1966). Essay on the origin of languages. In J. H. Moran & A. Gode (eds.), *On the origin of language: Two essays by Jean-Jacques Rousseau and Johann Gottfried Herder*. New York: Frederick Unger. (Original work published 1754–91)

Ruffman, T., Olson, D. R., & Astington, J. W. (1991). Children's understanding of visual ambiguity. *British Journal of Developmental Psychology*, *9*, 89–102.

Olson, D. R., & Torrance, N. (1990). *Young children's understanding of the relation between verbal ambiguity, visual ambiguity and false belief*. Unpublished paper, Centre for Applied Cognitive Science, Ontario Institute for Studies in Education, Toronto.

Saenger, P. (1982). Silent reading: Its impact on late medieval script and society. *Viator*, *13*, 367–414.

(1991). The separation of words and the physiology of reading. In D. R. Olson & N. Torrance (eds.), *Literacy and orality* (pp. 198–214). Cambridge: Cambridge University Press.

Sampson, G. (1985). *Writing systems*. Stanford, CA: Stanford University Press.

Sanders, B. (1991). Lie it as it plays: Chaucer becomes an author. In D. R. Olson & N. Torrance (eds.), *Literacy and orality* (pp. 111–128). Cambridge: Cambridge University Press.

Sarton, G. (1955). *The appreciation of ancient and medieval science during the Renaissance (1450–1600)*. Philadelphia: University of Pennsylvania Press.

Saussure, F. de (1983). *Course in general linguistics*. London: Duckworth. (Original work published 1916)

Scardamalia, M., & Bereiter, C. (1985). Development of dialectical processes in composition. In D. R. Olson, N. Torrance, & A. Hildyard (eds.), *Literacy, language, and learning: The nature and consequences of reading and writing* (pp. 307–329). Cambridge: Cambridge University Press.

Schama, S. (1987). *The embarrassment of riches: An interpretation of Dutch culture in the golden age*. New York: Alfred A. Knopf.

Schliemann, H. (1979). *Memoirs of Heinrich Schliemann*. New York: Harper and Row.

Schmandt-Bessarat, D. (1986). Tokens: Facts and interpretations. *Visible Language, 20*(3), 250–272.

(1987). *Oneness, twoness, threeness: How ancient accountants invented numbers*. New York: New York Academy of Sciences.

(1992). *Before writing*. Austin: University of Texas Press.

Scholes, R. J., & Willis, B. J. (1991). Linguists, literacy, and the intensionality of Marshall McLuhan's Western man. In D. R. Olson & N. Torrance (eds.), *Literacy and orality* (pp. 215–235). Cambridge: Cambridge University Press.

Scribner, S. (1975). Recall of classical syllogisms: A cross-cultural investigation of error on logical problems. In R. Falmagne (ed.), *Reasoning: Representation and process*. Hillsdale, NJ: Erlbaum.

& Cole, M. (1981). *The psychology of literacy*. Cambridge, MA: Harvard University Press.

Searle, J. R. (1969). *Speech acts*. Cambridge: Cambridge University Press.

(1983). *Intentionality*. Cambridge: Cambridge University Press.

Senner, W. M. (ed.). (1989). *The origins of writing*. Lincoln: University of Nebraska Press.

Serra, E. (1992). *Children's understanding of how writing reflects speech*. Unpublished paper, Centre for Applied Cognitive Science, Ontario Institute for Studies in Education, Toronto.

Shapin, S. (1984). Pomp and circumstance: Robert Boyle's literary technology. *Social Studies of Science, 14*, 481–520.

& Schaffer, S. (1985). *Leviathan and the air-pump: Hobbes, Boyle, and the experimental life*. Princeton, NJ: Princeton University Press.

Shultz, T. R., & Wells, D. (1985). Judging the intentionality of action-outcomes. *Developmental Psychology, 21*, 83–89.

Sinclair, H. (1978). Conceptualization and awareness in Piaget's theory and its relevance to the child's conception of language. In A. Sinclair, J. Jarvella, & W. Levelt (eds.), *The child's conception of language* (pp. 191–200). Berlin: Springer-Verlag.

Sinclair, J. M., & Coulthard, R. M. (1975). *Towards an analysis of discourse: The English used by teachers and pupils*. London: Oxford University Press.

Skelton, R. A. (1958). *Explorer's maps: Chapters in the cartographic record of geographical discovery*. London: Routledge & Kegan Paul.

(1965). *The Vinland map and the Tartar relation*. New Haven, CT: Yale University Press.

Slocum, J. (1900). *Sailing around the world*. New York: The Century Co.

Smalley, B. (1941). *The study of the Bible in the Middle Ages*. Oxford: Clarendon.

Smith, F. (1989). Overselling literacy. *Phi Delta Kappan*, *70*, 352–359.

Smith, M. E. (1973). *Picture writing from ancient southern Mexico*. Oklahoma: University of Oklahoma Press.

Snell, B. (1960). *The discovery of the mind: The Greek origins of European thought* (T. G. Rosenmeyer, trans.). New York: Harper & Row.

Sperber, D. (1975). *Rethinking symbolism*. Cambridge: Cambridge University Press.

Sprat, T. (1966). In J. I. Cope & H. W. Jones (eds.), *History of the Royal Society of London for the improving of natural knowledge*. St. Louis: Washington University Press. (Original work published 1667)

Stevenson, H. W., Stigler, J. W., Lucker, G. W., Lee, S. Y., Hsu, C. C., & Kitamura, S. (1982). Reading disabilities: The case of Chinese, Japanese, and English. *Child Development*, *53*, 1164–1181.

Stock, B. (1983). *The implications of literacy*. Princeton, NJ: Princeton University Press.

(1984–85). Medieval history, linguistic theory, and social organization. *New Literary History*, *16*, 13–29.

(1990). *Listening for the text: The uses of the past*. Baltimore, MD: Johns Hopkins University Press.

Strauss, G. (1978). *Luther's house of learning: Indoctrination of the young in the German Reformation*. Baltimore, MD: Johns Hopkins University Press.

Street, B. (1984). *Literacy in theory and practice*. Cambridge: Cambridge University Press.

Stross, B. (1974). Speaking of speaking: Tenejapa Tzeltal metalinguistics. In R. Bauman & J. Sherzer (eds.), *Explorations in the ethnography of speaking*. Cambridge: Cambridge University Press.

Tambiah, S. J. (1990). *Magic, science and religion and the scope of rationality*. Cambridge: Cambridge University Press.

Tannen, D. (1985). Relative focus on involvement in oral and written discourse. In D. R. Olson, N. Torrance, & A. Hildyard (eds.), *Literacy, language, and learning: The nature and consequences of reading and writing* (pp. 124–147). Cambridge: Cambridge University Press.

Thomas, R. (1989). *Oral tradition and written record in classical Athens*. Cambridge: Cambridge University Press.

Thornton, M. (1989). *Folk psychology: An introduction*. Toronto: University of Toronto Press.

Torrance, N., Lee, E., & Olson, D. (1992, April). *The development of the distinction between paraphrase and exact wording in the recognition of utterances.* Poster presentation at the meeting of the American Educational Research Association, San Francisco, CA. .

   & Olson, D. R. (1985). Oral and literate competencies in the early school years. In D. R. Olson, N. Torrance, & A. Hildyard (eds.), *Literacy, language, and learning: The nature and consequences of reading and writing* (pp. 256–284). Cambridge: Cambridge University Press.

Toulmin, S. (1972). *Human understanding.* Princeton, NJ: Princeton University Press.

Traugott, E., & Pratt, M. L. (1980). *Linguistics for students of literature.* New York: Harcourt Brace Jovanovich.

Treiman, R. (1991). The role of intrasyllabic units in learning to read. In L. Rieben & C. Perfetti (eds.), *Learning to read: Basic research and its implications* (pp. 149–160). Hillsdale, NJ: Erlbaum.

Tuman, M. C. (1987). *A preface to literacy: An inquiry into pedagogy, practice, and progress.* Tuscaloosa: The University of Alabama Press.

Tyson, G., & Wagonheim, S. (1986). *Print and culture in the Renaissance: Essays on the advent of Europe.* Newark: University of Delaware Press.

UNESCO (1975). *Final report for the International Symposium for Literacy.* Persepolis, Iran.

Unger, J. M., & deFrancis, J. (in press). Logographic and semasiographic writing systems: A critique of Sampson's classification. In I. Taylor & D. R. Olson (eds.), *Scripts and literacy: Reading and learning to read alphabets, syllabaries and characters.* Dordrecht: Kluwer.

Vansina, J. (1965). *Oral tradition: A study in historical methodology* (H. M. Wright, trans.). London: Routledge & Kegan Paul. (Original work published 1961)

Vendler, Z. (1970). Say what you think. In J. L. Cowan (ed.), *Studies in thought and language.* Tucson: University of Arizona Press.

   (1972). *Res cogitans.* Ithaca, NY: Cornell University Press.

Vygotsky, L. (1962). *Thought and language.* Cambridge, MA: MIT Press.

   (1978). *Mind in society: The development of higher psychological processes.* M. Cole, V. John-Steiner, S. Scribner, & E. Souberman (eds.). Cambridge, MA: Harvard University Press.

Watson, R., & Olson, D. R. (1987). From meaning to definition: A literate bias on the structure of meaning. In R. Horowitz & S. J. Samuels (eds.), *Comprehending oral and written language* (pp. 329–353). San Diego: Academic Press.

Watt, I. (1957). *The rise of the novel.* Harmondsworth: Penguin Books.

Weber, M. (1930). *The Protestant ethic and the spirit of capitalism* (T. Parson, trans.). London: Allen & Unwin. (Original work published 1905)

Webster, C. (1975). *The great instauration: Science, medicine and reform (1626–1660).* London: Duckworth.

Wellman, H. M. (1990). *The child's theory of mind.* Cambridge, MA: Bradford Books/MIT Press.

Whiten, A. (ed.). (1991). *Natural theories of mind.* Oxford: Blackwell.

Whorf, B. L. (1956). Science and linguistics. In *Selected writings of Benjamin Lee Whorf.* Cambridge, MA: MIT Press.

Wimmer, H., Hogrefe, J., & Sodian, B. (1988). A second stage in children's conception of mental life: Understanding informational accesses as origins of knowledge and belief. In J. W. Astington, P. L. Harris, & D. R. Olson (eds.), *Developing theories of mind* (pp. 173–192). Cambridge: Cambridge University Press.

& Perner, J. (1983). Beliefs about beliefs: Representation and constraining function of wrong beliefs in young children's understanding of deception. *Cognition, 13,* 103–128.

Wineburg, S. S. (1991). On the reading of historical texts: Notes on the breach between school and academy. *American Educational Research Journal, 28*(3), 495–519.

Winner, E. (1988). *The point of words.* Cambridge, MA: Harvard University Press.

& Leekam, S. (1991). Distinguishing irony from deception: Understanding the speaker's second-order intention. *British Journal of Developmental Psychology, 9*(2), 257–270.

Windmueller, G., Rosenblatt, E., Bosco, L., Best, E., & Gardner, H. (1987). Making sense of literal and nonliteral falsehood. *Metaphor and Symbolic Activity, 2,* 13–32.

Wittgenstein, L. (1958). *Philosophical investigations* (G. E. M. Anscombe, trans.). Oxford: Blackwell.

Wundt, W. (1916). *Elements of folk psychology* (E. L. Schaub, trans.). New York: Macmillan.

Yates, F. (1966). *The art of memory.* Chicago: University of Chicago Press.

NAME INDEX

SUBJECT INDEX